AFRICAN
AMERICANS
OPPOSING VIEWPOINTS®

P9-BZY-723

Other Books of Related Interest:

American History Series

The American Frontier
The American Revolution
Asian Americans
The Bill of Rights
The Civil Rights Movement
The Civil War
The Cold War
The Creation of the Constitution
The Great Depression
Immigration
Isolationism
The 1960s
Puritanism
Reconstruction
Slavery
The Women's Rights Movement
World War II

Opposing Viewpoints in American History

Volume I: From Colonial Times to Reconstruction
Volume II: From Reconstruction to the Present

Opposing Viewpoints Series

Race Relations
Interracial America

AFRICAN AMERICANS

OPPOSING VIEWPOINTS®

David L. Bender, *Publisher*
Bruno Leone, *Executive Editor*

William Dudley, *Series Editor*
John C. Chalberg, Ph.D., professor of history,
   Normandale Community College, *Consulting
   Editor*

William Dudley, *Book Editor*

Greenhaven Press, Inc.
San Diego, California

Cover illustrations, clockwise from top: 1) photograph of bus station, Durham, North Carolina, May 1940 (Library of Congress); 2) photograph of black voters at polling station in Harlem, New York City, November 3, 1936 (UPI/Bettmann); 3) photograph of Malcolm X at Nation of Islam rally in New York City, July 27, 1963 (AP/Wide World); 4) woodcut illustration of hold in slave-trading ship (Library of Congress)

Library of Congress Cataloging-in-Publication Data

African Americans : opposing viewpoints / William Dudley, book editor.
    p.   cm. — (American history series)
    Includes bibliographical references and index.
    ISBN 1-56510-521-4 (pap. : alk. paper). —
ISBN 1-56510-522-2 (lib. : alk. paper)
    1. Afro-Americans—History—Sources. I. Dudley, William, 1964- . II. Series: American history series (San Diego, Calif.)
E184.6.A34   1997   96-18328
973′.0496073—dc20   CIP

©1997 by Greenhaven Press, Inc., PO Box 289009,
San Diego, CA 92198-9009

Printed in the U.S.A.

"America was born of revolt, flourished in dissent, became great through experimentation."

Henry Steele Commager

Contents

Chapter 4: Booker T. Washington and His Critics

Chapter 5: The Great Migration and the Harlem Renaissance

Foreword

Aboard the *Arbella* as it lurched across the cold, gray Atlantic, John Winthrop was as calm as the waters surrounding him were wild. With the confidence of a leader, Winthrop gathered his Puritan companions around him. It was time to offer a sermon. England lay behind them, and years of strife and persecution for their religious beliefs were over, he said. But the Puritan abandonment of England, he reminded his followers, did not mean that England was beyond redemption. Winthrop wanted his followers to remember England even as they were leaving it behind. Their goal should be to create a new England, one far removed from the authority of the Anglican church and King Charles I. In Winthrop's words, their settlement in the New World ought to be "a city upon a hill," a just society for corrupt England to emulate.

A Chance to Start Over

One June 8, 1630, John Winthrop and his company of refugees had their first glimpse of what they came to call New England. High on the surrounding hills stood a welcoming band of fir trees whose fragrance drifted to the *Arbella* on a morning breeze. To Winthrop, the "smell off the shore [was] like the smell of a garden." This new world would, in fact, often be compared to the Garden of Eden. Here, John Winthrop would have his opportunity to start life over again. So would his family and his shipmates. So would all those who came after them. These victims of conflict in old England hoped to find peace in New England.

Winthrop, for one, had experienced much conflict in his life. As a Puritan, he was opposed to Catholicism and Anglicanism, both of which, he believed, were burdened by distracting rituals and distant hierarchies. A parliamentarian by conviction, he despised Charles I, who had spurned Parliament and created a private army to do his bidding. Winthrop believed in individual responsibility and fought against the loss of religious and political freedom. A gentleman landowner, he feared the rising economic power of a merchant class that seemed to value only money. Once Winthrop stepped aboard the *Arbella*, he hoped, these conflicts would not be a part of his American future.

Yet his Puritan religion told Winthrop that human beings are fallen creatures and that perfection, whether communal or individual, is unachievable on this earth. Therefore, he faced a paradox: On the one hand, his religion demanded that he attempt to live a perfect life in an imperfect world. On the other hand, it told him that he was destined to fail.

Soon after Winthrop disembarked from the *Arbella*, he came face-to-face with this maddening dilemma. He found himself presiding not over a utopia but over a colony caught up in disputes as troubling as any he had confronted in his English past. John Winthrop, it seems, was not the only Puritan with a dream of a heaven on earth. But others in the community saw the dream differently. They wanted greater political and religious freedom than their leader was prepared to grant. Often, Winthrop was able to handle this conflict diplomatically. For example, he expanded, participation in elections and allowed the voters of Massachusetts Bay greater power.

But religious conflict was another matter because it was grounded in competing visions of the Puritan utopia. In Roger Williams and Anne Hutchinson, two of his fellow colonists, John Winthrop faced rivals unprepared to accept his definition of the perfect community. To Williams, perfection demanded that he separate himself from the Puritan institutions in his community and create an even "purer" church. Winthrop, however, disagreed and exiled Williams to Rhode Island. Hutchinson presumed that she could interpret God's will without a minister. Again, Winthrop did not agree. Hutchinson was tried on charges of heresy, convicted, and banished from Massachusetts.

John Winthrop's Massachusetts colony was the first but far from the last American attempt to build a unified, peaceful community that, in the end, only provoked a discord. This glimpse at its history reveals what Winthrop confronted: the unavoidable presence of conflict in American life.

American Assumptions

From America's origins in the early seventeenth century, Americans have often held several interrelated assumptions about their country. First, people believe that to be American is to be free. Second, because Americans did not have to free themselves from feudal lords or an entrenched aristocracy, America has been seen as a perpetual haven from the troubles and disputes that are found in the Old World.

John Winthrop lived his life as though these assumptions were true. But the opposing viewpoints presented in the American History Series should reveal that for many Americans, these assumptions were and are myths. Indeed, for numerous Americans, liberty has not always been guaranteed, and disputes have been an integral, sometimes welcome part of their life.

The American landscape has been torn apart again and again by a great variety of clashes—theological, ideological, political, economic, geographical, and social. But such a landscape is not necessarily a hopelessly divided country. If the editors hope to prove anything during the course of this series, it is not that the United States has been destroyed by conflict but rather that it has been enlivened, enriched, and even strengthened by Americans who have disagreed with one another.

Thomas Jefferson was one of the least confrontational of Americans, but he boldly and irrevocably enriched American life with his individualistic views. Like John Winthrop before him, he had a notion of an American Eden. Like Winthrop, he offered a vision of a harmonious society. And like Winthrop, he not only became enmeshed in conflict but eventually presided over a people beset by it. But unlike Winthrop, Jefferson believed this Eden was not located in a specific community but in each individual American. His Declaration of Independence from Great Britain could also be read as a declaration of independence for each individual in American society.

Jefferson's Ideal

Jefferson's ideal world was composed of "yeoman farmers," each of whom was roughly equal to the others in society's eyes, each of whom was free from the restrictions of both government and fellow citizens. Throughout his life, Jefferson offered a continuing challenge to Americans: Advance individualism and equality or see the death of the American experiment. Jefferson believed that the strength of this experiment depended upon a society of autonomous individuals and a society without great gaps between rich and poor. His challenge to his fellow Americans to create—and sustain—such a society has itself produced both economic and political conflict.

A society whose guiding document is the Declaration of Independence is a society assured of the freedom to dream—and to disagree. We know that Jefferson hated conflict, both personal and political. His tendency was to avoid confrontations of any sort, to squirrel himself away and write rather than to stand up and speak his mind. It is only through his written words that we can grasp Jefferson's utopian dream of a society of independent farmers, all pursuing their private dreams and all leading lives of middling prosperity.

Jefferson, this man of wealth and intellect, lived an essentially happy private life. But his public life was much more troublesome. From the first rumblings of the American Revolution in the 1760s to the North-South skirmishes of the 1820s that ultimately produced the Civil War, Jefferson was at or near the center of American political history. The issues were almost too many—and too crucial—for one lifetime: Jefferson had to choose between sup-

11

porting or rejecting the path of revolution. During and after the ensuing war, he was at the forefront of the battle for religious liberty. After endorsing the Constitution, he opposed the economic plans of Alexander Hamilton. At the end of the century, he fought the infamous Alien and Sedition Acts, which limited civil liberties. As president, he opposed the Federalist court, conspiracies to divide the union, and calls for a new war against England. Throughout his life, Thomas Jefferson, slaveholder, pondered the conflict between American freedom and American slavery. And from retirement at his Monticello retreat, he frowned at the rising spirit of commercialism he feared was dividing Americans and destroying his dream of American harmony.

No matter the issue, however, Thomas Jefferson invariably supported the rights of the individual. Worried as he was about the excesses of commercialism, he accepted them because his main concern was to live in a society where liberty and individualism could flourish. To Jefferson, Americans had to be free to worship as they desired. They also deserved to be free from an over-reaching government. To Jefferson, Americans should also be free to possess slaves.

Harmony, an Elusive Goal

Before reading the articles in this anthology, the editors ask readers to ponder the lives of John Winthrop and Thomas Jefferson. Each held a utopian vision, one based upon the demands of community and the other on the autonomy of the individual. Each dreamed of a country of perpetual new beginnings. Each found himself thrust into a position of leadership and found that conflict could not be avoided. Harmony, whether communal or individual, was a forever elusive goal.

The opposing visions of Winthrop and Jefferson have been at the heart of many differences among Americans from many backgrounds through the whole of American history. Moreover, their visions have provoked important responses that have helped shape American society, the American character, and many an American battle.

The editors of the American History Series have done extensive research to find representative opinions on the issues included in these volumes. They have found numerous outstanding opposing viewpoints from people of all times, classes, and genders in American history. From those, they have selected commentaries that best fit the nature and flavor of the period and topic under consideration. Every attempt was made to include the most important and relevant viewpoints in each chapter. Obviously, not every notable viewpoint could be included. Therefore, a selective, annotated bibliography has been provided at the end of each book to aid readers in seeking additional information.

The editors are confident that as this series reveals past conflicts, it will help revitalize the reader's views of the American present. In that spirit, the American History Series is dedicated to the proposition that American history is more complicated, more fascinating, and more troubling than John Winthrop or Thomas Jefferson ever dared to imagine.

John C. Chalberg
Consulting Editor

Introduction

"One ever feels this twoness—an American, a Negro; two souls, two thoughts, two unreconciled strivings; two warring ideals in one dark body."

W.E.B. Du Bois, *The Souls of Black Folk*, 1903

Americans of African descent form the largest minority group in the United States. The 1990 U.S. census counted 29,986,060 Americans who defined themselves as "black"—about 12 percent of the total U.S. population. More than the size of their population, however, it is their history that makes African Americans distinct from other American ethnic groups.

The historical legacy that links African Americans together—despite the enormous economic and social diversity within this group—consists of several elements. These include the cultural heritage of Africa, the fact that slavery—not voluntary immigration—brought most Africans to America, and the reality that for most of American history African Americans have been viewed and treated as being racially inferior.

Because of their past, sociologist Bob Blauner argues, African Americans have the unusual and ambiguous position of being *both* a race and an ethnic group—that is, they are defined both by shared physical characteristics and by their shared ethnic and cultural heritage. Thus, questions of racial, ethnic, and national identity have been perennially important ones for African Americans. Because of the color of their skin, most African Americans have not had the option of voluntarily shedding their ethnic identity by changing their name from Gatz to Gatsby, Danielovitch to Daniels. (However, unknown numbers of light-skinned African Americans have "passed" for white, attaining rights and privileges denied to blacks, but at the cost of abandoning their families and, some would argue, of losing their identity.) African Americans' struggle to define their identity is revealed by the fact that "colored," "African," "Afro-American," "Negro," "black," and "African American," among other labels, have all been favored (and condemned) at different times.

Underlying the debate over names (and the "passing" phenomenon) is a deeper question: Can African Americans be "true"

Americans? Noted black intellectual and activist W.E.B. Du Bois wrote in 1897:

> No Negro who has given earnest thought to the situation of his people in America has failed . . . to ask himself at some time: What, after all, am I? Am I an American or am I a Negro? Can I be both?

These were questions debated not only by African Americans themselves but also by white Americans throughout the course of American history, many of whom have equated "American" with "white." In *The Federalist Papers*, John Jay wrote of the United States that "providence has been pleased to give this one connected country, to one united people, a people descended from the same ancestors"—an assertion that seemingly excludes descendants of Africa. Blacks, whether enslaved or free, have appeared to many a troublesome exception to the American "melting pot" of different ethnic groups.

The African Heritage

The ancestors of today's African Americans came from all parts of Africa; most, however, were West Africans from an area ranging from the Senegal River to the southern tip of present-day Angola. In the 1400s, when European exploration of Africa began with the Portuguese, this area of Africa was populated by a wide variety of tribes (Guinean, Ibo, Yoruba, and others) and societies, including powerful kingdoms such as Benin and the Songhai Empire. In many areas, West Africans had developed prosperous agricultural civilizations that included centralized governments, universities, and skilled crafts such as metalworking. Much of the richness of West African culture was unknown to or ignored by European explorers and slave traders, most of whom believed that Africans were uncivilized "savages."

The extent to which African culture has influenced African Americans past and present continues to be debated by historians. Obviously, one of the effects of the slave trade was severe culture shock and dislocation, as people were forcibly taken from their communities and kinship groups and brought to a new land, made to learn a new language and adjust to a life of slavery. The preservation of African culture was complicated by the diverse languages and cultures of Africans who were taken as slaves. Some historians and sociologists, such as E. Franklin Frazier and Robert E. Park, have argued that, due to these factors, the impact of African cultural heritage on African-American life has been minimal. Others, including anthropologist Melville J. Herskovits and social historian John Blassingame, have concluded that African culture has had significant influence on African-American (and American) life.

Slavery

At the time of Portuguese exploration in the 1400s, many African societies practiced some form of slavery. Typically war captives, slaves performed domestic service and were often absorbed into the extended family system. In some cases they could work to attain their freedom. In many respects African slavery was similar to that practiced in other societies throughout the world.

A different form of slavery was developed by Portugal and Spain in the 1500s. Black Africans were enslaved in great numbers not as household servants but as laborers for sugar plantations in colonies in the New World. By the end of the seventeenth century other European countries had joined in the lucrative slave trade. Europeans generally did not capture these slaves but purchased them from coastal African merchants and chiefs, who captured the slaves in Africa's interior.

Relatively few blacks lived in the American colonies before 1700. At that time most of the colonies had begun enacting laws establishing lifetime hereditary slavery for blacks. From 1700 until the American Revolution, large numbers of Africans were imported. Of the estimated ten million Africans brought to the New World in the three centuries following Christopher Columbus's 1492 voyage, between three and six hundred thousand were taken to what is now the United States. It is this group that became the ancestors of most of today's African Americans. (Some African Americans are descended from immigrants from Jamaica and other West Indian islands whose African ancestors came to the islands as slaves. There is also a growing population of recent immigrants from Africa and their descendants.)

When the thirteen British colonies declared independence from Great Britain in 1776, one-fifth of their population consisted of blacks, most of whom were held under a system of chattel slavery. Slave marriages were not recognized by law and slaveowners had virtually unlimited authority over their property. Stringent slave codes were developed by colonies in response to slave rebellions and runaways. The result was a social and legal system that divided the American population by race. Historian Winthrop D. Jordan writes in *White over Black:*

> Slaves were forbidden to wander off their plantation without a "ticket" from their master or overseer. They were never to be allowed to congregate in large numbers, carry clubs or arms, or strike a white person. . . . All white persons were authorized to apprehend any Negro unable to give a satisfactory account of himself.

Slavery remained the central aspect of African-American history until the Civil War. Blacks came to this country not as potential

American citizens but as alien laborers; their legal and social status would continue to be affected by their race up to and beyond the abolition of slavery in 1865.

The Racial Divide

Slavery was abolished in the United States following decades of a national debate over slavery that culminated in the Civil War—a conflict in which blacks played prominent roles as abolitionists, escaped slaves, and soldiers. In 1868, the Fourteenth Amendment to the Constitution, reversing previous Supreme Court pronouncements, officially established blacks as U.S. citizens. However, the racial divide between white and black remained. Many Americans shared the opinions expressed by the *New York Times* on September 3, 1865: The freed slaves were "degraded negroes" who threatened the viability of America's government and society. The effort slaves and free blacks had waged to resist and/or escape from slavery was replaced by a struggle for equal rights and freedom in the face of racial repression.

During the century following the Civil War, African Americans were subject to laws and customs restricting their economic and political power and their social contact with whites. Racial repression reached its extreme form in the South around the turn of the century. There states established a thorough system of racial segregation (called "Jim Crow") that separated blacks from whites in courts, parks, trains, and other public places. Black children were educated in segregated schools with inferior funding and facilities. African Americans were prevented from voting, depriving them of political influence. The economic aspirations of many blacks were thwarted by laws and discriminatory practices preventing them from owning businesses, entering the professions, or joining labor unions. Violence was an integral part of this system of racial repression: Black Americans were kept constantly aware that they might become victims of lynchings or white mob attacks on black communities.

Such conditions also existed, to a less systematic degree, outside the South, and they persisted through much of the twentieth century. In northern states, residential discrimination kept blacks confined to ghettos, while workplace discrimination kept them in unskilled jobs and domestic work. Among the clearest examples of official racial prejudice were the laws many states passed banning interracial marriage (the Supreme Court finally overturned such laws in 1967).

These laws and customs were based on certain stereotypical views of the black "character"—views that many whites shared. Writer Wallace Stegner, in this passage written in 1945, provides a good summary of these beliefs, as well as an antiracist refutation:

In spite of Negro achievements in many fields, it is a common faith that there is a definable Negro "character." The Negro, according to this folk belief, is a child, with a child's emotional equipment, dependence, and lack of judgment. Like a child, he has to be watched on every job. He can't do really skilled work. He never thinks beyond the moment—give him a dollar and he'll chuck everything to go blow it. He lacks moral sense, is loose in his sex life, quick to anger and violence, and so on.

Such generalizations, of course, are absurd. There is no such thing as the abstract "Negro" any more than there is such a thing as the abstract "white." No tests have ever proved that one race is lower than another, or that any race does not contain about the same quota of fools and freaks and criminals and geniuses and ordinary mortals as any other race.

Black Nationalism vs. Assimilation

African Americans have responded in various ways to white racism, to their status as second-class citizens, and to W.E.B. Du Bois's question of whether they could become true Americans. Two general views can be categorized: black nationalism and assimilation. These differing schools of thought, which can be seen throughout most of African-American history, are exemplified in the following two extracts, both written during the Civil War. Black abolitionist Frederick Douglass asserted in 1863:

> The question is: Can the white and colored people of this country be blended into a common nationality, and enjoy together, in the same country, under the same flag, the inestimable blessings of life, liberty, and the pursuit of happiness, neighborly citizens of a common country? I answer most unhesitatingly, I believe they can.

In contrast to Douglass's confidence in a common nationality, missionary and educator Edward W. Blyden argued in 1862 that blacks needed to form their own nation:

> We shall never receive the respect of other races until we establish a powerful nationality. We should not content ourselves with living among other races, simply by their permission or their endurance, as Africans live in this country [the United States]. We must build up Negro states. . . . The heart of every true Negro yearns after a distinct and separate nationality.

Such drastically different visions of blacks as American citizens are evident in the debates over whether blacks should emigrate from the United States to Africa or Central America, in the bitter controversies surrounding black nationalist leader Marcus Garvey during the 1920s, and in the contrasting visions expressed in the 1960s by Martin Luther King Jr. and Malcolm X. These divisions can also be seen within the life of one man—Du Bois, who agitated for first-class citizenship for African Americans for many years before renouncing his U.S. citizenship and moving to Ghana toward the end of his life.

Part of American History

In the end, it seems, Du Bois answered his question of whether it was possible to be both black and American in the negative. Whether he was ultimately correct or not remains, for many, an open question. Yet Du Bois was also the person who wrote that African Americans "have woven ourselves into the very warp and woof of this nation" and that "there are no truer exponents of the pure human spirit of the Declaration of Independence than the American Negroes." The viewpoints in this volume present a sampling of the debates concerning this racial and ethnic group that, in the words of black historian Lerone Bennett, has "helped make America what it was and what it is."

CHAPTER 1

A Founding Father's Views on Race

Chapter Preface

In the Declaration of Independence, the Second Continental Congress justified its decision to form a new nation by revolution on the grounds that "all men are created equal" and are endowed with the rights of "life, liberty, and the pursuit of happiness"—rights that Great Britain was violating, according to the Congress.

Many in America's enslaved black population believed that these words applied to them as well. As early as 1777, black slaves in Massachusetts were petitioning the state legislature for their freedom, expressing "astonishment that it has never been considered that every principle from which America has acted in the course of their unhappy difficulties with Great Britain pleads stronger than a thousand arguments in favor of your petitioners." Blacks who were active in the abolitionist movement in the nineteenth century cited the Declaration of Independence in arguing that slavery and racial discrimination were inconsistent with America's founding principles. A black convention in New York in 1831 expressed the sentiment of many African Americans when it declared that "the time will come when the Declaration of Independence will be felt in the heart, as well as uttered from the mouth, and when the rights of all shall be properly acknowledged and appreciated."

The questions raised by these black abolitionists are debated to this day. Why, in fighting the British on grounds of freedom, did Americans continue to enslave the black population? Why did the U.S. Constitution, created in 1787 to institute a national government that would "secure the blessings of liberty," sanction and protect slavery in states that wanted it? Some answers can be found by examining the views of Thomas Jefferson, the author of the Declaration of Independence. The noted advocate of liberty, who became the nation's third president, was also an owner of slaves. This contradiction between Jefferson's ideas and actions reflected the paradoxical beliefs and realities of the nation as a whole.

From the beginning of his public career Jefferson was an opponent of slavery. In 1769, his first act after being elected to Virginia's House of Burgesses was to introduce a measure for the gradual emancipation of slaves. In 1774, in his first printed work, *A Summary of the Rights of British Americans*, he asserted that the abolition of slavery was greatly desired in the colonies. In his

21

1821 autobiography, Jefferson wrote of slaves, "Nothing is more certainly written in the book of fate, than that these people are to be free."

Yet Jefferson owned slaves; and unlike some noted slaveowners (such as George Washington), he did not free them during his lifetime or in his will. Furthermore, in his writings Jefferson expressed doubts about whether African slaves could ever become American citizens and share the same land and rights with white Americans. Blacks, Jefferson believed, had "odious peculiarities" resulting either from biological inferiority or from the degradation wrought by slavery. Consequently, Jefferson advocated the abolition of slavery, followed by the removal of blacks from the United States. Immediately following the passage from his autobiography quoted above, Jefferson wrote:

> [It is no] less certain that the two races, equally free, cannot live in the same government. Nature, habit, opinion have drawn indelible lines of distinction between them. It is still in our power to direct the process of emancipation and deportation, peaceably, and in slow degree, so that the evil will wear off insensibly.

The following chapter presents one of Jefferson's extended writings on race and equality. In response, Benjamin Banneker, one of the young nation's most famous African Americans, calls on Jefferson to fully embrace the principles of the Declaration of Independence.

VIEWPOINT 1

"I advance it . . . as a suspicion only, that the blacks . . . are inferior to the whites in the endowments both of body and mind."

Blacks Are Inferior to Whites

Thomas Jefferson (1743–1826)

Thomas Jefferson's famous words in the Declaration of Independence that "all men are created equal" and are endowed with the rights of "life, liberty, and the pursuit of happiness" have been frequently repeated by many African Americans in arguing for their own liberty and equality in the United States. Whether Jefferson meant for his words to apply to blacks as well as whites is questionable, as the following viewpoint indicates. Excerpted from a chapter of *Notes on the State of Virginia*, which was written by Jefferson beginning in 1781 and which was first published in English in 1787, the essay is one of Jefferson's few extended writings on race.

The excerpt begins with a description of how the Virginia legislature revised its laws during the American Revolution, when Jefferson was governor. Among the proposed revisions was a plan for the gradual emancipation of slaves and their subsequent removal from Virginia. In defending this emancipation scheme (which was never enacted), Jefferson describes what he believes to be fundamental differences between blacks and whites. He concludes that the two races could never coexist as equals in the new nation.

From Thomas Jefferson, *Notes on the State of Virginia* (London: n.p., 1787).

Many of the laws which were in force during the monarchy being relative merely to that form of government, or inculcating principles inconsistent with republicanism, the first assembly which met after the establishment of the commonwealth appointed a committee to revise the whole code, to reduce it into proper form and volume, and report it to the assembly. This work has been executed by three gentlemen, and reported; but probably will not be taken up till a restoration of peace shall leave to the legislature leisure to go through such a work. . . .

Emancipation and Colonization

[It was proposed] to emancipate all slaves born after the passing the act. The bill reported by the revisers does not itself contain this proposition; but an amendment containing it was prepared, to be offered to the legislature whenever the bill should be taken up, and farther directing, that they should continue with their parents to a certain age, then to be brought up, at the public expense, to tillage, arts, or sciences, according to their geniuses, till the females should be eighteen, and the males twenty-one years of age, when they should be colonized to such place as the circumstances of the time should render most proper, sending them out with arms, implements of household and of the handicraft arts, seeds, pairs of the useful domestic animals, &c., to declare them a free and independent people, and extend to them our alliance and protection, till they have acquired strength; and to send vessels at the same time to other parts of the world for an equal number of white inhabitants; to induce them to migrate hither, proper encouragements were to be proposed. It will probably be asked, Why not retain and incorporate the blacks into the State, and thus save the expense of supplying by importation of white settlers, the vacancies they will leave? Deep-rooted prejudices entertained by the whites; ten thousand recollections, by the blacks, of the injuries they have sustained; new provocations; the real distinctions which nature has made; and many other circumstances, will divide us into parties, and produce convulsions, which will probably never end but in the extermination of the one or the other race. To these objections, which are political, may be added others, which are physical and moral. The first difference which strikes us is that of color. Whether the black of the negro resides in the reticular membrane between the skin and scarf-skin [outer layer], or in the scarf-skin itself; whether it proceeds from the color of the blood, the color of the bile, or from that of some other secretion, the difference is fixed in nature, and is as real as if its seat and cause were better known to us. And is this difference of no importance? Is it not the foundation of a greater or less share of beauty in the two races? Are not the fine mixtures of red and white, the expressions of every passion by greater or less suffusions of color in the one, preferable to that eternal monotony, which reigns in the countenances, that immovable veil of black which covers the emotions of the other race? Add to these, flowing hair, a more elegant symmetry of form, their own judgment in favor of the whites, declared by their preference of them, as uniformly as is the preference of the Oranootan [Orangutan] for the black woman over those of his own species. The circumstance of superior beauty, is thought worthy attention in the propagation of our horses, dogs, and other domestic animals; why not in that of man? Besides those of color, figure, and hair, there are other physical distinctions proving a difference of race. They have less hair on the face and body. They secrete less by the kidneys, and more by the glands of the skin, which gives them a very strong and disagreeable odor. This greater degree of transpiration, renders them more tolerant of heat, and less so of cold than the whites. Perhaps, too, a difference of structure in the pulminary apparatus, which a late ingenious experimentalist has discovered to be the principal regulator of animal heat, may have disabled them from extricating, in the act of inspiration, so much of that fluid from the outer air, or obliged them in expiration, to part with more of it. They seem to require less sleep. A black after hard labor through the day, will be induced by the slightest amusements to sit up till midnight, or later, though knowing he must be out with the first dawn of the morning. They are at least as brave, and more adventuresome. But this may perhaps proceed from a want of forethought, which prevents their seeing a danger till it be present. When present, they do not go through it with more coolness or steadiness than the whites. They are more ardent after their female; but love seems with them to be more an eager desire, than a tender delicate mixture of sentiment and sensation. Their griefs are transient. Those numberless afflictions, which render it doubtful whether heaven has given life to us in mercy or in wrath, are less felt, and sooner forgotten with them. In general, their existence appears to participate more of sensation than reflection. To this must be ascribed their disposition to sleep when abstracted from their diversions, and unemployed in labor. An animal whose body is at rest, and who does not reflect, must be disposed to sleep of course. Comparing them by their faculties of memory, reason, and imagination, it appears to me that in memory they are equal to the whites; in reason much inferior, as I think one could scarcely be found capable of tracing and comprehending the investigations of Euclid; and that in imagination they are dull, tasteless, and anomalous. It would be unfair to

25

follow them to Africa for this investigation. We will consider them here, on the same stage with the whites, and where the facts are not apochryphal on which a judgment is to be formed. It will be right to make great allowances for the difference of condition, of education, of conversation, of the sphere in which they move. Many millions of them have been brought to, and born in America. Most of them, indeed, have been confined to tillage, to their own homes, and their own society; yet many have been so situated, that they might have availed themselves of the conversation of their masters; many have been brought up to the handicraft arts, and from that circumstance have always been associated with the whites. Some have been liberally educated, and all have lived in countries where the arts and sciences are cultivated to a considerable degree, and all have had before their eyes samples of the best works from abroad. The Indians, with no advantages of this kind, will often carve figures on their pipes not destitute of design and merit. They will crayon out an animal, a plant, or a country, so as to prove the existence of a germ in their minds which only wants cultivation. They astonish you with strokes of the most sublime oratory; such as prove their reason and sentiment strong, their imagination glowing and elevated. But never yet could I find that a black had uttered a thought above the level of plain narration; never saw even an elementary trait of painting or sculpture. In music they are more generally gifted than the whites with accurate ears for tune and time, and they have been found capable of imagining a small catch. Whether they will be equal to the composition of a more extensive run of melody, or of complicated harmony, is yet to be proved. Misery is often the parent of the most affecting touches in poetry. Among the blacks is misery enough, God knows, but no poetry. Love is the peculiar œstrum of the poet. Their love is ardent, but it kindles the senses only, not the imagination. Religion, indeed, has produced a Phyllis Whately [Wheatley]; but it could not produce a poet. The compositions published under her name are below the dignity of criticism. The heroes of the Dunciad are to her, as Hercules to the author of that poem. Ignatius Sancho [a black English writer] has approached nearer to merit in composition; yet his letters do more honor to the heart than the head. They breathe the purest effusions of friendship and general philanthropy, and show how great a degree of the latter may be compounded with strong religious zeal. He is often happy in the turn of his compliments, and his style is easy and familiar, except when he affects a Shandean fabrication of words. But his imagination is wild and extravagant, escapes incessantly from every restraint of reason and taste, and, in the course of its vagaries, leaves a tract of thought as incoherent and eccentric, as is the course of a meteor through the sky. His

Lincoln on Racial Equality

Thomas Jefferson's view that blacks were inferior to whites was shared to some extent by many of America's famous leaders, including Abraham Lincoln. The following passage on racial equality is excerpted from an address delivered on September 18, 1858, when Lincoln was campaigning for the U.S. Senate.

While I was at the hotel to-day an elderly gentleman called upon me to know whether I was really in favor of producing a perfect equality between the negroes and white people. [Great laughter.] While I had not proposed to myself on this occasion to say much on that subject, yet as the question was asked me I thought I would occupy perhaps five minutes in saying something in regard to it. I will say then that I am not, nor ever have been in favor of bringing about in any way the social and political equality of the white and black races, [applause]—that I am not nor ever have been in favor of making voters or jurors of negroes, nor of qualifying them to hold office, nor to intermarry with white people; and I will say in addition to this that there is a physical difference between the white and black races which I believe will for ever forbid the two races living together on terms of social and political equality. And inasmuch as they cannot so live, while they do remain together there must be the position of superior and inferior, and I as much as any other man am in favor of having the superior position assigned to the white race.

subjects should often have led him to a process of sober reasoning; yet we find him always substituting sentiment for demonstration. Upon the whole, though we admit him to the first place among those of his own color who have presented themselves to the public judgment, yet when we compare him with the writers of the race among whom he lived and particularly with the epistolary class in which he has taken his own stand, we are compelled to enrol him at the bottom of the column. This criticism supposes the letters published under his name to be genuine, and to have received amendment from no other hand; points which would not be of easy investigation. The improvement of the blacks in body and mind, in the first instance of their mixture with the whites, has been observed by every one, and proves that their inferiority is not the effect merely of their condition of life. We know that among the Romans, about the Augustan age especially, the condition of their slaves was much more deplorable than that of the blacks on the continent of America. The two sexes were confined in separate apartments, because to raise a child cost the master more than to buy one. Cato, for a very restricted indulgence to his slaves in this particular, took from them a certain price. But in this country the slaves multiply as fast as the free inhabitants. Their situation and manners place the commerce between the two sexes almost without restraint. The same Cato, on a principle of economy, always sold his sick and superannuated slaves. He gives it as a standing precept to a master visiting his farm, to sell his old oxen, old wagons, old tools, old and diseased servants, and everything else become useless. . . .

The American slaves cannot enumerate this among the injuries and insults they receive. . . . We are told of a certain Vedius Pollio, who, in the presence of Augustus, would have given a slave as food to his fish, for having broken a glass. With the Romans, the regular method of taking the evidence of their slaves was under torture. Here it has been thought better never to resort to their evidence. When a master was murdered, all his slaves, in the same house, or within hearing, were condemned to death. Here punishment falls on the guilty only, and as precise proof is required against him as against a freeman. Yet notwithstanding these and other discouraging circumstances among the Romans, their slaves were often their rarest artists. They excelled too in science, insomuch as to be usually employed as tutors to their master's children. Epictetus, Terence, and Phædrus, were slaves. But they were of the race of whites. It is not their condition then, but nature, which has produced the distinction. Whether further observation will or will not verify the conjecture, that nature has been less bountiful to them in the endowments of the head, I believe that in those of the heart she will be found to have done them justice. That disposition to theft with which they have been branded, must be ascribed to their situation, and not to any depravity of the moral sense. The man in whose favor no laws of property exist, probably feels himself less bound to respect those made in favor of others. When arguing for ourselves, we lay it down as a fundamental, that laws, to be just, must give a reciprocation of right; that, without this, they are mere arbitrary rules of conduct, founded in force, and not in conscience; and it is a problem which I give to the master to solve, whether the religious precepts against the violation of property were not framed for him as well as his slave? And whether the slave may not as justifiably take a little from one who has taken all from him, as he may slay one who would slay him? . . .

Notwithstanding these considerations which must weaken their respect for the laws of property, we find among them numerous instances of the most rigid integrity, and as many as among their better instructed masters, of benevolence, gratitude, and unshaken fidelity. The opinion that they are inferior in the faculties of reason and imagination, must be hazarded with great diffidence. To justify a general conclusion, requires many observations, even where the subject may be submitted to the anatomical knife, to optical glasses, to analysis by fire or by solvents. How much more then where it is a faculty, not a substance, we are examining; where it eludes the research of all the senses; where the conditions of its existence are various and variously combined; where the effects of those which are present or absent bid defiance to calculation; let me add too, as a circumstance of great tenderness, where our conclusion would degrade a whole race of men from the rank in the scale of beings which their Creator may perhaps have given them. To our reproach it must be said, that though for a century and a half we have had under our eyes the races of black and of red men, they have never yet been viewed by us as subjects of natural history. I advance it, therefore, as a suspicion only, that the blacks, whether originally a distinct race, or made distinct by time and circumstances, are inferior to the whites in the endowments both of body and mind. It is not against experience to suppose that different species of the same genus, or varieties of the same species, may possess different qualifications. Will not a lover of natural history then, one who views the gradations in all the races of animals with the eye of philosophy, excuse an effort to keep those in the department of man as distinct as nature has formed them? This unfortunate difference of color, and perhaps of faculty, is a powerful obstacle to the emancipation of these people. Many of their advocates, while they wish to vindicate the liberty of human nature, are anxious also to preserve its dignity and beauty. Some of these, embarrassed by the question, "What further is to be done with them?" join themselves in opposition with those who are actuated by sordid avarice only. Among the Romans emancipation required but one effort. The slave, when made free, might mix with, without staining the blood of his master. But with us a second is necessary, unknown to history. When freed, he is to be removed beyond the reach of mixture.

*"One universal Father hath given being to us all; and
. . . afforded us all the same sensations and endowed us
all with the same faculties."*

Blacks Are Not
Inferior to Whites

Benjamin Banneker (1731–1806)

Benjamin Banneker was one of a vanguard of free African
Americans to gain national prominence following the American
Revolution. The child of free black parents and the inheritor of a
Maryland tobacco farm, Banneker taught himself astronomy and
surveying and became America's first noted black scientist. His
work surveying the boundaries for the District of Columbia in
1791 and his writing of an astronomical almanac were both hailed
by local abolitionist groups as testimony to the mental capabili-
ties of blacks—and a refutation of the racial views expressed by
Thomas Jefferson in his *Notes on the State of Virginia*.

Banneker presented a manuscript for his astronomical almanac
to Jefferson (then secretary of state) in 1791. The following viewpoint is taken from Banneker's accompanying letter to Jefferson,
in which he argues for the natural equality of the races and de-
cries the injustice of slavery. Banneker's letter and Jefferson's reply were published together as a pamphlet in 1792.

I am fully sensible of that freedom, which I take with you in
the present occasion; a liberty which seemed to me scarcely al-
lowable, when I reflected on that distinguished and dignified sta-

From Benjamin Banneker, *Letter from Benjamin Banneker to the Secretary of State* (Philadelphia,
n.p., 1792).

tion in which you stand, and the almost general prejudice and prepossession, which is so prevalent in the world against those of my complexion.

I suppose it is a truth too well attested to you, to need a proof here, that we are a race of beings, who have long labored under the abuse and censure of the world; that we have long been looked upon with an eye of contempt and that we have long been considered rather as brutish than human, and scarcely capable of mental endowments.

Sir, I hope I may safely admit, in consequence of that report which hath reached me, that you are a man less inflexible in sentiments of this nature, than many others; that you are measurably friendly, and well disposed towards us; and that you are willing and ready to lend your aid and assistance to our relief, from those many distresses, and numerous calamities, to which we are reduced.

Eradicate False Ideas

Now Sir, if this is founded in truth, I apprehend you will embrace every opportunity, to eradicate that train of absurd and false ideas and opinions, which so generally prevails with respect to us; and that your sentiments are concurrent with mine, which are, that one universal Father hath given being to us all; and that he hath not only made us all of one flesh, but that he hath also, without partiality, afforded us all the same sensations and endowed us all with the same faculties; and that however variable we may be in society or religion, however diversified in situation or color, we are all in the same family and stand in the same relation to him.

Sir, if these are sentiments of which you are fully persuaded, I hope you cannot but acknowledge, that it is the indispensable duty of those, who maintain for themselves the rights of human nature, and who possess the obligations of Christianity, to extend their power and influence to the relief of every part of the human race, from whatever burden or oppression they may unjustly labor under; and this, I apprehend, a full conviction of the truth and obligation of these principles should lead all to.

Sir, I have long been convinced, that if your love for yourselves, and for those inestimable laws, which preserved to you the rights of human nature, was founded on sincerity, you could not but be solicitous, that every individual, of whatever rank or distinction, might with you equally enjoy the blessings thereof; neither could you rest satisfied short of the most active effusion of your exertions, in order to the promotion from any state of degradation, to which the unjustifiable cruelty and barbarism of men may have reduced them.

Sir, I freely and cheerfully acknowledge, that I am of the African race, and in that color which is natural to them of the deepest dye; and it is under a sense of the most profound gratitude to the Supreme Ruler of the Universe, that I now confess to you, that I am not under that state of tyrannical thraldom, and inhuman captivity, to which too many of my brethren are doomed, but that I have abundantly tasted of the fruition of those blessings, which proceed from that free and unequalled liberty with which you are favored; and which, I hope, you will willingly allow you have mercifully received, from the immediate hand of that Being, from whom proceedeth every good and perfect Gift.

Jefferson's Reply

Thomas Jefferson's reply to Benjamin Banneker, dated August 30, 1791, is reprinted here.

I thank you, sincerely, for your letter of the 19th instant, and for the Almanac it contained. No body wishes more than I do, to see such proofs as you exhibit, that nature has given to our black brethren talents equal to those of the other colors of men; and that the appearance of the want of them, is owing merely to the degraded condition of their existence, both in Africa and America. I can add with truth, that no body wishes more ardently to see a good system commenced, for raising the condition, both of their body and mind, to what it ought to be, as far as the imbecility of their present existence, and other circumstances, which cannot be neglected, will admit.

I have taken the liberty of sending your Almanac to Monsieur de Condozett, Secretary of the Academy of Sciences at Paris, and Member of the Philanthropic Society, because I considered it as a document, to which your whole color had a right for their justification, against the doubts which have been entertained of them.

Sir, suffer me to recall to your mind that time, in which the arms and tyranny of the British crown were exerted, with every powerful effort, in order to reduce you to a state of servitude: look back, I entreat you, on the variety of dangers to which you were exposed; reflect on that time, in which every human aid appeared unavailable, and in which even hope and fortitude wore the aspect of inability to the conflict, and you cannot but be led to a serious and grateful sense of your miraculous and providential preservation; you cannot but acknowledge, that the present freedom and tranquility which you enjoy you have mercifully received, and that it is the peculiar blessing of Heaven.

This, Sir, was a time when you clearly saw into the injustice of a state of slavery, and in which you had just apprehensions of the horror of its condition. It was now that your abhorrence thereof was so excited, that you publicly held forth this true and invaluable doctrine, which is worthy to be recorded and remembered in all succeeding ages: 'We hold these truths to be self-evident, that all men are created equal; that they are endowed by their Creator with certain unalienable rights, and that among these are, life, liberty, and the pursuit of happiness.'

Here was a time, in which your tender feelings for yourselves had engaged you thus to declare, you were then impressed with proper ideas of the great violation of liberty, and the free possession of those blessings, to which you were entitled by nature; but, Sir, how pitiable is it to reflect, that although you were so fully convinced of the benevolence of the Father of Mankind, and of his equal and impartial distribution of these rights and privileges, which he hath conferred upon them, that you should at the same time counteract his mercies, in detaining by fraud and violence so numerous a part of my brethren, under groaning captivity, and cruel oppression, that you should at the same time be found guilty of that most criminal act, which you professedly detested in others, with respect to yourselves.

I suppose that your knowledge of the situation of my brethren, is too extensive to need a recital here; neither shall I presume to prescribe methods by which they may be relieved, otherwise than by recommending to you and all others, to wean yourselves from those narrow prejudices which you have imbibed with respect to them, and as Job proposed to his friends, 'put your soul in their souls' stead'; thus shall your hearts be enlarged with kindness and benevolence towards them; and thus shall you need neither the direction of myself or others, in what manner to proceed herein.

The Almanac

And now, Sir, although my sympathy and affection for my brethren hath caused my enlargement thus far, I ardently hope, that your candor and generosity will plead with you in my behalf, when I make known to you, that it was not originally my design; but having taken up my pen in order to direct to you, as a present, a copy of my Almanac, which I have calculated for the succeeding year, I was unexpectedly and unavoidably led thereto.

This calculation is the product of my arduous study, in this most advanced stage of life; for having long had unbounded desires to become acquainted with the secrets of nature, I have had to gratify my curiosity herein through my own assiduous application to Astronomical Study, in which I need not recount to you the many difficulties and disadvantages which I have had to encounter.

And although I had almost declined to make my calculation for the ensuing year, in consequence of that time which I had allotted therefor, being taken up at the Federal Territory, by the request of Mr. Andrew Ellicott, yet finding myself under several engagements to Printers of this State, to whom I had communicated my design, on my return to my place of residence, I industriously applied myself thereto, which I hope I have accomplished with correctness and accuracy; a copy of which I have taken the liberty to direct to you, and which I humbly request you will favorably receive; and although you may have the opportunity of perusing it after its publication; yet I choose to send it to you in manuscript previous thereto, that thereby you might not only have an earlier inspection, but that you might also view it in my own hand writing.

CHAPTER 2

Blacks in the Era of Slavery and Abolitionism

Chapter Preface

From 1619, when a Dutch ship brought twenty Africans to the Virginia settlement of Jamestown, until the Civil War, the history of blacks in America was almost synonymous with the history of slavery in America. The vast majority of blacks were held as slaves, while the minority of blacks who were free were greatly affected by the laws and customs that had developed around slavery. The viewpoints in this chapter date from the early and middle decades of the nineteenth century, a time when slavery had been almost entirely abolished in the northern states but was the very foundation of the South's plantation society and cotton-exporting economy. During this period America was in the throes of a growing national debate over the institution of slavery and the future of blacks in America—a debate that blacks, both free and slave, strongly influenced with their words and actions.

By 1830 the number of blacks in the United States had grown to approximately 2 million slaves and 300,000 free blacks, together constituting 18 percent of the U.S. population. Because the slave trade was outlawed by the federal government in 1808 (although slave smuggling would persist until the Civil War), by 1830 most African Americans were one or more generations removed from Africa.

The lives of blacks under slavery were depicted in various ways. Abolitionists such as former slave Peter Randolph decried slavery as a "system of robbery and cruel wrong, from beginning to end. It robs men and women of their liberty, lives, property, affections, and virtue." Defenders of slavery argued that black slaves fared better than the people remaining in Africa, who were "unblessed by the lights of civilization or Christianity," in the words of South Carolina governor George McDuffie. "Our slaves are cheerful, contented, and happy," he asserted in an 1835 speech, "except where those foreign intruders and fatal ministers of mischief, the emancipationists, . . . have tempted them to aspire above the condition to which they have been assigned in the order of Providence."

Regardless of the supposed contentedness of slaves, southern leaders found it necessary to pass numerous codes regulating slaves' behavior. Slaves were prohibited from owning weapons, receiving an education, meeting in groups, traveling without the permission of their masters, and testifying against white people in court. Many of these provisions were made to prevent slave insurrections, and they were tightened after the 1831 Nat Turner–led slave uprising in Virginia, in which sixty whites were killed.

Slaves demonstrated resistance to their oppressed condition in numerous ways, including open rebellion (of which the Nat Turner rebellion was the most extreme example). Some slaves feigned illness or otherwise resisted injunctions to work. Many ran away, in some cases temporarily to visit family members, in other cases permanently; by 1855 as many as 60,000 had fled north to freedom.

Free blacks in the United States prior to the Civil War faced different conditions. In the South the "slaves without masters" were often viewed as a threat to the region's social order. Required to carry certificates of freedom at all times, they were subject to many of the same harsh laws and limitations as were slaves. Free blacks could not move from place to place, did not stand as equals with whites in court, were required to observe nighttime curfews, and in some states were forced to report to white guardians.

Blacks in the North did not have to cope with most of the restrictive laws of the South (although they did face some racial barriers, including laws passed by some western states and territories restricting black immigration). They were able to form mutual aid societies and to hold political conventions. They also organized their own churches in response to continuing segregation and discrimination within established church denominations. *Freedom's Journal*, the first black newspaper, was started in New York City in 1827. Most free blacks remained mindful of the plight of slaves in the South. "The free people of Color, with few exceptions," observed British abolitionist John Scoble in 1853, "are true to their brethren in bond, and determined to remain by them whatever the cost." Free blacks played significant roles in the abolitionist movement. Escaped slaves, such as Frederick Douglass and Sojourner Truth, gained prominence as abolitionists by speaking and writing of their lives in bondage.

The concept of black emigration from the United States and colonization elsewhere found support from abolitionists, slavery defenders, free blacks, and slaves during these tumultuous years. The idea also found opposition from all these quarters. Some whites saw colonization as a way to rid the country of free blacks and strengthen the institution of slavery—an argument that many free blacks saw as reason to oppose colonization. However, some slaves and free blacks believed that leaving America was the only way to attain freedom and dignity for themselves. Emigration was one of many much-debated issues African Americans confronted prior to the momentous events of the Civil War.

"Strange, indeed, is the idea that [slavery] . . . should ever have found a place in . . . a country, the very soil of which is said to be consecrated to liberty."

Slavery Must Be Abolished in America

Nathaniel Paul (dates unknown)

On July 4, 1827, ten thousand slaves in the state of New York were freed as slavery was officially abolished (due to emancipation laws passed some years before). Many celebrations were held by blacks in honor of this event. The following viewpoint is taken from an address delivered by Nathaniel Paul at a commemorative gathering in Albany, New York, on July 5, 1827. Paul, a pioneering black Baptist minister, expounds on the evils of slavery, predicts its eventual complete abolition, and calls for freed blacks to educate themselves and to use their freedom wisely. The abolitionist movement, for which Paul lectured in the 1830s and 1840s, made use of many of his themes and arguments.

Through the long lapse of ages it has been common for nations to record whatever was peculiar or interesting in the course of their history. . . . And as the nations which have already passed away have been careful to select the most important events, peculiar to themselves, and have recorded them for the good of the people that should succeed them, so will we place it upon our history; and we will tell the good story to our children and to our children's children, down to the latest posterity, that on the

From Nathaniel Paul, *An Address Delivered on the Celebration of the Abolition of Slavery in the State of New York, July 5, 1827* (Albany: n.p., 1827).

Fourth Day of July, in the year of our Lord 1827, slavery was abolished in the state of New York.

Seldom, if ever, was there an occasion which required a public acknowledgment, or that deserved to be retained with gratitude of heart to the all-wise disposer of events, more than the present on which we have assembled. . . .

In contemplating the subject before us, in connection with the means by which so glorious an event has been accomplished, we find much which requires our deep humiliation and our most exalted praises. We are permitted to behold one of the most pernicious and abominable of all enterprises, in which the depravity of human nature ever led man to engage, entirely eradicated. The power of the tyrant is subdued, the heart of the oppressed is cheered, liberty is proclaimed to the captive, and the opening of the prison to those who were bound, and he who had long been the miserable victim of cruelty and degradation, is elevated to the common rank in which our benevolent Creator first designed that man should move,—all of which have been effected by means the most simple, yet perfectly efficient. Not by those fearful judgments of the almighty, which have so often fallen upon the different parts of the earth, which have overturned nations and kingdoms, scattered thrones and scepters, nor is the glory of the achievement tarnished with the horrors of the field of battle. We hear not the cries of the widow and the fatherless; nor are our hearts affected with the sight of garments rolled in blood; but all has been done by the diffusion and influence of the pure, yet powerful principles of benevolence, before which the pitiful impotency of tyranny and oppression is scattered and dispersed, like the chaff before the rage of the whirlwind.

The Injustice of Slavery

I will not, on this occasion, attempt fully to detail the abominable traffic to which we have already alluded. Slavery, with its concomitants and consequences, in the best attire in which it can possibly be presented, is but a hateful monster, the very demon of avarice and oppression, from its first introduction to the present time; it has been among all nations the scourge of heaven, and the curse of the earth. It is so contrary to the laws which the God of nature has laid down as the rule of action by which the conduct of man is to be regulated towards his fellow man, which binds him to love his neighbor as himself, that it ever has, and ever will meet the decided disapprobation of heaven.

In whatever form we behold it, its visage is satanic, its origin the very offspring of hell, and in all cases its effects are grievous.

On the shores of Africa, the horror of the scene commences; here, the merciless tyrant, divested of everything human except the form, begins the action. The laws of God and the tears of the oppressed are alike disregarded; and with more than savage barbarity, husbands and wives, parents and children are parted to meet no more: and, if not doomed to an untimely death, while on the passage, yet are they for life consigned to a captivity still more terrible; a captivity, at the very thought of which, every heart, not already biassed with unhallowed prejudices, or callous to every tender impression, pauses and revolts; exposed to the caprice of those whose tender mercies are cruel; unprotected by the laws of the land, and doomed to drag out miserable existence, without the remotest shadow of a hope of deliverance, until the king of terrors shall have executed his office, and consigned them to the kinder slumbers of death. But its pernicious tendency may be traced still farther: not only are its effects of the most disastrous character, in relation to the slave, but it extends its influence to the slaveholder; and in many instances it is hard to say which is most wretched, the slave or the master.

By 1860 approximately four million slaves resided in the United States. This photograph of slave farmers was taken in 1862 in South Carolina.

After the fall of man, it would seem that God, foreseeing that pride and arrogance would be the necessary consequences of the apostacy, and that man would seek to usurp undue authority over his fellow, wisely ordained that he should obtain his bread by the sweat of his brow; but contrary to this sacred mandate of heaven, slavery has been introduced, supporting the one in all the absurd luxuries of life, at the expense of the liberty and independence of the other. Point me to any section of the earth where slavery, to any considerable extent exists, and I will point you to a people whose morals are corrupted; and when pride, vanity and profusion are permitted to range unrestrained in all their desolating effects, and thereby idleness and luxury are promoted, under the influence of which, man, becoming insensible of his duty to his God and his fellow creature; and indulging in all the pride and vanity of his own heart, says to his soul, thou hast much goods laid up for many years. But while thus sporting, can it be done with impunity? Has conscience ceased to be active? Are there no forebodings of a future day of punishment, and of meeting the merited avenger? Can he retire after the business of the day and repose in safety? Let the guards around his mansions, the barred doors of his sleeping room, and the loaded instruments of death beneath his pillow, answer the question. . . .

Thus have we hinted at some of the miseries connected with slavery. And while I turn my thoughts back and survey what is past, I see our forefathers seized by the hand of the rude ruffian, and torn from their native homes and all that they held dear or sacred. I follow them down the lonesome way, until I see each safely placed on board the gloomy slave ship; I hear the passive groan, and the clanking of the chains which bind them. I see the tears which follow each other in quick succession adown the dusky cheek.

I view them casting the last and longing look towards the land which gave them birth, until at length the ponderous anchor is weighed, and the canvas spread to catch the favored breeze; I view them wafted onward until they arrive at the destined port; I behold those who have been so unfortunate as to survive the passage, emerging from their loathsome prison, and landing amidst the noisy rattling of the massy fetters which confine them; I see the crowd of traffickers in human flesh gathering, each anxious to seize the favored opportunity of enriching himself with their toils, their tears and their blood. I view them doomed to the most abject state of degraded misery, and exposed to suffer all that unrestrained tyranny can inflict, or that human nature is capable of sustaining.

Tell me, ye mighty waters, why did ye sustain the ponderous load of misery? Or speak, ye winds, and say why it was that ye executed your office to waft them onward to the still more dismal state; and ye proud waves, why did you refuse to lend your aid and to have overwhelmed them with your billows? Then should they have slept sweetly in the bosom of the great deep, and so have been hid from sorrow. And, oh thou immaculate God, be not angry with us, while we come into this thy sanctuary, and make the bold inquiry in this thy holy temple, why it was that thou didst look on with the calm indifference of an unconcerned spectator when thy holy law was violated, thy divine authority despised and a portion of thine own creatures reduced to a state of mere vassalage and misery? Hark! while he answers from on high: hear Him proclaiming from the skies—Be still, and know that I am God! Clouds and darkness are round about me; yet righteousness and judgment are the habitation of my throne. I do my will and pleasure in the heavens above, and in the earth beneath; it is my sovereign prerogative to bring good out of evil, and cause the wrath of man to praise me, and the remainder of that wrath I will restrain.

Slavery in the United States

Strange, indeed, is the idea that such a system, fraught with such consummate wickedness, should ever have found a place in this the otherwise happiest of all countries—a country, the very soil of which is said to be consecrated to liberty, and its fruits the equal rights of man. But strange as the idea may seem, or paradoxical as it may appear to those acquainted with the constitution of the government, or who have read the bold declaration of this nation's independence; yet it is a fact that can neither be denied or controverted, that in the United States of America, at the expiration of fifty years after its becoming a free and independent nation, there are no less than fifteen hundred thousand human beings still in a state of unconditional vassalage.

Yet America is first in the profession of the love of liberty, and loudest in proclaiming liberal sentiments towards all other nations, and feels herself insulted, to be branded with anything bearing the appearance of tyranny or oppression. Such are the palpable inconsistencies that abound among us and such is the medley of contradictions which stain the national character, and renders the American republic a byword, even among despotic nations. But while we pause and wonder at the contradictory sentiments held forth by the nation, and contrast its profession and practice, we are happy to have it in our power to render an apology for the existence of the evil, and to offer an excuse for the framers of the constitution. It was before the sons of Columbia felt the yoke of their oppressors, and rose in their strength to put it off that this land became contaminated with slavery. Had this not been the case, led by the spirit of pure republicanism that then possessed the souls of those patriots who were struggling for liberty, this soil would have been sufficiently guarded against its intrusion, and the people of these United States to this day

42

would have been strangers to so great a curse. It was by the permission of the British parliament that the human species first became an article of merchandise among them, and as they were accessory to its introduction, it well becomes them to be first, as a nation, in arresting its progress and effecting its expulsion. It was the immortal [Thomas] Clarkson, a name that will be associated with all that is sublime in mercy, until the final consummation of all things, who first looking abroad, beheld the sufferings of Africa, and looking at home, he saw his country stained with her blood. He threw aside the vestments of the priesthood, and consecrated himself to the holy purpose of rescuing a continent from rapine and murder, and of erasing this one sin from the book of his nation's iniquities. Many were the difficulties to be encountered, many were the hardships to be endured, many were the persecutions to be met with; formidable, indeed, was the opposing party. . . . But the cause of justice and humanity were not to be deserted by him and his fellow philanthropists on account of difficulties. We have seen them for twenty years persevering against all opposition and surmounting every obstacle they found in their way. Nor did they relax aught of their exertions until the criers of the oppressed having roused the sensibility of the nation, the island empress rose in her strength and said to this foul traffic, "Thus far thou hast gone, but thou shalt go no farther." Happy for us, my brethren, that the principles of benevolence were not exclusively confined to the isle of Great Britain. There have lived, and there still do live, men in this country who are patriots and philanthropists, not merely in name, but in heart and practice; men whose compassions have long since led them to pity the poor and despised sons of Africa. They have heard their groans, and have seen their blood, and have looked with an holy indignation upon the oppressor; nor was there anything except the power to have crushed the tyrant and liberated the captive. Through their instrumentality, the blessings of freedom have long since been enjoyed by all classes of people throughout New England, and through their influence, under the Almighty, we are enabled to recognize the fourth day of the present month as the day in which the cause of justice and humanity have triumphed over tyranny and oppression, and slavery is forever banished from the State of New York. . . .

From what has already taken place, we look forward with pleasing anticipation to that period when it shall no longer be said that in a land of freemen there are men in bondage, but when this foul stain will be entirely erased and this worst of evils will be forever done away. The progress of emancipation, though slow, is nevertheless certain. It is certain, because that God who has made of one blood all nations of men, and who is said to be no respecter of persons, has so decreed; I therefore have no hesitation in declaring from this sacred place that not only throughout the United States of America, but throughout every part of the habitable world where slavery exists, it will be abolished. However great may be the opposition of those who are supported by the traffic, yet slavery will cease. The lordly planter who has his thousands in bondage may stretch himself upon his couch of ivory and sneer at the exertions which are made by the humane and benevolent, or he may take his stand upon the floor of Congress and mock the pitiful generosity of the East or West for daring to meddle with the subject and attempting to expose its injustice; he may threaten to resist all efforts for a general or a partial emancipation even to a dissolution of the Union. But still I declare that slavery will be extinct; a universal and not a partial emancipation must take place; nor is the period far distant. The indefatigable exertions of the philanthropists in England to have it abolished in their West India Islands, the recent revolutions in South America, the catastrophe and exchange of power in the Isle of Hayti, the restless disposition of both master and slave in the Southern States, the Constitution of our government, the effects of literary and moral instruction, the generous feelings of the pious and benevolent, the influence and spread of the holy religion of the cross of Christ, and the irrevocable decrees of Almighty

Frederick Douglass on Slavery and the Fourth of July

A quarter century after Nathaniel Paul's 1827 oration, Frederick Douglass, an escaped slave who became a leading abolitionist activist and speaker, attacks American hypocrisy while delivering an address at Rochester, New York, on July 4, 1852.

What, to the American slave, is your 4th of July? I answer; a day that reveals to him, more than all other days in the year, the gross injustice and cruelty to which he is the constant victim. To him, your celebration is a sham; your boasted liberty, an unholy license; your national greatness, swelling vanity; your sounds of rejoicing are empty and heartless; your denunciation of tyrants, brass fronted impudence; your shouts of liberty and equality, hollow mockery; your prayers and hymns, your sermons and thanksgivings, with all your religious parade and solemnity, are, to Him, mere bombast, fraud, deception, impiety, and hypocrisy—a thin veil to cover up crimes which would disgrace a nation of savages. There is not a nation on the earth guilty of practices more shocking and bloody than are the people of the United States, at this very hour.

God, all combine their efforts, and with united voice declare that the power of tyranny must be subdued, the captive must be liberated, the oppressed go free, and slavery must revert back to its original chaos of darkness, and be forever annihilated from the earth. Did I believe that it would always continue, and that man to the end of time would be permitted with impunity to usurp the same undue authority over his fellow, I would disallow any allegiance or obligation I was under to my fellow creatures, or any submission that I owed to the laws of my country; I would deny the superintending power of divine Providence in the affairs of this life; I would ridicule the religion of the Savior of the world, and treat as the worst of men the ministers of the everlasting gospel; I would consider my Bible as a book of false and delusive fables, and commit it to the flames; nay, I would still go farther; I would at once confess myself an atheist, and deny the existence of a holy God.

But slavery will cease, and the equal rights of man will be universally acknowledged. Nor is its tardy progress any argument against its final accomplishment. But do I hear it loudly responded—this is but a mere wild fanaticism, or at best but the misguided conjecture of an untutored descendant of Africa. Be it so. I confess my ignorance, and bow with due deference to my superiors in understanding; but if in this case I err, the error is not peculiar to myself; if I wander, I wander in a region of light from whose political hemisphere the sun of liberty pours forth his refulgent rays, around which dazzle the starlike countenances of Clarkson, . . . [George] Washington, [John] Adams, [Thomas] Jefferson, [John] Hancock and [Benjamin] Franklin; if I err, it is their sentiments that have caused me to stray. For these are the doctrines which they taught while with us; nor can we reasonably expect that since they have entered the unbounded space of eternity, and have learned more familiarly the perfections of that God who governs all things that their sentiments have altered. Could they now come forth among us, they would tell that what they have learned in the world of spirits has served only to confirm what they taught while here; they would tell us that all things are rolling on according to the sovereign appointment of the eternal Jehovah, who will overturn and overturn until he whose right it is to reign shall come and the period will be ushered in; when the inhabitants of the earth will learn by experience what they are now slow to believe—that our God is a God of justice and no respecter of persons. But while, on the one hand, we look back and rejoice at what has already taken place, and, on the other, we look forward with pleasure to that period when men will be respected according to their characters, and not according to their complexion, and when their vices alone will render them contemptible;

while we rejoice at the thought of this land's becoming a land of freemen, we pause, we reflect. What, we would ask, is liberty without virtue? It tends to lasciviousness; and what is freedom but a curse, and even destruction, to the profligate? Not more desolating in its effects is the mountain torrent, breaking from its lofty confines and rushing with vast impetuosity upon the plains beneath, marring as it advances all that is lovely in the works of nature and of art, than the votaries of vice and immorality, when permitted to range unrestrained. Brethren, we have been called into liberty; only let us use that liberty as not abusing it. This day commences a new era in our history; new scenes, new prospects open before us, and it follows as a necessary consequence that new duties devolve upon us; duties, which if properly attended to, cannot fail to improve our moral condition and elevate us to a rank of respectable standing with the community; or if neglected, we fall at once into the abyss of contemptible wretchedness. . . . We do well to remember, that every act of ours is more or less connected with the general cause of the people of color, and with the general cause of emancipation. Our conduct has an important bearing, not only on those who are yet in bondage in this country, but its influence is extended to the isles of India, and to every part of the world where the abomination of slavery is known. Let us then relieve ourselves from the odious stigma which some have long since cast upon us, that we were incapacitated by the God of nature for the enjoyment of the rights of freemen, and convince them and the world that although our complexion may differ, yet we have hearts susceptible of feeling, judgment capable of discerning, and prudence sufficient to manage our affairs with discretion, and by example prove ourselves worthy the blessings we enjoy. . . .

A Call to Action

There remains much to be done, and there is much to encourage us to action. The foundation for literary, moral and religious improvement, we trust, is already laid in the formation of the public and private schools for the instruction of our children, together with the churches of different denominations already established. From these institutions we are encouraged to expect the happiest results; and while many of us are passing down the declivity of life, and fast hastening to the grave, how animating the thought that the rising generation is advancing under more favorable auspices than we were permitted to enjoy, soon to fill the places we now occupy; and in relation to them vast is the responsibility that rests upon us; much of their future usefulness depends upon the discharge of the duties we owe them. They are advancing, not to fill the place of slaves, but of freemen; and in order to fill such a station with honor to themselves, and with good to the public, how necessary their education, how important the moral and religious cultivation of their minds! . . . The God of Nature has endowed our children with intellectual powers surpassed by none; nor is there anything wanting but their careful cultivation in order to fit them for stations the most honorable, sacred, or useful. And may we not, without becoming vain in our imaginations, indulge the pleasing anticipation that within the little circle of those connected with our families there may hereafter be found the scholar, the statesman, or the herald of the cross of Christ. Is it too much to say, that among that little number there shall yet be one found like to the wise legislator of Israel, who shall take his brethren by the hand and lead them forth from worse than Egyptian bondage to the happy Canaan of civil and religious liberty; or one whose devotedness towards the cause of God, and whose zeal for the salvation of Africa, shall cause him to leave the land which gave him birth, and cross the Atlantic, eager to plant the standard of the cross upon every hill of that vast continent, that has hitherto ignobly submitted to the baleful crescent, or crouched under the iron bondage of the vilest superstition. Our prospects brighten as we pursue the subject, and we are encouraged to look forward to that period when the moral desert of Africa shall submit to cultivation, and verdant groves and fertile valleys, watered by the streams of Siloia, shall meet the eye that has long surveyed only the widespread desolations of slavery, despotism, and death. How changed shall then be the aspect of the moral and political world! Africa, elevated to more than her original dignity, and redressed for the many aggravated and complicated wrongs she has sustained, with her emancipated sons, shall take her place among the other nations of the earth. The iron manacles of slavery shall give place to the still stronger bonds of brotherly love and affection, and justice and equity shall be the governing principles that shall regulate the conduct of men of every nation. Influenced by such motives, encouraged by such prospects, let us enter the field with a fixed determination to live and to die in the holy cause.

"Where two races . . . distinguished by color and other physical differences . . . are brought together, the relation now existing in the slaveholding states between the two is . . . a positive good."

Slavery Must Not Be Abolished in America

John C. Calhoun (1782–1850) and
William Harper (1790–1847)

Prior to the Civil War the lives of the vast majority of blacks in the United States were defined by slavery, which remained firmly entrenched in the southern cotton-growing states. Responding in part to abolitionist attacks on slavery's immorality, slavery defenders argued that slavery, far from evil, was a moral and constructive institution. A main theme of many proslavery writings was the belief that blacks were racially inferior to whites, as can be seen in the following two-part viewpoint. Part I is excerpted from a February 1837 Senate speech by John C. Calhoun. The South Carolina senator, then in the middle of a long political career in which he became recognized as the leading spokesman for the South, defends slavery in that region as being necessary to ensure social peace and economic prosperity. He argues that slavery has been an uplifting experience for blacks brought from Africa. Part II is excerpted from William Harper's *Memoir on Slavery*, considered by many a classic of proslavery literature. In his defense of slavery, written in 1837, Harper focuses on what he considers to be important racial differences between whites and blacks. Harper, appointed chancellor of the Missouri Territory in 1819, later served as a U.S. senator and as a judge in South Carolina.

From John C. Calhoun, speech before the U.S. Senate, February 1837, in *Speeches of John C. Calhoun* (New York: Harper & Brothers, 1843). From William Harper, *Memoir on Slavery*, 1837; reprinted in *The Pro-Slavery Argument* (Charleston, SC: n.p., 1852).

I

We of the South will not, cannot surrender our institutions. To maintain the existing relations between the two races inhabiting that section of the Union is indispensable to the peace and happiness of both. It cannot be subverted without drenching the country in blood and extirpating one or the other of the races. Be it good or bad, it has grown up with our society and institutions and is so interwoven with them that to destroy it would be to destroy us as a people. But let me not be understood as admitting, even by implication, that the existing relations between the two races, in the slaveholding states, is an evil. Far otherwise: I hold it to be a good, as it has thus far proved itself to be, to both, and will continue to prove so, if not disturbed by the fell spirit of Abolition.

Civilizing the Black Race

I appeal to facts. Never before has the black race of Central Africa, from the dawn of history to the present day, attained a condition so civilized and so improved, not only physically but morally and intellectually. It came among us in a low, degraded, and savage condition, and, in the course of a few generations, it has grown up under the fostering care of our institutions, as reviled as they have been, to its present comparative civilized condition. This, with the rapid increase of numbers, is conclusive proof of the general happiness of the race, in spite of all the exaggerated tales to the contrary.

In the meantime, the white or European race has not degenerated. It has kept pace with its brethren in other sections of the Union where slavery does not exist. It is odious to make comparison; but I appeal to all sides whether the South is not equal in virtue, intelligence, patriotism, courage, disinterestedness, and all the high qualities which adorn our nature. I ask whether we have not contributed our full share of talents and political wisdom in forming and sustaining this political fabric; and whether we have not constantly inclined most strongly to the side of liberty and been the first to see and first to resist the encroachments of power. In one thing only are we inferior—the arts of gain. We acknowledge that we are less wealthy than the Northern section of this Union, but I trace this mainly to the fiscal action of this government, which has extracted much from and spent little among us. Had it been the reverse—if the exaction had been from the other section and the expenditure with us—this point of superiority would not be against us now, as it was not at the formation of this government.

49

But I take higher ground. I hold that, in the present state of civilization, where two races of different origin and distinguished by color and other physical differences, as well as intellectual, are brought together, the relation now existing in the slaveholding states between the two is, instead of an evil, a good—a positive good. I feel myself called upon to speak freely upon the subject, where the honor and interests of those I represent are involved. I hold, then, that there never has yet existed a wealthy and civilized society in which one portion of the community did not, in point of fact, live on the labor of the other. Broad and general as is this assertion, it is fully borne out by history.

The Negro Is an Inferior Species of Man

John H. Van Evrie, a physician in Washington, D.C., made scientific arguments espousing the inferiority of blacks in his 1853 book Negroes and Negro Slavery: the First, an Inferior Race—the Latter, Its Normal Condition.

The Negro is a man, but a different and inferior *species* of man, who could no more originate from the same source as ourselves, than the owl could from the eagle, or the shad from the salmon, or the cat from the tiger; and who can no more be forced by *human power* to manifest the faculties, or perform the purposes assigned by the Almighty Creator to the Caucasian man, than can either of these forms of life be made to manifest faculties other than those inherent, *specific,* and eternally impressed upon their organization....

The Caucasian brain measures 92 cubic inches—with the cerebrum, the centre of the intellectual functions, relatively predominating over the cerebellum, the centre of the animal instincts; thus, it is capable of indefinite progression, and transmits the knowledge or experience acquired by one generation to subsequent generations—the record of which is history.

The Negro brain measures from 65 to 70 cubic inches—with the cerebellum, the centre of the animal instincts relatively predominating over the cerebrum, the centre of the intellectual powers; thus, its acquisition of knowledge is limited to a single generation, and incapable of transmitting this to subsequent generations, *it can have no history.* A single glance at eternal and immutable *facts,* which perpetually separate these forms of human existence will be sufficient to cover the whole ground—thus, could the deluded people who propose to improve on the works of the Creator, and *elevate* the Negro to the standard of the white, actually perform an act of omnipotence, and, add 25 or 30 per cent. to the totality of the Negro brain, they would still be at as great a distance as ever from their final object, while the relations of the anterior and posterior portions of the brain remained as at present.

This is not the proper occasion, but, if it were, it would not be difficult to trace the various devices by which the wealth of all civilized communities has been so unequally divided and to show by what means so small a share has been allotted to those by whose labor it was produced, and so large a share given to the nonproducing class. The devices are almost innumerable, from the brute force and gross superstition of ancient times to the subtle and artful fiscal contrivances of modern. I might well challenge a comparison between them and the more direct, simple, and patriarchal mode by which the labor of the African race is among us commanded by the European. I may say, with truth, that in few countries so much is left to the share of the laborer and so little exacted from him or where there is more kind attention to him in sickness or infirmities of age. Compare his condition with the tenants of the poorhouses in the most civilized portions of Europe—look at the sick and the old and infirm slave, on one hand, in the midst of his family and friends, under the kind superintending care of his master and mistress, and compare it with the forlorn and wretched condition of the pauper in the poorhouse.

But I will not dwell on this aspect of the question. I turn to the political; and here I fearlessly assert that the existing relation between the two races in the South, against which these blind fanatics are waging war, forms the most solid and durable foundation on which to rear free and stable political institutions. It is useless to disguise the fact. There is, and always has been, in an advanced stage of wealth and civilization, a conflict between labor and capital. The condition of society in the South exempts us from the disorders and dangers resulting from this conflict; and which explains why it is that the political condition of the slaveholding states has been so much more stable and quiet than those of the North. The advantages of the former, in this respect, will become more and more manifest if left undisturbed by interference from without, as the country advances in wealth and numbers. We have, in fact, but just entered that condition of society where the strength and durability of our political institutions are to be tested; and I venture nothing in predicting that the experience of the next generation will fully test how vastly more favorable our condition of society is to that of other sections for free and stable institutions, provided we are not disturbed by the interference of others or shall have sufficient intelligence and spirit to resist promptly and successfully such interference.

The Consequences of Emancipation

It rests with ourselves to meet and repel them. I look not for aid to this government or to the other states; not but there are kind feelings toward us on the part of the great body of the nonslaveholding states; but, as kind as their feelings may be, we may rest assured that no political party in those states will risk their ascendency for our safety. If we do not defend ourselves, none will defend us; if we yield, we will be more and more pressed as we recede; and, if we submit, we will be trampled underfoot. Be assured that emancipation itself would not satisfy these fanatics; that gained, the next step would be to raise the Negroes to a social and political equality with the whites; and, that being effected, we would soon find the present condition of the two races reversed. They, and their Northern allies, would be the masters, and we the slaves; the condition of the white race in the British West India Islands, as bad as it is, would be happiness to ours; there the mother country is interested in sustaining the supremacy of the European race. It is true that the authority of the former master is destroyed, but the African will there still be a slave, not to individuals, but to the community—forced to labor, not by the authority of the overseer but by the bayonet of the soldiery and the rod of the civil magistrate.

Surrounded as the slaveholding states are with such imminent perils, I rejoice to think that our means of defense are ample if we shall prove to have the intelligence and spirit to see and apply them before it is too late. All we want is concert, to lay aside all party differences, and unite with zeal and energy in repelling approaching dangers. Let there be concert of action, and we shall find ample means of security without resorting to secession or disunion. I speak with full knowledge and a thorough examination of the subject, and, for one, see my way clearly.

One thing alarms me—the eager pursuit of gain which overspreads the land and which absorbs every faculty of the mind and every feeling of the heart. Of all passions, avarice is the most blind and compromising—the last to see and the first to yield to danger. I dare not hope that anything I can say will arouse the South to a due sense of danger. I fear it is beyond the power of mortal voice to awaken it in time from the fatal security into which it has fallen.

II

That the African negro is an inferior variety of the human race, is, I think, now generally admitted, and his distinguishing characteristics are such as peculiarly mark him out for the situation which he occupies among us. And these are no less marked in their original country, than as we have daily occasion to observe them. The most remarkable is their indifference to personal liberty. In this they have followed their instincts since we have any knowledge of their continent, by enslaving each other; but contrary to the experience of every race, the possession of slaves has no material effect in raising the character, and promoting the civilization of the master. Another trait is the want of domestic affections, and insensibility to the ties of kindred. . . . They are, however, very submissive to authority, and seem to entertain great reverence for chiefs, priests, and masters. No greater indignity can be offered an individual, than to throw opprobrium on his parents. On this point of their character I think I have remarked, that, contrary to the instinct of nature in other races, they entertain less regard for children than for parents, to whose authority they have been accustomed to submit. . . . Let me ask if this people do not furnish the very material out of which slaves ought to be made, and whether it be not an improving of their condition to make them the slaves of civilized masters? There is a variety in the character of the tribes. Some are brutally and savagely ferocious and bloody, whom it would be mercy to enslave. From the travellers' account, it seems not unlikely that the negro race is tending to extermination, being daily encroached on and overrun by the superior Arab race. It may be, that when they shall have been lost from their native seats, they may be found numerous, and in no unhappy condition, on the continent to which they have been transplanted.

Racial Differences

The opinion which connects form and features with character and intellectual power, is one so deeply impressed on the human mind, that perhaps there is scarcely any man who does not almost daily act upon it, and in some measure verify its truth. Yet in spite of this intimation of nature, and though the anatomist and physiologist may tell them that the races differ in every bone and muscle, and in the proportion of brain and nerves, yet there are some who, with a most bigoted and fanatical determination to free themselves from what they have prejudged to be prejudice, will still maintain that this physiognomy, evidently tending to that of the brute, when compared to that of the Caucasian race, may be enlightened by as much thought, and animated by as lofty sentiment. We who have the best opportunity of judging, are pronounced to be incompetent to do so, and to be blinded by our interest and prejudices—often by those who have no opportunity at all—and we are to be taught to distrust or disbelieve that which we daily observe, and familiarly know, on such authority. Our prejudices are spoken of. But the truth is, that, until very lately, since circumstances have compelled us to think for ourselves, we took our opinions on this subject, as on every other, ready formed from the country of our origin. And so deeply rooted were they, that we adhered to them, as most men will do to deeply rooted opinions, even against the evidence of our own observation, and our own senses. If the inferiority exists, it is attributed to the apathy and degradation produced by Slavery. Though of the hundreds of thousands scattered over other countries, where the laws impose no disability upon them, none has given evidence of an approach to even mediocrity of intellectual excellence; this, too, is attributed to the slavery of a portion of their race. They are regarded as a servile caste, and degraded by opinion, and thus every generous effort is repressed. Yet though this should be the general effect, this very estimation is calculated to produce the contrary effect in particular instances. It is observed by [Francis] Bacon, with respect to deformed persons and eunuchs, that though in general there is something of perversity in the character, the disadvantage often leads to extraordinary displays of virtue and excellence. "Whoever hath any thing fixed in his person that doth induce contempt, hath also a perpetual spur in himself, to rescue and deliver himself from scorn." So it would be with them, if they were capable of European aspirations—genius, if they possessed it, would be doubly fired with noble rage to rescue itself from this scorn. Of course, I do not mean to say that there may not be found among them some of superior capacity to many white persons; but that great intellectual powers are, perhaps, never found among them, and that in general their capacity is very limited, and their feelings animal and coarse—fitting them peculiarly to discharge the lower, and merely mechanical offices of society.

And why should it not be so? We have among domestic animals infinite varieties, distinguished by various degrees of sagacity, courage, strength, swiftness, and other qualities. And it may be observed, that this is no objection to their being derived from a common origin, which we suppose them to have had. Yet these accidental qualities, as they may be termed, however acquired in the first instance, we know that they transmit unimpaired to their posterity for an indefinite succession of generations. It is most important that these varieties should be preserved, and that each should be applied to the purposes for which it is best adapted. No philo-zoost, I believe, has suggested it as desirable that these varieties should be melted down into one equal, undistinguished race of curs or road horses.

The Benefits of Slavery

Slavery, as it is said in an eloquent article published in a Southern periodical work [*Southern Literary Messenger*, January 1835], to which I am indebted for other ideas, "has done more to elevate a degraded race in the scale of humanity; to tame the savage; to civilize the barbarous; to soften the ferocious; to enlighten the ignorant, and to spread the blessings of Christianity among the heathen, than all the missionaries that philanthropy and religion have ever sent forth." Yet unquestionable as this is, and though human ingenuity and thought may be tasked in vain to devise any other means by which these blessings could have been conferred, yet a sort of sensibility which would be only mawkish and contemptible, if it were not mischievous, affects still to weep over the wrongs of "injured Africa." Can there be a doubt of the immense benefit which has been conferred on the race, by transplanting them from their native, dark, and barbarous regions, to the American continent and islands? There, three-fourths of the race are in a state of the most deplorable personal Slavery. And those who are not, are in a scarcely less deplorable condition of political Slavery, to barbarous chiefs—who value neither life nor any other human right, or enthralled by priests to the most abject and atrocious superstitions. . . . It was a useful and beneficent work, approaching the heroic, to tame the wild horse, and subdue him to the use of man; how much more to tame the nobler animal that is capable of reason, and subdue him to usefulness?

"We have fully discovered . . . the great political disease with which we are affected. . . . We propose for this disease a remedy. That remedy is Emigration."

Blacks Should Emigrate from the United States

Martin R. Delany (1812–1885) et al.

The mass emigration of blacks from the United States to colonize areas in Africa or Central America was a scenario that was seriously proposed and debated by many white and black Americans as early as 1714, when a pamphlet written under the pseudonym "Native American" suggested it. In 1816 the American Colonization Society (ACS) was founded by prominent white political leaders, including Henry Clay and John Randolph, to sponsor the resettlement of freed blacks to Africa. Colonization was supported by some whites who wished to abolish slavery but who did not support granting political equality to freed slaves. The ACS purchased land on Africa's west coast and founded the colony of Liberia in 1821, and over the next forty years it sent eleven thousand blacks there. However, the idea of emigration sparked much opposition among the free black population of the United States. An 1817 meeting of free blacks in Philadelphia, Pennsylvania, issued a strongly worded condemnation of the colonization idea that was restated by similar meetings held in other cities. Colonization was also opposed by William Lloyd Garrison and other abolitionists.

In the 1850s, a renewed interest in and debate over colonization emerged within the African American community. This resulted in part from disappointing political developments for blacks seeking freedom for slaves and political equality for all African Americans. Among these developments were the 1850 Fugitive

From Martin R. Delany, "Political Destiny of the Colored Race on the American Continent," in *Proceedings of the National Emigration Convention of Colored People, Cleveland, 1854* (Pittsburgh: A.A. Anderson, 1854).

Slave Act, which jeopardized the freedom of blacks in northern states, and the 1857 Supreme Court *Dred Scott* decision decreeing that blacks could never be considered American citizens.

A leading figure in the debate over emigration was Martin R. Delany, a physician, editor, and disillusioned black abolitionist. In a book published in 1852, *The Condition, Elevation, Emigration, and Destiny of the Colored People of the United States, Politically Considered*, Delany argued that blacks were "a nation within a nation" and recommended emigration. He remained critical of Liberia and the ACS, which he believed were under the control of whites, and sought instead the formation of a black-led emigration movement. The following viewpoint is taken from a "State Paper" produced by a National Emigration Convention held in Cleveland, Ohio, in 1854. The address, written by a convention committee headed by Delany, argues that blacks will never attain true citizenship and equality in America and should therefore emigrate. This viewpoint provides an interesting early example of black nationalism.

TO THE COLORED INHABITANTS OF THE UNITED STATES

Fellow-Countrymen!—The duty assigned us is an important one, comprehending all that pertains to our destiny and that of our posterity—present and prospectively. And while it must be admitted, that the subject is one of the greatest magnitude, requiring all that talents, prudence and wisdom might adduce, and while it would be folly to pretend to give you the combined result of these three agencies, we shall satisfy ourselves with doing our duty to the best of our ability, and that in the plainest, most simple and comprehensive manner.

Our object, then, shall be to place before you our true position in this country—the United States,—the improbability of realizing our desires, and the sure, practicable and infallible remedy for the evils we now endure.

We Are Not Citizens

We have not addressed you as *citizens*—a term desired and ever cherished by us—because such you have never been. We have not addressed you as *freemen*,—because such privileges have never been enjoyed by any colored man in the United States. Why then should we flatter your credulity, by inducing you to believe that which neither has now, nor never before had an existence. Our oppressors are ever gratified at our manifest satisfaction, especially when that satisfaction is founded upon false premises; an assumption on our part, of the enjoyment of rights and privileges which never have been conceded, and which, according to the present system of the United States policy, we never can enjoy.

The *political policy* of this country was solely borrowed from, and shaped and moddled after, that of Rome. This was strikingly the case in the establishment of immunities, and the application of terms in their Civil and Legal regulations.

The term Citizen—politically considered—is derived from the Roman definition—which was never applied in any other sense—*Cives Ingenui*; which meant, one exempt from restraint of any kind. (*Cives*, a citizen; one who might enjoy the highest honors in his own free town—the town in which he lived—and in the country or commonwealth; and *Ingenui, freeborn*—of GOOD EXTRACTION.) All who were deprived of citizenship—that is, the right of enjoying positions of honor and trust—were termed *Hostes* and *Peregrini*; which are public and private *enemies*, and foreigners, or *aliens* to the country. (*Hostis*, a public—and sometimes—private enemy: and *Peregrinus*, an *alien, stranger*, or *foreigner*.)

The Romans, from a national pride, to distinguish their inhabitants from those of other countries, termed them all "citizens," but consequently, were under the necessity of specifying four classes of citizens: none but the *Cives Ingenui* being unrestricted in their privileges. There was one class, called the *Jus Quiritium*, or the wailing or *supplicating* citizen—that is, one who was continually *moaning, complaining, or crying for aid or succor*. This class might also include within themselves, the *jus suffragii*, who had the privilege of *voting*, but no other privilege. They could vote for one of their superiors—the *Cives Ingenui*—but not for themselves.

Such, then, is the condition, precisely, of the black and colored inhabitants of the United States: in some of the States they answering to the latter class, having the privilege of *voting*, to elevate their superiors to positions to which they need never dare aspire, or even hope to attain.

There has, of late years, been a false impression obtained, that the privilege of *voting* constitutes, or necessarily embodies, the *rights of citizenship*. A more radical error never obtained favor among an oppressed people. Suffrage is an ambiguous term, which admits of several definitions. But according to strict political construction, means simply "a vote, voice, approbation." Here, then, you have the whole import of the term suffrage. To have the "right of suffrage," as we rather proudly term it, is simply to have the *privilege*—there is no *right* about it—of giving our *approbation* to that which our *rulers may do*, without the privilege, on our part, of doing the same thing. Where such privileges are granted—privileges which are now exercised in but few of the States by colored men—we have but the privilege granted of saying, in common with others, who shall, for the time being, exercise *rights*, which in him, are conceded to be *inherent* and *inviolate*. . . .

Much might be adduced on this point to prove the insignificance of the black man, politically considered in this country, but we deem it wholly unnecessary at present, and consequently proceed at once to consider another feature of this important subject.

Let it then be understood, as a great principle of political economy, that no people can be free who themselves do not constitute an essential part of the *ruling element* of the country in which they live. Whether this element be founded upon a true or false, a just or an unjust basis; this position in community is necessary to personal safety. The liberty of no man is secure, who controls not his own political destiny. What is true of an individual, is true of a family; and that which is true of a family, is also true concerning a whole people. To suppose otherwise, is that delusion which at once induces its victim, through a period of long suffering, patiently to submit to every species of wrong; trusting against probability, and hoping against all reasonable grounds of expectation, for the granting of privileges and enjoyment of rights, which never will be attained. This delusion reveals the true secret of the power which holds in peaceable subjection, all the oppressed in every part of the world.

We Must Be Our Own Rulers

A people, to be free, must necessarily be *their own rulers*: that is, *each individual* must, in himself, embody the *essential ingredient*—so to speak—of the *sovereign principle* which composes the *true basis* of his liberty. This principle, when not exercised by himself, may, at his pleasure, be delegated to another—his true representative.

Said a great French writer: "A free agent, in a free government, should be his own governor," that is, he must possess within himself the *acknowledged right to govern*: this constitutes him a *governor* though he may delegate to another the power to govern himself.

No one, then, can delegate to another a power he never possessed; that is, he cannot *give an agency* in that which he never had a right. Consequently, the colored man in the United States, being deprived of the right of inherent sovereignty, cannot *confer* a suffrage, because he possesses none to confer. Therefore, where there is no suffrage, there can neither be *freedom* nor *safety* for the disfranchised. And it is a futile hope to suppose that the agent of another's concerns, will take a proper interest in the affairs of those to whom he is under no obligations. Having no favors to ask or expect, he therefore has none to lose.

In other periods and parts of the world—as in Europe and Asia—the people being of one common, direct origin of race, though established on the presumption of difference by birth, or what was termed *blood*, yet the distinction between the superior classes and common people, could only be marked by the difference in the dress and education of the two classes. To effect this, the interposition of government was necessary; consequently, the costume and education of the people became a subject of legal restriction, guarding carefully against the privileges of the common people. . . .

In Europe, when an inferior is elevated to the rank of equality with the superior class, the law first comes to his aid, which, in its decrees, entirely destroys his identity as an inferior, leaving no trace of his former condition visible.

In the United States, among the whites, their color is made, by law and custom, the mark of distinction and superiority; while the color of the blacks is a badge of degradation, acknowledged by statute, organic law, and the common consent of the people.

With this view of the case—which we hold to be correct—to elevate to equality the degraded subject of law and custom, it can only be done, as in Europe, by an entire destruction of the identity of the former condition of the applicant. Even were this desirable—which we by no means admit—with the deep seated prejudices engendered by oppression, with which we have to contend, ages incalculable might reasonably be expected to roll around, before this could honorably be accomplished; otherwise, we should encourage and at once commence an indiscriminate concubinage and immoral commerce, of our mothers, sisters, wives and daughters, revolting to think of, and a physical curse to humanity. . . .

The Disease and the Cure

But we have fully discovered and comprehended the great political disease with which we are affected, the cause of its origin and continuance; and what is now left for us to do, is to discover and apply a sovereign remedy—a healing balm to a sorely diseased body—a wrecked but not entirely shattered system. We propose for this disease a remedy. That remedy is Emigration. This Emigration should be well advised, and like remedies applied to remove the disease from the physical system of man, skillfully and carefully applied, within the proper time, directed to operate on that part of the system, whose greatest tendency shall be, to benefit the whole.

Several geographical localities have been named, among which rank the Canadas. These we do not object to as places of tempo-

rary relief, especially to the fleeing fugitive—which, like a palia-
tive, soothes for the time being the misery—but cannot commend
them as permanent places upon which to fix our destiny, and that
of our children, who shall come after us. . . .

Blacks Have No Future in the United States

*In the decade prior to the Civil War, James Theodore Holly, a black
Episcopal minister in New Haven, Connecticut, wrote numerous
tracts and articles advocating emigration to Haiti. The following passage, arguing that blacks have a greater future in areas where they are
in the majority, is excerpted from an article in the August 1859 issue
of the* Anglo-African Magazine. *Holly later settled in Haiti.*

Link by link the chain of oppression is being broken asunder
throughout all the West-Indies, Central and South America, and the
black man is assuming his unquestionable status in society as the
equal of the white. An illimitable field of human progress, therefore,
opens up before the meanest slave now delving in the tobacco-fields
of Cuba, or diving for precious gems in the rivers of Brazil. That
progress is secure to him just where he is, by the irresistible force of
circumstances that his numerical strength gives him: and which is
wafting him on to the national glories of a boundless future. But in
the United States the numerical weakness of the colored people; the
public sentiment of the dominant race against them, stronger than
law; and the social repellancy which the whites manifest towards
the blacks, stronger than the attractions of Christian love; place the
black man under such odious barriers of caste as he will never be
able to surmount. The social ostracism of the colored people in the
United States is complete and irremediable. The political death of
Slavery already broods over them; and this curse will only cease to
prey upon their vitals here, when they shall be entirely removed beyond the borders of America; or utter annihilation shall leave the
world to think of the black man in the United States as a being that
one was. When the highest conception of political justice, as developed in the American Declaration of Independence; and the freest
field for the untrammelled operation of religion, as secured by the
American Constitution fail to improve public sentiment, and to correct social prejudices after the operations of nearly three generations, then we have nothing to look for in this nation, but God's terrible judgment which he promises to visit upon those who neglect
to obey his commandments, unto the third and fourth generations.

The odds are against us, because the ruling element there, as in
the United States, is, and ever must be, white—the population
now standing, in all British America, two and a half millions of
whites, to but forty thousand of the black race; or sixty-one and a
fraction, whites, to one black!—the difference being eleven times

61

greater than in the United States—so that colored people might never hope for anything more than to exist politically by mere suffrance—occupying a secondary position to the whites of the Canadas. The Yankees from this side of the lakes are fast settling in the Canadas, infusing, with industrious success, all the malignity and Negro-hate, inseparable from their very being, as Christian Democrats and American advocates of equality.

Then, to be successful, our attention must be turned in a direction towards those places where the blacks and colored man comprise, by population, and constitute by necessity of numbers, the *ruling element* of the body politic. And where, when occasion shall require it, the issue can be made and maintained on this basis. Where our political enclosure and national edifice can be reared, established, walled, and proudly defended on this great elementary principle of original identity. Upon this solid foundation rests the fabric of every substantial political structure in the world, which cannot exist without it; and so soon as a people or nation lose their original identity, just so soon must that nation or people become extinct.—Powerful though they may have been, they must fall. Because the nucleus which heretofore held them together, becoming extinct, there being no longer a centre of attraction, or basis for a union of the parts, a dissolution must as naturally ensue, as the result of the nutrality of the basis of adhesion among the particles of matter.

This is the secret of the eventful downfall of Egypt, Carthage, Rome, and the former Grecian States, once so powerful—a loss of original identity; and with it, a loss of interest in maintaining their fundamental principles of nationality.

This, also, is the great secret of the present strength of Great Britain, Russia, the United States, and Turkey; and the endurance of the French nation, whatever its strength and power, is attributable only to their identity as Frenchmen. . . .

Nor is this the only important consideration. Were we content to remain as we are, sparsely interspersed among our white fellow-countrymen, we never might be expected to equal them in any honorable or respectable competition for a livelihood. For the reason that, according to the customs and policy of the country, we for ages would be kept in a secondary position, every situation of respectability, honor, profit or trust, either as mechanics, clerks, teachers, jurors, councilmen, or legislators, being filled by white men, consequently, our energies must become paralysed or enervated for the want of proper encouragement.

This example upon our children, and the colored people generally, is pernicious and degrading in the extreme. And how could it otherwise be, when they see every place of respectability filled and occupied by the whites, they pandering to their vanity, and existing among them merely as a thing of conveniency.

Our friends in this and other countries, anxious for our elevation, have for years been erroneously urging us to lose our identity as a distinct race, declaring that we were the same as other people; while at the very same time their own representative was traversing the world and propagating the doctrine in favor of a *universal Anglo-Saxon predominence.* The "Universal Brotherhood," so ably and eloquently advocated by that Polyglot Christian Apostle [Elihu Burritt] of this doctrine, had established as its basis, a universal acknowledgment of the Anglo-Saxon rule.

The truth is, we are not identical with the Anglo-Saxon or any other race of the Caucasian or pure white type of the human family, and the sooner we know and acknowledge this truth, the better for ourselves and posterity.

The English, French, Irish, German, Italian, Turk, Persion, Greek, Jew, and all other races, have their native or inherent peculiarities, and why not our race? We are not willing, therefore, at all times and under all circumstances to be moulded into various shapes of eccentricity, to suit the caprices and conveniences of every kind of people. We are more suitable to everybody than everybody is suitable to us; therefore, no more like other people than others are like us.

Our Inherent Traits

We have then inherent traits, attributes—so to speak—and native characteristics, peculiar to our race—whether pure or mixed blood—and all that is required of us is to cultivate these and develope them in their purity, to make them desirable and emulated by the rest of the world.

That the colored races have the highest traits of civilization, will not be disputed. They are civil, peaceable and religious to a fault. In mathematics, sculpture and architecture, as arts and sciences, commerce and internal improvements as enterprises, the white race may probably excel; but in languages, oratory, poetry, music and painting as arts and sciences, and in ethics, metaphysics, theology and legal jurisprudence; in plain language—in the true principles of morals, correctness of thought, religion, and law or civil government, there is no doubt but the black race will yet instruct the world.

It would be duplicity longer to disguise the fact, that the great issue, sooner or later, upon which must be disputed the world's destiny, will be a question of black and white; and every individual will be called upon for his identity with one or the other. The blacks and colored races are four-sixths of all the population of the world; and these people are fast tending to a common cause with each other. The white races are but one-third of the population of the globe—or one of them to two of us—and it cannot much longer continue, that two-thirds will passively submit to the universal domination of this one-third. And it is notorious that the only progress made in territorial domain, in the last three centuries, by the whites, has been a usurpation and encroachment on the rights and native soil of some of the colored races. . . .

We regret the necessity of stating the fact—but duty compels us to the task—that for more than two thousand years, the determined aim of the whites has been to crush the colored races wherever found. With a determined will, they have sought and pursued them in every quarter of the globe. The Anglo-Saxon has taken the lead in this work of universal subjugation. But the Anglo-American stands pre-eminent for deeds of injustice and acts of oppression, unparalleled perhaps in the annals of modern history.

We admit the existence of great and good people in America, England, France, and the rest of Europe, who desire a unity of interests among the whole human family, of whatever origin or race.

But it is neither the moralist, Christian, nor philanthropist whom we now have to meet and combat, but the politician—the civil engineer and skillful economist, who direct and control the machinery which moves forward with mighty impulse, the nations and powers of the earth. We must, therefore, if possible, meet them on vantage ground, or, at least, with adequate means for the conflict.

Should we encounter an enemy with artillery, a prayer will not stay the cannon shot; neither will the kind words nor smiles of philanthropy shield his spear from piercing us through the heart. We must meet mankind, then, as they meet us—prepared for the worst, though we may hope for the best. Our submission does not gain us an increase of friends nor respectability—as the white race will only respect those who oppose their usurpation, and acknowledge as equals those who will not submit to their rule. This may be no new discovery in political economy, but it certainly is a subject worthy the consideration of the black race. . . .

Our Future in the United States

Having glanced hastily at our present political position in the world generally, and the United States in particular—the fundamental disadvantages under which we exist, and the improbability of ever attaining citizenship and equality of rights in this country—we call your attention next, to the places of destination to which we shall direct Emigration.

The West Indies, Central and South America, are the countries of our choices, the advantages of which shall be made apparent to your entire satisfaction.

Though we have designated them as countries, they are in fact but one country—relatively considered—a part of this, the Western Continent. . . .

There is but one question presents itself for our serious consideration, upon which we *must* give a decisive reply—Will we transmit as an inheritance to our children, the blessings of unrestricted civil liberty, or shall we entail upon them, as our only political legacy, the degradation and oppression left us by our fathers?

Shall we be persuaded that we can live and prosper nowhere but under the authority and power of our North American white oppressors, that this (the United States) is the country most—if not the only one—favorable to our improvement and progress? Are we willing to admit that we are incapable of self-government, establishing for ourselves such political privileges and making such internal improvements as we delight to enjoy, after American white men have made them for themselves?

No! Neither is it true that the United States is the country best adapted to *our* improvement. But that country is the best in which our manhood—morally, mentally and physically—can be *best developed*—in which we have an untrammeled right to the enjoyment of civil and religious liberty; and the West Indies, Central and South America, present now such advantages, superiorly preferable to all other countries. . . .

You will doubtless be asked—and that, too, with an air of seriousness—why, if desirable to remain on this continent, not be content to remain *in* the United States. The objections to this—and potent reasons, too, in our estimation—have already been clearly shown.

But notwithstanding all this, were there still any rational, nay, even the most futile grounds for hope, we still might be stupid enough to be content to remain, and yet through another period of unexampled patience and suffering, continue meekly to drag the galling yoke and clank the chain of servility and degradation. But whether or not in this, God is to be thanked and Heaven blessed, we are not permitted, despite our willingness and stupidity, to indulge even the most distant glimmer of a hope of attaining to the level of a well protected slave.

For years, we have been studiously and jealously observing the course of political events and policy, on the part of this country, both in a national and individual State capacity, as pursued toward the colored people. And he who, in the midst of them, can live with observation, is either excusably ignorant, or reprehensibly deceptious and untrustworthy. . . .

When the condition of the inhabitants of any country is fixed by legal grades of distinction, this condition can never be changed except by express legislation. And it is the height of folly to expect such express legislation, except by the inevitable force of some irresistible internal political pressure. The force necessary to this imperative demand on our part, we never can obtain, because of our numerical feebleness.

Were the interests of the common people identical with ours, we, in this, might succeed, because we, as a class, would then be numerically the superior. But this is not a question of the rich against the poor, nor the common people against the higher classes but a question of white against black—every white person, by legal right, being held superior to a black or colored person. . . .

Should anything occur to prevent a successful emigration to the South—Central, South America and the West Indies—we have no hesitancy, rather than remain in the United States, the merest subordinates and serviles of the whites, should the Canadas still continue separate in their political relations from this country, to recommend to the great body of our people, to remove to Canada West, where being politically equal to the whites, physically united with each other by a concentration of strength; when worse comes to worse, we may be found, not as a scattered, weak and impotent people, as we now are separated from each other throughout the Union, but a united and powerful body of freemen, mighty in politics, and terrible in any conflict which might ensue, in the event of an attempt at the disturbance of our political relations, domestic repose, and peaceful firesides.

Now, fellow-countrymen, we have done. Into your ears have we recounted your own sorrows; before your own eyes have we exhibited your wrongs; into your own hands have we committed your own cause. If there should prove a failure to remedy this dreadful evil, to assuage this terrible curse which has come upon us; the fault will be yours and not ours; since we have offered you a healing balm for every sorely aggravated wound.

Martin R. Delany, Pa.
William Webb, Pa.
Augustus R. Green, Ohio
Edward Butler, Mo.
H.S. Douglass, La.
A. Dudley, Wis.
Conaway Barbour, Ky.
Wm. J. Fuller, R.I.
Wm. Lambert, Mich.
J. Theodore Holly, N.Y.
T.A. White, Ind.
John A. Warren, Canada

"No one idea has given rise to more oppression and persecution toward the colored people of this country, than that which makes Africa, not America, their home."

Blacks Should Not Emigrate from the United States

Frederick Douglass (1817–1895)

As early as 1817 northern free blacks had strongly opposed back-to-Africa schemes that were being proposed by white organizations such as the American Colonization Society. Black opposition to colonization persisted despite the efforts of some black leaders, such as Martin R. Delany, to promote black migration from the United States in the 1850s. A consistent and formidable opponent of colonization during this time was Frederick Douglass, an escaped slave who had gained national and international renown as a lecturer and writer for the abolitionist movement.

The following viewpoint is taken from an article in the February 1859 issue of *Douglass' Monthly*, a newspaper published, edited, and largely written by Douglass. In the article Douglass responds specifically to questions posed by Henry Highland Garnet, a black abolitionist and minister who in 1858 helped found and became president of the African Civilization Society. The organization, unlike other colonization groups, officially rejected *mass* emigration of blacks; its stated goals included the uplifting of Africa and the curtailment of the slave trade through the selective emigration to Africa of black Americans—emigrants who could then prove to whites their ability to govern and run societies free of white domination. Douglass, however, argues that

From Frederick Douglass, "African Civilization Society," *Douglass' Monthly*, February 1859.

even such a limited colonization program would harm blacks in America by distracting them from the fundamental goal of abolishing slavery and by enabling whites to persist in the idea that blacks can never be true Americans.

"But I entreated you to tell your readers what your objections are to the civilization and christianization of Africa. What objection have you to colored men in this country engaging in agriculture, lawful trade, and commerce in the land of my forefathers? What objection have you to an organization that shall endeavor to check and destroy the African slave-trade, and that desires to co-operate with anti-slavery men and women of every grade in our own land, and to toil with them for the overthrow of American slavery?—Tell us, I pray you, tell us in your clear and manly style. 'Gird up thy loins, and answer thou me, if thou canst.'"—Letter from Henry Highland Garnet.

Hitherto we have allowed ourselves but little space for discussing the claims of this new scheme for the civilization of Africa, doing little more than indicating our dissent from the new movement, yet leaving our columns as free to its friends as to its opponents. We shall not depart from this course, while the various writers bring good temper and ability to the discussion, and shall keep themselves within reasonable limits. We hope the same impartiality will be shown in the management of the *Provincial Freeman*, the adopted organ of the African Civilization Society. We need discussion among ourselves, discussion to rouse our souls to intenser life and activity.—"Communipaw" did capital service when he gave the subtle brain of Wm. Whipper a little work to do, and our readers the pleasure of seeing it done. Anything to promote earnest thinking among our people may be held as a good thing in itself, whether we assent to or dissent from the proposition which calls it forth.

We say this much before entering upon a compliance with the request of our friend Garnet, lest any should infer that the discussion now going on is distasteful to us, or that we desire to avoid it. The letter in question from Mr. Garnet is well calculated to make that impression. He evidently enjoys a wholesome confidence, not only in the goodness of his own cause but in his own ability to defend it.—Sallying out before us, as if in "complete steel," he entreats us to appear "in manly style," to *"gird up our loins,"* as if the contest were one requiring all our strength and activity. "Answer thou me if thou canst?"—As if an answer were impossible. Not content with this, he reminds us of his former similar entreaties, thus making it our duty to reply to him, if for no better reason than respect and courtesy towards himself.

The first question put to us by Mr. Garnet is a strange and almost preposterous one. He asks for our "objections to the civilization and christianization of Africa." The answer we have to make here is very easy and very ready, and can be given without even taking the trouble to observe the generous advice to "gird up our loins." We have not, dear brother, the least possible objection either to the civilization or to the christianization of Africa, and the question is just about as absurd and ridiculous as if you had asked us to "gird up our loins," and tell the world what objection Frederick Douglass has to the abolition of slavery, or the elevation of the free people of color in the United States! We not only have no objection to the civilization and christianization of Africa, but rejoice to know that through the instrumentality of commerce, and the labors of faithful missionaries, those very desirable blessings are already being realized in the land of my fathers Africa.

We Prefer America

Brother Garnet is a prudent man, and we admire his tact and address in presenting the issue before us, while we cannot assent entirely to its fairness. *"I did not ask you for a statement of your preference of America to Africa."* That is very aptly said, but is it impartially said? Does brother Garnet think such a preference, in view of all the circumstances, a wise and proper one? Or is he wholly indifferent as to the preference or the other? He seems to think that our preferences have nothing to do with the question between us and the African Civilization Society, while we think that this preference touches the very bone of contention. The African Civilization Society says to us, go to Africa, raise cotton, civilize the natives, become planters, merchants, compete with the slave States in the Liverpool cotton market, and thus break down American slavery. To which we simply and briefly reply, "we prefer to remain in America"; and we do insist upon it, in very face of our respected friend, that that is both a direct and candid answer. There is no dodging, no equivocation, but so far as we are concerned, the whole matter is ended. *You* go there, *we* stay here, is just the difference between us and the African Civilization Society, and the true issue upon which co-operation with it or opposition to it must turn.

Brother Garnet will pardon us for thinking it somewhat cool in him to ask us to give our objections to this new scheme. Our objections to it have been stated in substance, repeatedly. It has been no fault of ours if he has not read them.

As long ago as last September, we gave our views at large on this subject, in answer to an eloquent letter from Benjamin Coates, Esq., the real, but not the ostensible head of the African Civilization movement.

We Are Americans

Responding to proposals for American blacks to immigrate to Haiti, Frederick Douglass writes in the July 1861 issue of Douglass' Monthly *why he believes blacks should stay in the United States.*

I assume that more than two hundred years have demonstrated the ability of black people to live and flourish in the temperate climate of the United States; that we are now more than four millions in number, and that no mode of emigration contemplating our entire removal can possibly succeed; that we are Americans, speaking the same language, adopting the same customs, holding the same general opinions as to religion and government, and shall rise or fall with Americans; that upon the whole our history here has been one of progress and improvement, and in all the likelihoods of the case, will become more so; that the lines of social and political distinction, marking unjust and unnatural discriminations against us, are gradually being effaced; and that upon the fall of slavery, as fall it must, these discriminations will disappear still more rapidly. I hold that all schemes of wholesale emigration tend to awaken and keep alive and confirm the popular prejudices of the whites against us. They serve to kindle hopes of getting us out of the country; and while they thus naturally produce in the whites indifference to our welfare, they promote distrust and destroy in ourselves one very important element of progress—namely, the element of permanent location. 'A rolling stone gathers no moss.' No people will much improve a land from which they are momentarily expecting to be excluded, or from which they are to go speedily of their own accord. Permanence, a local habitation, as well as a name, is essential to our progress.

Meanwhile we will state briefly, for the benefit of friend Garnet, seven considerations, which prevent our co-operation with the African Civilization Society.

1. No one idea has given rise to more oppression and persecution toward the colored people of this country, than that which makes Africa, not America, their home. It is that wolfish idea that elbows us off the side walk, and denies us the rights of citizenship. The life and soul of this abominable idea would have been thrashed out of it long ago, but for the jesuitical and persistent teaching of the American Colonization Society. The natural and unfailing tendency of the African Civilization Society, by sending *"around the hat"* in all our towns and cities for money to send colored men to Africa, will be to keep life and power in this narrow,

bitter and persecuting idea, that Africa, not America, is the Negro's true home.

2. The abolition of American slavery, and the moral, mental and social improvement of our people, are objects of immediate, pressing and transcendent importance, involving a direct and positive issue with the pride and selfishness of the American people. The prosecution of this grand issue against all the principalities and powers of church and state, furnishes ample occupation for all our time and talents; and we instinctively shrink from any movement which involves a substitution of a doubtful and indirect issue, for one which is direct and certain, for we believe that the demand for the abolition of slavery now made in the name of humanity, and according to the law of the Living God, though long delayed, will, if faithfully pressed, certainly triumph.—The African Civilization Society proposes to plant its guns too far from the battlements of slavery for us. Its doctrines and measures are those of doubt and retreat, and it must land just where the American Colonization movement landed, upon the lying assumption, that white and black people can never live in the same land on terms of equality. Detesting this heresy as we do, and believing it to be full of all "deceivableness" of unrighteousness, we shun the paths that lead to it, no matter what taking names they bear, or how excellent the men who bid us to walk in them.

The Slave Trade

3. Among all the obstacles to the progress of civilization and of christianity in Africa, there is not one so difficult to overcome as the African slave trade. No argument is needed to make this position evident. The African Civilization Society will doubtless assent to its truth. Now, so regarding the slave trade, and believing that the existence of slavery in this country is one of the strongest props of the African slave trade, we hold that the best way to put down the slave trade, and to build up civilization in Africa, is to stand our ground and labor for the abolition of slavery in the U.S. But for slavery here, the slave trade would have been long since swept from the ocean by the united navies of Great Britain, France and the United States. The work, therefore, to which we are naturally and logically conducted, as the one of primary importance, is to abolish slavery. We thus get the example of a great nation on the right side, and break up, so far as America is concerned, a demand for the slave trade. More will have been done. The enlightened conscience of our nation, through its church and government, and its press, will be let loose against slavery and the slave trade wherever practiced.

4. One of the chief considerations upon which the African Civilization Society is recommended to our favorable regard, is its

tendency to break up the slave trade. We have looked at this recommendation, and find no reason to believe that any one man in Africa can do more for the abolition of that trade, while living in Africa, than while living in America. If we cannot make Virginia, with all her enlightenment and christianity, believe that there are better uses for her energies than employing them in breeding slaves for the market, we see not how we can expect to make Guinea, with its ignorance and savage selfishness, adopt our notions of political economy. Depend upon it, the savage chiefs on the western coast of Africa, who for ages have been accustomed to selling their captives into bondage, and pocketing the ready cash for them, will not more readily see and accept our moral and economical ideas, than the slave-traders of Maryland and Virginia. We are, therefore, less inclined to go to Africa to work against the slave-trade, than to stay here to work against it. Especially as the means for accomplishing our object are quite as promising here as there, and more especially since we are here already, with constitutions and habits suited to the country and its climate, and to its better institutions.

5. There are slaves in the United States to the number of four millions. They are stigmatized as an inferior race, fit only for slavery, incapable of improvement, and unable to take care of themselves. Now, it seems plain that here is the place, and we are the people to meet and put down these conclusions concerning our race. Certainly there is no place on the globe where the colored man can speak to a larger audience, either by precept or by example, than in the United States.

6. If slavery depended for its existence upon the cultivation of cotton, and were shut up to that single production, it might even then be fairly questioned whether any amount of cotton culture in Africa would materially affect the price of that article in this country, since demand and supply would go on together. But the case is very different. Slave labor can be employed in raising anything which human labor and the earth can produce. If one does not pay, another will. Christy says "Cotton is King," and our friends of the African Civilization movement are singing the same tune; but clearly enough it must appear to common sense, that "King Cotton" in America has nothing to fear from King Cotton in Africa.

7. We object to enrolling ourselves among the friends of that new Colonization scheme, because we believe that our people should be let alone, and given a fair chance to work out their own destiny where they are. We are perpetually kept, with wandering eyes and open mouths, looking out for some mighty revolution in our affairs here, which is to remove us from this country. The consequence is, that we do not take a firm hold upon the advantages and opportunities about us. Permanent location is a mighty ele-

ment of civilization. In a savage state men roam about, having no continued abiding place. They are *"going, going, going."* Towns and cities, houses and homes, are only built up by men who halt long enough to build them. There is a powerful motive for the cultivation of an honorable character, in the fact that we have a country, a neighborhood, a home. The full effect of this motive has not hitherto been experienced by our people. When in slavery, we were liable to perpetual sales, transfers and removals; and now that we are free, we are doomed to be constantly harassed with schemes to get us out of the country. We are quite tired of all this, and wish no more of it.

To all this it will be said that Douglass is opposed to our following the example of white men. They are pushing East, West, North and South. They are going to Oregon, Central America, Australia, South Africa and all over the world. Why should we not have the same right to better our condition that other men have and exercise? Any man who says that we deny this right, or even object to its exercise, only deceives the ignorant by such representations.

A Public Issue

If colored men are convinced that they can better their condition by going to Africa, or anywhere else, we shall respect them if they will go, just as we respect others who have gone to California, Fraser Island, Oregon and the West Indies. They are self-moved, self-sustained, and their success or failure is their own individual concern. But widely different is the case, when men combine, in societies, under taking titles, send out agents to collect money, and call upon us to help them travel from continent to continent to promote some selfish or benevolent end. In the one case, it is none of our business where our people go.—They are of age, and can act for themselves.—But when they ask the public to go, or for money, sympathy, aid, or co-operation, or attempt to make it appear anybody's duty to go, the case ceases to be a private individual affair, and becomes a public question, and he who believes that he can make a better use of his time, talents, and influence, than such a movement proposes for him, may very properly say so, without in any measure calling in question the equal right of our people to migrate.

Again it may be said that we are opposed to sending the Gospel to benighted Africa; but this is not the case. The *American Missionary Society*, in its rooms at 48 Beekman Street, has never had occasion to complain of any such opposition, nor will it have such cause. But we will not anticipate the objections which may be brought to the foregoing views. They seem to us sober, rational, and true; but if otherwise, we shall be glad to have them honestly criticised.

CHAPTER 3

Reconstruction and the Rise of Jim Crow

Chapter Preface

The Civil War marks a clear dividing line in African-American history. Prior to the conflict, most blacks lived in slavery, a condition that shaped their whole lives. During the Civil War thousands of slaves escaped behind Union lines and supported the war effort against the Confederacy as spies, laborers, and soldiers. Their efforts were rewarded in December 1865, months after the last Confederate forces had surrendered, when slavery was formally abolished in the United States by the Thirteenth Amendment to the Constitution. An era had ended, and Americans now faced fundamental questions concerning the role and status of the four million former slaves. Historians Benjamin Quarles and Leslie H. Fishel write that to many white Americans the newly freed slave

> was an unknown quantity, largely uneducated, grossly stereotyped, crudely visible, practically untried in a free society, and a potential threat to the existing political, economic, and social alignments. If allowed to vote, which party would he support? If allowed to compete in a free market, whose jobs would he take? If permitted to intermix with whites, what social complications would follow?

The viewpoints in this chapter examine some of the debates over these questions.

The era of Reconstruction (1865–1877) was a time of significant political gain and achievement by African Americans. With the passage of the 1866 Civil Rights Act and the Fourteenth Amendment to the Constitution, the former slaves were recognized as U.S. citizens possessing full citizenship rights. Black men gained the vote after the Fifteenth Amendment, which forbade states from disfranchising their citizens on the basis of race, was passed in 1870. On the state level, blacks played important roles in the reorganization of most of the former Confederate states. Blacks were politically influential in these states because federal military rule provided some measure of protection for black leaders and voters against local white backlash and because many whites had been disfranchised for participating in the Confederate rebellion. Sixteen African Americans—all of whom were members of the Republican Party, as were most black voters—were elected to Congress over the next decade, and hundreds more served in state legislatures and local offices.

However, many whites resented the growth of black political power. The Ku Klux Klan and other secret organizations launched campaigns of terror, injuring or assassinating local black and white Republican leaders as well as black citizens who voted or asserted their political rights. In part because of such violent tactics (and also because many ex-Confederates were pardoned and enfranchised), the conservative white leadership of the Democratic Party, which had dominated the South prior to the Civil War, was able to reclaim state governments, beginning with Virginia in 1869. Black political power was further eroded by the withdrawal of federal troops from the South in 1877. In the 1890s many southern states revised their constitutions to restrict blacks' ability to vote, thereby cementing white one-party rule in the region. The Supreme Court facilitated these developments with narrow interpretations of the Fourteenth and Fifteenth Amendments that upheld most state laws dealing with race.

Besides losing political power, African Americans in the South following 1877 lost ground in education, social mobility, and economic advancement. Former slaves who had left their masters to seek work elsewhere found themselves barred from labor unions and excluded from skilled trades. Many became tenant farmers and sharecroppers. Some were entrapped by debt peonage and the convict-lease system, in which blacks arrested on minor charges were rented out to plantation owners. African Americans made significant gains in education (the black literacy rate rose from 19 percent in 1870 to 43 percent by 1890), but by 1878 most southern states had segregated school systems, with black schools receiving much less funding than white schools. Laws mandating racial segregation spread to transportation and other areas of social contact. The net result of all these developments was the creation in the South of the "Jim Crow" society of rigid racial segregation.

The viewpoints in this chapter examine some of the issues concerning African Americans in the decades following the abolition of slavery.

"The Freedmen's Bureau, or any agency to interfere between the freedman and his former master, is only productive of mischief."

The Freedmen's Bureau Is Harmful

James D.B. De Bow (1820–1867)

The months and years immediately following the Civil War were dominated by the question of how to integrate the four million slaves emancipated by the conflict into American society. The United States government struggled with this question while at the same time trying to govern the former Confederate states, reunite the nation, and recover from the Civil War's destruction. Significant differences of opinion soon developed between President Andrew Johnson and Republicans in Congress over how to deal with these issues. The president generally supported cooperation with the local southern white leadership and opposed both immediate suffrage for blacks and massive social reform within the South. A faction of the Republican Party, known as Radical Republicans, sought to use the federal government to secure the franchise and other civil rights for blacks. One area of dispute between President Johnson and Radical Republicans in Congress was the work and function of the Freedmen's Bureau, a federal agency created by Congress in March 1865, whose responsibilities included supervising the education and labor arrangements of the former slaves.

To oversee the development of policy during this crucial time, Congress in December 1865 established the Joint Committee on Reconstruction. One of the committee's tasks was to gather information on conditions in the South. From January to May 1866 the committee (divided into four subcommittees) took testimony

From James D.B. De Bow, *Reports of the Committees of the House of Representatives*, 39th Cong., 1st sess., March 28, 1866.

from a wide variety of witnesses, including Union and Confederate army officers, travelers, journalists, and former slaves.

The following viewpoint is taken from testimony by James D.B. De Bow, one of the prominent ex-Confederates questioned. De Bow was the founder and editor of *De Bow's Review*, a journal that received national recognition prior to the Civil War for its economic and political analyses of the South and for its strong advocacy of slavery. During the Civil War De Bow worked for the Confederacy as a cotton purchasing agent. His opinions expressed here on the work of the Freedmen's Bureau and on blacks in general are representative of many ex-Confederates who did not favor the granting of suffrage and other citizenship rights to blacks. De Bow was questioned by George H. Williams, a senator from Oregon who was part of the Republican Party's Radical wing.

Question. State if you have been, at any time since the cessation of hostilities, in the State of Louisiana and if so, how long, and what opportunities you have had to ascertain the temper and disposition of the people towards the general government.

Answer. I spent five or six weeks of the present year in Louisiana, and was in intimate association with the citizens there of all classes. I am a resident of that State, and of course largely acquainted, and having been absent during the war, after the surrender of the city, I met a great many of the people on my return. I have also just returned from a general tour at the south.

Question. What are the views and feelings of the people there as to the late war and its results, and as to the future condition of that State in its relations to the federal government?

Answer. There seems to be a general—you may say universal—acquiescence in the results. There is a great deal of dissatisfaction as to the course in reference to their condition pursued by the federal government. I think the people having fairly tried the experiment of secession are perfectly satisfied with the result, and that there is no disposition in any quarter, in any shape or form, to embarrass the United States government, or to refrain from the most complete performance of all the duties of citizenship. I saw nothing of that sort. All parties, those who were opposed to the war and those who were in favor of the war, are now agreed that it is for the best interest of the State to perform all the duties of citizenship, and to accept whatever the government has effected in reference to the negro, as well as in reference to other questions. . . .

Question. What is your opinion of the necessity or utility of the

Freedmen's Bureau, or of any agency of that kind?

Answer. I think if the whole regulation of the negroes, or freedmen, were left to the people of the communities in which they live, it will be administered for the best interest of the negroes as well as of the white men. I think there is a kindly feeling on the part of the planters towards the freedmen. They are not held at all responsible for anything that has happened. They are looked upon as the innocent cause. In talking with a number of planters, I remember some of them telling me they were succeeding very well with their freedmen, having got a preacher to preach to them and a teacher to teach them, believing it was for the interest of the planter to make the negro feel reconciled; for, to lose his services

Freedmen's Bureau Encourages Trouble

Among the former Confederate officials who testified before the Joint Committee on Reconstruction in 1866 was Caleb G. Forshey, founder and superintendent of the Texas Military Institute and Confederate army engineer during the Civil War.

Question. What is your opinion as to the necessity and advantages of the Freedmen's Bureau, or an agency of that kind, in Texas?

Answer. My opinion is that it is not needed; my opinion is stronger than that—that the effect of it is to irritate, if nothing else. While in New York City recently I had a conversation with some friends from Texas, from five distant points in the state. We met together and compared opinions; and the opinion of each was the same, that the Negroes had generally gone to work since January; that except where the Freedmen's Bureau had interfered, or rather encouraged troubles, such as little complaints, especially between Negro and Negro, the Negro's disposition was very good, and they had generally gone to work, a vast majority of them with their former masters. I was very gratified to learn that from districts where I feared the contrary. Still this difference was made, particularly by Mr. Carpenter, from Jefferson, the editor of the *Jefferson Herald*. He said that in two or three counties where they had not been able to organize the Freedmen's Bureau, there had been no trouble at all; nearly all the Negroes had gone to work. The impression in Texas at present is that the Negroes under the influence of the Freedmen's Bureau do worse than without it.

I want to state that I believe all our former owners of Negroes are the friends of the Negroes; and that the antagonism paraded in the papers of the North does not exist at all. I know the fact is the very converse of that; and good feeling always prevails between the masters and the slaves. But the Negroes went off and left them in the lurch; my own family was an instance of it. But they came back after a time, saying they had been free enough and wanted a home.

as a laborer for even a few months would be very disastrous. The sentiment prevailing is, that it is for the interest of the employer to teach the negro, to educate his children, to provide a preacher for him, and to attend to his physical wants. And I may say I have not seen any exception to that feeling in the south. Leave the people to themselves, and they will manage very well. The Freedmen's Bureau, or any agency to interfere between the freedman and his former master, is only productive of mischief. There are constant appeals from one to the other and continual annoyances. It has a tendency to create dissatisfaction and disaffection on the part of the laborer, and is in every respect in its result most unfavorable to the system of industry that is now being organized under the new order of things in the south. I do not think there is any difference of opinion upon this subject.

Question. Do you think the white men of the south would do justice by the negroes in making contracts and in paying them for their labor?

Answer. Before these negroes were freed, there were some two or three hundred thousand free negroes in the south, and some four or five hundred thousand of them in the country. There were a great many in Louisiana. There were in New Orleans some free negroes among the wealthiest men we had. I made a comparison when I was superintendent of the United States census in 1850, and found that the condition of the free negroes in the south, their education, &c., was better; that as a class they were immeasurably better off than the free people of the north. I never heard any cause of complaint of our treatment of these people in the south before the war, even from northern sources, and I do not presume there would be more cause of complaint now. If we performed our duty to this same class of population when the great mass of negroes were held by us as slaves, I think it should go very far to indicate that we should not be lacking in our duties to them now. There are free negroes in Louisiana who owned fifty or a hundred slaves, and plantations on the coast, and there were hundreds of them who owned more or less property.

Slavery vs. Free Labor

Question. What is your opinion as to the relative advantages to the blacks of the present system of free labor, as compared with that of slavery as it heretofore existed in this country?

Answer. If the negro would work, the present system is much cheaper. If we can get the same amount of labor from the same persons, there is no doubt of the result in respect to *economy*. Whether the same amount of labor can be obtained, it is too soon yet to decide. We must allow one summer to pass first. They are working now very well on the plantations. That is the general testimony. The negro women are not disposed to field work as they formerly were, and I think there will be less work from them in the future than there has been in the past. The men are rather inclined to get their wives into other employment, and I think that will be the constant tendency, just as it is with the whites. Therefore, the real number of agricultural laborers will be reduced. I have no idea the efficiency of those who work will be increased. If we can only keep up their efficiency to the standard before the war, it will be better for the south, without doubt, upon the mere money question, because it is cheaper to hire the negro than to own him. Now a plantation can be worked without any outlay of capital by hiring the negro and hiring the plantation.

Question. What, in your opinion, is to be the effect upon the blacks?

Answer. I think it will be disastrous to them. I judge that because of the experience of other countries, and not from any experience we have had ourselves. I judge by their shiftless character, and their disposition to crowd into the cities. It is what I see all over the south. You will find large numbers of them in every city, crowded together in miserable shanties, eking out a very uncertain subsistence; and, so far, the mortality has been very great among them. They were not disposed to enter upon any regular work before the 1st of January. They were confident in the expectation that the lands were to be divided among them up to that time. But after the 1st of January they became satisfied they were not to get the lands, and they very generally went to work.

Question. What arrangements are generally made among the landholders and the black laborers in the south?

Answer. I think they generally get wages. A great many persons, however, think it better to give them an interest in the crops. That is getting to be very common.

Civil Rights and Education

Question. What do you find the disposition of the people as to the extension of civil rights to the blacks—the right to sue and enforce their contracts and to hold property, real and personal, like white people?

Answer. I think there is a willingness to give them every right except the right of suffrage. It is believed they are unfit to exercise that. The idea is entertained by many that they will eventually be endowed with that right. It is only a question of time; but the universal conviction is that if it ever be conceded, it will be necessary to prepare for it by slow and regular means, as the white race was prepared. I believe everybody unites in the belief that it would be disastrous to give the right of suffrage now. Time and circumstances may alter the case. There is no difference of opinion upon this subject now.

Question. Suppose the negroes were to vote now, what would be the influences operating upon them as to the exercise of that vote?

Answer. The negro would be apt to vote with his employer if he was treated well. That is his character. They generally go with their employer; but it is probable they would be tampered with a great deal. There would be emissaries sent among them to turn their minds; so that, although I understand some prominent men think the negro would generally vote with his master, I doubt it. I think the tendency would be in that direction; but that they would be drawn off by emissaries sent there for malicious purposes, though a great many would, no doubt, go with their former masters. You cannot make any rule. I find that northern men who have come to the south, purchased land, and gone to cultivating cotton or anything else, talk now very much as we do on these questions. Their views upon all these questions, with the little experience they have had, are very much the same as those of southern men. They say our experience, in regard to these questions, is worth more than their theories.

Question. What facilities are the people disposed to give the freedmen in becoming educated?

Answer. I think they generally laugh at the idea of the negro learning. They have been accustomed to the idea that the negroes are pretty stupid. I do not think there would be any opposition to their becoming educated. We have schools all about for them, but the people sometimes laugh at the idea of the negroes learning much. Under the institution of slavery we used to teach them everything nearly except to read. On almost every plantation they were taught the Bible, the catechism, prayers, hymns, &c. But in regard to their being educated, so far as they are capable, I think the people regard it as for their best interest to afford them every facility—that is, the better informed people.

Question. Do the employers of negroes in the south claim or exercise the right of physical compulsion to enforce their contracts?

Answer. No, sir, I know of no such claim—nothing of the kind.

VIEWPOINT 2

"The withdrawal of the Freedmen's Bureau would be followed by a condition of anarchy and bloodshed."

The Freedmen's Bureau Is Essential

Thomas Conway (1840–1887)

The Freedmen's Bureau was created by Congress in March 1865 to provide for the welfare of the newly freed slaves. In addition to dispensing food and medical care, its agents helped establish schools, brokered labor agreements between former slaves and owners, and in a few cases resettled freed slaves on confiscated land. The bureau's presence was resented by many white southerners and was a subject of dispute between President Andrew Johnson and Republicans in Congress.

The following viewpoint on the Freedmen's Bureau and on post–Civil War race relations is excerpted from the testimony of Thomas Conway before the Joint Committee on Reconstruction. Established by Congress in December 1865, the committee held hearings and conducted investigations into conditions in the South in 1866. Conway, an Irish-born Baptist minister, was a Union army chaplain during the Civil War. Following the war he became a Freedmen's Bureau agent in Louisiana. Responding to questions by George H. Williams, a Republican senator from Oregon, Conway paints a bleak picture of race relations in Louisiana and asserts that the Freedmen's Bureau is necessary to shield blacks from violent retribution by local whites. He also argues in favor of black suffrage and education.

From Thomas Conway, *Reports of the Committees of the House of Representatives*, 39th Cong., 1st sess., February 22, 1866.

In 1866 Congress passed a law (over Johnson's veto) extending the life and expanding the power of the Freedmen's Bureau. However, the agency remained chronically short of funds and officials and ceased most of its activities by 1870. Conway himself, as Louisiana's state superintendent of schools, helped establish fifteen hundred schools for African Americans.

Question. What, in your judgment, would be the effect of the withdrawal of the Freedmen's Bureau or some organization or system like that from Louisiana?

Answer. I should expect in Louisiana, as in the whole southern country, that the withdrawal of the Freedmen's Bureau would be followed by a condition of anarchy and bloodshed, and I say that much in the light of as large an experience upon the subject as any man in the country. I have been in the army since the 19th of April, 1861; I have been over the whole country, almost from Baltimore to the Gulf. I was one of the first who held any official position in regard to the freedmen, and I am pained at the conviction I have in my own mind that if the Freedmen's Bureau is withdrawn the result will be fearful in the extreme. What it has already done and is now doing in shielding these people, only incites the bitterness of their foes. They will be murdered by wholesale, and they in their turn will defend themselves. It will not be persecution merely; it will be slaughter; and I doubt whether the world has ever known the like. These southern rebels, when the power is once in their hands, will stop with nothing short of extermination. Governor [James M.] Wells himself told me that he expected in ten years to see the whole colored race exterminated, and that conviction is shared very largely among the white people of the south. It has been threatened by leading men there that they would exterminate the freedmen. They have said so in my hearing. In reply I said that they could not drive the freedmen out of the nation, because, in the first place, they would not go; and for another reason, that they had no authority to drive them out; and for a third reason, that they were wanted in the south as laborers. To that they replied, that, if necessary, they would get their laborers from Europe; that white laborers would be more agreeable to them; that the negro must be gotten rid of in some way, and that, too, as speedily as possible. I have heard it so many times, and from so many different quarters, that I believe it is a fixed determination, and that they are looking anxiously to the extermination of the whole negro race from the country. There is an agent here now, with letters from the governor of Louisiana to parties in New York, with a view of entering at once upon negotiations to secure laborers from various parts of Europe. There are other parties endeavoring to get coolies into the south, and in various places there are immense efforts made to obtain white labor to supplant that of the negro. It is a part of the immense and desperate programme which they have adopted and expect to carry out within ten years. It is the same determination to which I referred in my report. I said the negro race would be exterminated unless protected by the strong arm of the government; no weak arm will do. The very strongest arm of the government is needed to shield them. The wicked work has already commenced, and it could be shown that the policy pursued by the government is construed by the rebels as not being opposed to it.

Blacks in Danger

Several African Americans testified before the Joint Committee on Reconstruction in 1866. Among them was Daniel Norton, a physician who moved from New York to Yorktown, Virginia, during the Civil War, who gave this account of conditions facing blacks.

Question. How do the returned rebels treat the colored people?

Answer. They have in some cases treated them well, but in more cases they have not. A number of persons living in the country have come into Yorktown and reported to the Freedmen's Bureau that they have not been treated well; that they worked all the year and had received no pay, and were driven off on the first of January. They say that the owners with whom they had been living rented out their places, sold their crops, and told them they had no further use for them, and that they might go to the Yankees. . . .

Question. In case of the removal of the military force from among you, and also of the Freedmen's Bureau, what would the whites do with you?

Answer. I do not think that the colored people would be safe. They would be in danger of being hunted and killed. The spirit of the whites against the blacks is much worse than it was before the war; a white gentleman with whom I was talking made this remark: he said he was well disposed toward the colored people, but that finding that they took up arms against him, he had come to the conclusion that he never wanted to have anything to do with them, or to show any spirit of kindness toward them. These were his sentiments.

Question. State, if you please, what you know as to the views and feelings of the white people in that region of country—those who have heretofore been rebels—as to the authority of the general government, and also as to whether any change in their views and feelings are manifest since hostilities ceased; if so, what that change is, and what has been the occasion of it, in your opinion.

Answer. In the neighborhood of New Orleans, comprising about twenty parishes in Louisiana, which we have mostly controlled since the time of General [Benjamin] Butler's arrival, there has been, to my knowledge, a considerable loyal element—not an element which became loyal since the occupation of the district by our troops, but men who were loyal previously. With those who sympathized with and participated in the rebellion, (and I think I know them all) I was brought in contact, and with nearly every propertyholder in the State. My communication with them, and my knowledge of their actions, convinced me that at heart they were not changed, but were opposed to us and opposed to our government—not willing to make their opposition physical, but secret and quiet. They do now, and always have thrown every possible obstacle in the way of our work—men, too, with whom I had expected better things. Some of the leading officers of the State down there—men who do much to form and control the opinions of the masses—instead of doing as they promised, and quietly submitting to the authority of the government are engaged in issuing slave codes and in promulgating them to their subordinates, ordering them to carry them into execution, and this to the knowledge of State officials of a higher character, the governor and others. And the men who issued them were not punished except as the military authorities punish them. The governor inflicted no punishment on them while I was there, and I don't know that, up to this day, he has ever punished one of them. These rules were simply the old black code of the State, with the word "slave" expunged and "negro" substituted. The most odious features of slavery were preserved in them. . . .

Forced Labor

Question. Are the people there disposed to resort to personal violence or chastisement to compel the negroes to work now?

Answer. They are so disposed in nearly every instance. A resort to violence is the first thought that I have seen exhibited when freedmen did not act exactly to suit the employer. The planters frequently came to me with requests (in fact, it was almost daily) to be allowed to correct the laborers on their own plantations. It is the universal conviction, and the universal purpose with them, too, to do that so far as they are allowed to do it; and, so far as they can, they will do it. The only constraint put upon them in regard to it is through the agency of the Freedmen's Bureau. Without that, I am satisfied, they would very rapidly return to the old system of slavery. In some portions of the State of Louisiana, now, they have organized patrols of militiamen, who go up and down the roads the same as if they were scouting in time of war, to prevent the negroes from going from one place to another. I am satisfied, from the most reliable reports, that under the most strict rules of evidence it could be proved that in portions of the State these acts are being done the same as under the old system; that, except as regards buying and selling, the old system of slavery is being carried on in all its essential features, and that there is a deep-rooted determination, arising from the old habits of treating the negro, to continue the same treatment and the same restrictions that existed prior to the war. The Freedmen's Bureau was regarded by the planters in Louisiana in the language of one of their leaders, as a "conservative machine." This arose from the conduct of General Fullerton, whom the President sent to relieve me.

Question. What is your opinion as to the extent of general knowledge among the freedmen; and what is their capacity for understanding their rights and the questions that are being agitated in the country?

Answer. I have taken a great deal of pains to secure, for my own satisfaction, accurate information on that subject, and I have questioned the lowest and meanest of them as to their ideas of liberty and their duty as citizens; and I have never yet found any view expressed by them, or any evidence through their answers or conduct, which led me to think they were any lower or more ignorant than the lower order of the white people who live down there or that they had any less accurate knowledge of government and duty toward it than the lower class of white people. I have seen very ignorant white people there who had all the privileges of citizenship. I have seen them go to the polls and vote, when they had no better idea of the questions at issue in the election, or the importance of the act they were performing, than the lowest negro I ever saw. The great majority of colored people understand very well and have a very accurate idea of what their personal liberty is, and how far it is to be regulated in order to be a blessing to them, and a very good idea of their duty as citizens. They have one idea which underlies every other, and that is, that notwithstanding the treatment they receive at the hands of the government, and the want of complete protection and complete liberty the government has so far caused them to suffer, they believe that it will yet secure them full protection, full liberty, and a full enjoyment of all their rights as citizens and as men; and they are working very energetically in Louisiana for the attainment of that purpose. They have their societies and clubs, in which they canvass very carefully every act of the government in regard to them, and in regard to the rebels who live all around them. They read the newspapers pretty generally. I believe two-thirds of the negroes in Louisiana can read. They publish a newspaper there, read it, and sustain it. With the use of schools, and the diligence in learning among them, which arises partly from the suddenness of the opportunity presented, and in part from a desire to ascertain precisely what the government is doing for them, and how they can best live as men and citizens ought to live. These reasons, I think, mainly explain the causes of the desire they manifest in this regard, and the result will, I think, be their nearly all becoming quite intelligent in a short time.

The Right to Vote

Question. What, in your opinion, would be the effect upon whites, blacks, and all concerned, of giving the negro the right to vote?

Answer. I do not think the effect would be to inaugurate a war of races there, for this reason: The negroes are so numerous, and they would be so intensely determined to enjoy what rights they have in that respect, that the whites would submit, seeing the impossibility of preventing it, and for the purpose of avoiding collisions and bloodshed in the country. The lives and safety of loyal white men require the protection and assistance that would grow from the negro's vote. I think the troops should be retained, and that small squads of them should be stationed all through the country, so as to shield the freedmen in the enjoyment of this right till the whites have become familiar with it. The militia forces should not be organized in the south during this generation. These things being done, my judgment is that there would be no trouble at all. On the contrary, it would, in a more speedy and thorough manner than any other, secure permanent peace and prosperity to the country. In the present condition of things there they cannot hope for peace or prosperity, because loyal men cannot remain without the protection of the government, and the negroes have no safety in the protection of their white foes. When the negroes come to see that their own life and liberty are to be sacrificed, they will struggle manfully against such a result, and they will importune the government, and call upon mankind to be their witness, until liberty and safety are insured them; they will persevere devotedly until their rights are accomplished. There are so many of them, and so many white people to help them, I don't see how the government can resist giving them every protection warranted by the Constitution.

"This bill . . . will, more or less, bring about an antagonism of the races; and that state of things would not be best for the colored man."

A Federal Civil Rights Bill Is Dangerous

Robert B. Vance (1828–1899)

During Reconstruction, Congress passed two major laws and three constitutional amendments dealing with the civil rights of blacks. The Thirteenth Amendment, passed in Congress shortly before the end of the Civil War, abolished slavery. The Civil Rights Act of 1866 declared all blacks to be citizens and forbade states from discriminating on the basis of race. The law was designed to counteract special laws (Black Codes) which were passed by many southern states in 1865 and 1866 in an attempt to legally bind former slaves in restrictive labor contracts and to curtail their freedoms in other ways. It was to protect the 1866 law from possible future congressional repeal and/or Supreme Court invalidation that Congress passed the Fourteenth Amendment, ratified in July 1868. The Fifteenth Amendment, ratified in 1870, made it illegal for states to deny citizens the right to vote because of race.

The second major civil rights law, passed in 1875, was first introduced in 1870 by Charles Sumner, Republican senator from Massachusetts. Sumner was among those who believed that despite the 1866 law and the three new amendments to the Constitution, many African Americans were still being denied their full civil rights. Among the provisions in the bill were statutes banning segregated schools and calling for "the full and equal enjoyment of all the accommodations . . . of inns, public conveyances . . . , theaters, and other places of public amusement."

From Robert B. Vance, *Congressional Record*, 43rd Cong., 1st sess., January 10, 1874.

This second civil rights bill received much criticism, especially from white southern Democrats, who by the early 1870s were re-taking control of southern state governments and congressional seats from the Republican Party. The following viewpoint is by Robert B. Vance, a former Civil War Confederate officer who was a Democratic representative from North Carolina from 1873 to 1885. Vance, speaking before Congress in January 1874, professes personal concern for blacks and argues that Sumner's civil rights bill would cause them much harm by jeopardizing peaceful race relations in the South.

Mr. Speaker, having been unable to obtain the floor on the civil-rights bill, I propose to devote a portion of my time to the discussion of that subject; and I think I can do so without preju-dice and without subjecting myself truthfully to the charge of ha-tred toward the colored race. In the will of my grandfather (who was one of those who struggled for liberty upon the heights of King's Mountain) he enjoined it upon his children and his grand-children to treat kindly the colored people upon the plantation. I hope never to forget a sentiment so noble and so worthy of obedi-ence. In fact, as a southern man, as one who has sympathized from my earliest time of knowledge with the South in all the great principles and struggles which have interested her, I have felt it my duty to advance in every laudable way the interests of the col-ored race in this country. I have even taught a colored Sunday-school of one hundred and fifty scholars. I have endeavored in every way possible to advance the interests of that race. I feel, therefore, that I can speak upon this subject without prejudice.

The charge has been made against the people of the South that their opposition to such measures as the civil-rights bill has arisen from prejudice and hatred. This charge is unfounded; it is untrue. Before the war—in the days past and gone—in the days when there were four million slaves in the South, the churches of the South sent missionaries into the cotton plantations, and down into the orange groves, and out upon the rolling prairies of Texas. Into all parts of the country where great numbers of colored peo-ple were collected the churches sent their missionaries, and held up there the standard of the Cross, instructing them in the sub-lime principles which relate to questions vastly more important than mere earthly things.

I have yet to meet the southern man (and I thank God for it) who does not in his heart rejoice that the colored man is free. In my intercourse with the people of my own land, in my travels through the "sunny South," I have found the feeling everywhere one of gratitude and thankfulness that the chains of the colored man have been broken; that he is now permitted to walk the earth a free man.

Sir, the people of the South were not to blame for the introduction of slavery among them. It came from elsewhere, and became incorporated as a part of our institutions. The old colored women nursed the white children of the South, while kindness and friendship were maintained between the two races. Such an institution could not be readily abolished. It could probably only be done by the shock of arms.

Every southern man who will call to mind the fact that after the thunder of artillery had ceased, when the clang of arms was no more heard in the country, the southern people rallied and took the oath to support the proclamations of Mr. Lincoln, in order that the colored man might be free. Those proclamations, Mr. Speaker, were regarded at the time as unconstitutional; yet the southern people were willing that the colored man should enjoy his freedom, and all over the South they came forward and took the oath to support those proclamations.

Following hard upon that, the conventions of the Southern States assembled, and by a solemn act ratified the freedom of the colored man, confirming it forever by statute upon the records of their governments.

What else did they do? They went to work and secured the colored man in all his civil rights, or what may properly be termed civil rights. The people there consented that he should vote; they consented he should hold office; they consented he should serve upon juries; they consented that he should hold property, and that he should be a witness in court. All the real rights properly known as civil rights were guaranteed to the colored man in that section; and the charge cannot justly be made against this people that they are opposed to according civil rights to the colored man on account of any prejudice or hatred, for it is not in their hearts.

Civil Rights and Social Rights

Why, then, do we oppose the civil-rights bill? That is the question; and speaking as I do, and feeling as I speak, without prejudice, I will show what is the real objection to the bill known as the civil-rights bill. I think gentlemen of the House will bear me out when I say the title of the bill we had before us ought to be changed, and made to read thus: "A bill to protect the colored people in their social rights." That is the way it should read.

Now, Mr. Speaker the distinguished gentleman from Massachusetts [Benjamin Butler] laid down the law, and it has not been controverted, that all men are entitled under the law to the right to go to a hotel, to ride in a public railway carriage, to interment, and to be taught in the public schools sustained by moneys raised by taxation.

It is laid down as the common law of the land. Now, let us see for a few minutes, Mr. Speaker, how the case stands. There is no railway car in all the South which the colored man cannot ride in. That is his civil right. This bill proposes that he should have the opportunity or the right to go into a first-class car and sit with white gentlemen and white ladies. I submit if that is not a social right. There is a distinction between the two. Now, there is not a hotel in the South where the colored man cannot get entertainment such as food and lodgings. That is his civil right. The bill of the committee provides that there shall be no distinction. Even if he is allowed to go into the dining-room, and is placed at a separate table because of his color, it will be a violation of this law. Placing him, therefore, at the same table with the whites is a social right.

Now, sir, provision has been made for free schools in my own native State of North Carolina. We have cheerfully taxed ourselves there for the education of our people, including the colored race; but separate schools are organized for the instruction of the latter. One of the civil rights of the colored man undoubtedly is the right to be educated out of moneys raised by taxation. His children, under the law, have that right; but this bill goes further, and provides that colored children shall go into the same school with white children, mixing the colored children and the white children in the same schools. I submit to the House whether that is not a social right instead of a civil right. Therefore it is I say this bill ought to be changed, or rather its title ought to be changed. The real objection, then, to civil rights, so called, is that it is not best for both races, that in fact it will be detrimental to the interests of both races.

Now, Mr. Speaker, I propose to show briefly how that will be. In the first place, the true policy in regard to the intercourse of mankind all over this broad earth is in the recognition of the fact that such intercourse is one made up of mutual interests. It is the interest of the hotel-keeper to entertain his guests, it is the interest of the railway company to transport passengers; the interests are mutual; and that is the true policy all the world over. But whenever you undertake to force persons of color into their social rights, then, in my judgment, you have done the colored man a serious damage. Let the people of the South alone, sir, and this thing will adjust itself. It will come out all right. In coming to this city the other day colored men were sitting in first-class cars with their wives, where they were admitted by the managers of the road; and I am told in this city one of the first hotels admits colored men as guests. It will adjust itself if let alone; but if you undertake to coerce society before it is ready, you will damage the

Segregation Justified in *Plessy v. Ferguson*

In the late 1800s the Supreme Court of the United States issued several rulings that were bitterly criticized by African Americans and those supportive of their civil rights. In 1883 the Court invalidated major sections of the 1875 Civil Rights Act, arguing that Congress had no power to outlaw discriminatory actions by private individuals and businesses. In the famous 1896 case of Plessy v. Ferguson, *the Supreme Court upheld a Louisiana law mandating racial segregation for railroad passengers. The following passage is an excerpt from Chief Justice Henry B. Brown's majority opinion in* Plessy.

So far, then, as a conflict with the Fourteenth Amendment is concerned, the case reduces itself to the question whether the statute of Louisiana is a reasonable regulation, and with respect to this there must necessarily be a large discretion on the part of the legislature. In determining the question of reasonableness it is at liberty to act with reference to the established usages, customs and traditions of the people, and with a view to the promotion of their comfort, and the preservation of the public peace and good order. Gauged by this standard, we cannot say that a law which authorizes or even requires the separation of the two races in public conveyances is unreasonable, or more obnoxious to the Fourteenth Amendment than the acts of Congress requiring separate schools for colored children in the District of Columbia, the constitutionality of which does not seem to have been questioned, or the corresponding acts of state legislatures.

We consider the underlying fallacy of the plaintiff's argument to consist in the assumption that the enforced separation of the two races stamps the colored race with a badge of inferiority. If this be so, it is not by reason of anything found in the act, but solely because the colored race chooses to put that construction upon it. . . . The argument also assumes that social prejudices may be overcome by legislation, and that equal rights cannot be secured to the negro except by an enforced commingling of the two races. We cannot accept this proposition. If the two races are to meet upon terms of social equality, it must be the result of natural affinities, a mutual appreciation of each other's merits and a voluntary consent of individuals. . . . Legislation is powerless to eradicate racial instincts or to abolish distinctions based upon physical differences, and the attempt to do so can only result in accentuating the difficulties of the present situation. If the civil and political rights of both races be equal one cannot be inferior to the other civilly or politically. If one race be inferior to the other socially, the Constitution of the United States cannot put them upon the same plane.

colored man in all his interests, and at the same time do damage to the white race.

There are between four and five millions of colored people in the South, whose interests are intimately and closely connected with those of the white people. The one cannot well do without the other. Where does the colored man get his place to live, where does he obtain employment? In a great measure from the white men of the country, and almost entirely from those opposed to this bill. And I tell the House now, through you, Mr. Speaker, that the great majority of the people of the Southern States, of all political shades of opinion, are opposed to anything like force in this matter.

Look at my own State, sir. As I went home from the capital during the holidays I met with republican members of the Legislature of North Carolina who stated that we ought to oppose this bill. Republicans do not want it. They think it is wrong. A resolution was introduced into the Legislature of North Carolina in regard to this subject, and it received a very small vote. It did not receive the vote of the republican party. And, sir, it is my opinion that the colored people of the South *en masse* do not want it. They do not want to be brought into apparent antagonism to the white people, because their interests are closely connected together. The colored man cannot do well in the South, he cannot prosper, unless he has the sympathies, unless he has the fostering hand, unless he has the kind care, of the white man extended to him; his interests will suffer if this should not be the case.

And, sir, it is necessary anyhow in this world of ours that there should be kindness running from heart to heart. There has been enough trouble and enough sorrow in this world already. War has stamped its foot upon human sympathies. It has left its scars upon every human heart, sir; and now there ought to be sympathy, there ought to be kindness, there ought to be oneness of interest pervading the whole land. And these people need that thing. You rob the colored man by the passage of this bill more or less of the friendship of the owners of the soil in the South. And you rob him, sir, of the opportunity of education. Gentlemen may treat this statement lightly. The distinguished gentleman from Massachusetts said the other day that he would not act under a threat. He regarded the declaration made here that the schools would be broken up as a threat. It was not a threat, sir, it is a solemn fact.

I ask the attention of the House to this fact: the University of South Carolina was one of the most honored in all the land. That university has turned out some of the most eminent men of this country—Presidents, Senators, governors, and distinguished military chieftains. Where, sir, is it now? In what condition is the University of South Carolina? A law was passed in South Carolina that colored students should be received into that institution. What has been the effect? Some time since there were only from six to nine scholars in the University of South Carolina; while the professors are paid out of moneys raised from the people by taxation. This is no threat, sir. It is a plain, simple truth, that in passing bills of this kind and having mixed schools you destroy the school system of the South. That is to be the effect; and you thereby lessen the chances of the colored children for an education.

Racial Antagonisms

There is another point to which I ask the attention of the House. A bill like this gives rise to an antagonism of races. If the people are let alone in the South they will adjust these things and there will be peace in the country. But by passing a bill of this kind you place a dangerous power in the hands of the vicious. Here comes a vicious colored man and presents himself at a hotel and demands that he be permitted to go to the table with the whites, and that he shall have his choice of rooms. The hotel-keeper, acting upon his right as he understands it, handed down from all ages, that "every man's house is his castle;" that no man can come into his house without his consent, recognizing that as being the old Anglo-Saxon law of our ancestors, may refuse. Then you have it placed in the power of this man to have the hotel-keeper arrested, tried, and fined a sum not less than $100 no more than $5,000. And that, sir, would be placing a dangerous power in the hands of the vicious.

This bill, Mr. Speaker, will, more or less, bring about an antagonism of the races; and that state of things would not be best for the colored man. I submit it in good faith, that if the question is ever presented in the South, shall this country be ruled by white men or ruled by colored men? the colored man is not able to stand any such an antagonism as that; he will necessarily, sir, go down. I ask what race has ever been able to stand before the Caucasian? Look at the history of the world. Where is the Indian? Why, sir, less than two centuries ago on this spot the Indian reared his wigwam and stood upon these hills and looked upon the broad, beautiful Potomac, or his eye swept over the hunting grounds of the West; and he had the title to this magnificent country. Where is he now? He has gone back, step by step, before the advancing march of the white man. No race, sir, in the world has been able to stand before the pure Caucasian. An antagonism of races will not be good for the colored man.

There is another objection to this bill. It begets hopes and raises an ambition in the minds of the colored man that can never be realized. It is true, sir, that we can find some ten or twelve members of Congress here from densely-populated regions of the South where the colored race is dominant. But how is it in other States? Where is the colored man from Massachusetts? Is he here? Where is even Fred Douglass, who is acknowledged to be a man of ability? Is he here? No, sir; he has not found his way into this House. This bill, therefore, as I have said, begets in the minds of these people hopes and an ambition that can never be realized; and in that view of the case it is unfortunate for them. And I say, sir, that it is not for the best interest of the white race that this bill should pass. And why? Because if the common schools are to be destroyed, which are beneficial to the colored man, their destruction will also be against the interests of the whites, and the poor white children of the South will fail to receive those educational advantages which they ought to have; and in that respect it will not be best for the white race.

Another view of this question, Mr. Speaker, is this: that by placing the colored race and the white race continually together, by throwing them into social contact, the result will be more or less that the distinction between them will be broken down, and that miscegenation and an admixture of the races will follow. Sir, it must necessarily follow on such close intercommunication. I presume that no man will stand upon this floor and say that it is best for all the races of men on the face of the earth to become one by amalgamation.

Let us look for a moment and see how it is. We are told that colored men have not succeeded in this country because they had been borne down by chains and slavery. I admit, sir, that the colored man when in a state of servitude had not much opportunity to develop his mind and expand the powers that God has given him; but will any gentleman on this floor undertake to say that the colored race has not had an equal chance in the world with the white race? I suppose no man will controvert the theory that colored men were at the tower of Babel, and that when God confounded the languages of men and sent them forth into the world the colored race was among them. Some went one way and some went another. Some went north and some south, some east and some west; they went into all portions of the world. Well, sir, what has been the history of the Caucasian race? It has gone on progressing; it has whitened every ocean on the globe with the sails of commerce; it has reared monuments which will be everlasting; it has stamped its language on the world—the strong German, the elegant French, the soft Italian, and the ever-living and ever-spoken English. What language has the colored man given to the world? He started on an equal footing with the white race—what has he done? Look at Africa. There she is, bowed down by superstition and under the shadow of death.

Sir, it is absurd for gentlemen to talk about the equality of the races. But let us give to the colored man the opportunity of improvement; let us give him an education. I for one will vote cheerfully and gladly for the appropriation of a portion of the proceeds of the splendid domain of this country for the education of the colored race; but I think it ought to be done in separate schools. Sir, we have already given him the opportunity to be educated; we have allowed him to hold office; we have seen and heard colored men on this floor; they are here now.

I Would Not Beg

The bill ought not to pass; the matter ought to be left to the States. I will not undertake to argue the constitutionality of this question; that has been done by others, and well done. I have only spoken to the effect of the passage of such a measure, and what is best for the interests of both races; and I submit in concluding my remarks that we have really extended to the colored man everything that I think he ought to ask at our hands. If I belonged to the colored race I would not stand here and ask the passage of a law to force me into what are termed my civil rights. If I belonged to the colored race I would come up by my own merit. I would wait for time and opportunity, and I would not ask any help from Congress. I would not stand here as a beggar asking for these social rights; I would depend on my own merits. Sir, it reminds me of an anecdote that I heard up in the mountains of my own district which illustrates this point. There was a camp-meeting up there, and it was a very good time, and there were a great many shouting. The presiding elder went up to an old colored man and said to him, "Shout on, brother; shout on, if you feel like it; we shall all be white in heaven." The old fellow replied, "Bless the Lord, I feel the white coming now." [Laughter.] Now the rights of the colored man are coming on, and if he will place himself in a proper attitude he will secure them.

"We come here, five millions of people . . . asking that unjust discriminations against us be forbidden."

A Federal Civil Rights Bill Is Necessary

Richard H. Cain (1825–1887)

Richard H. Cain was one of sixteen African Americans elected to Congress during Reconstruction. Born free in Virginia and educated at Wilberforce University in Ohio, Cain worked as a minister for the African Methodist Episcopal Church. In 1865 he was sent as a missionary and teacher to South Carolina, where he was a delegate to the 1867 state constitutional convention and was a state senator from 1868 to 1872. Cain, a Republican, represented South Carolina in Congress from 1873 to 1875 and again from 1877 to 1879. In 1880 he was appointed a presiding bishop of the African Methodist Episcopal Church.

The following viewpoint is taken from an 1874 speech Cain delivered to Congress in support of a civil rights bill originally introduced in 1870 by Massachusetts senator Charles Sumner. Sumner's bill, which would have mandated integration of schools and public facilities, was attacked by some for attempting to interfere too much with established social practices. In his speech, Cain responds to arguments by one of the bill's critics, North Carolina representative Robert B. Vance. Cain argues that African Americans should have the full protection of their civil rights based on the U.S. Constitution and its Fourteenth and Fifteenth Amendments. As further reasons for supporting the civil rights bill, Cain cites the American ideal of equality as well as blacks' past contributions to the nation.

From Richard H. Cain, *Congressional Record*, 43rd Cong., 1st sess., January 10, 1874.

A weakened version of Sumner's bill permitting segregated schools was passed in Congress in February 1875. The Supreme Court declared much of the bill unconstitutional in 1883. Eight decades would elapse before Congress would again pass civil rights legislation.

———————

Mr. Speaker, I feel called upon more particularly by the remarks of the gentleman from North Carolina [Robert B. Vance] on civil rights to express my views. For a number of days this question has been discussed, and various have been the opinions expressed as to whether or not the pending bill should be passed in its present form or whether it should be modified to meet the objections entertained by a number of gentlemen whose duty it will be to give their votes for or against its passage. It has been assumed that to pass this bill in its present form Congress would manifest a tendency to override the Constitution of the country and violate the rights of the States.

Whether it be true or false is yet to be seen. I take it, so far as the constitutional question is concerned, if the colored people under the law, under the amendments to the Constitution, have become invested with all the rights of citizenship, then they carry with them all rights and immunities accruing to and belonging to a citizen of the United States. If four, or nearly five, million people have been lifted from the thralldom of slavery and made free; if the Government by its amendments to the Constitution has guaranteed to them all rights and immunities, as to other citizens, they must necessarily therefore carry along with them all the privileges enjoyed by all other citizens of the Republic.

Sir, the gentleman from North Carolina who spoke on the questions stated some objections, to which I desire to address a few words of reply. He said it would enforce social rights, and therefore would be detrimental to the interests of both the whites and the blacks of the country. My conception of the effect of this bill, if it be passed into a law, will be simply to place the colored men of this country upon the same footing with every other citizen under the law, and will not at all enforce social relationship with any other class of persons in the country whatsoever. It is merely a matter of law. What we desire is that our civil rights shall be guaranteed by law as they are guaranteed to every other class of persons; and when that is done all other things will come in as a necessary sequence, the enforcement of the rights following the enactment of the law.

Sir, social equality is a right which every man, every woman, and every class of persons have within their own control. They have a right to form their own acquaintances, to establish their own social relationships. Its establishment and regulation is not within the province of legislation. No laws enacted by legislators can compel social equality. Now, what is it we desire? What we desire is this: inasmuch as we have been raised to the dignity, to the honor, to the position of our manhood, we ask that the laws of this country should guarantee all the rights and immunities belonging to that proud position, to be enforced all over this broad land.

Sir, the gentleman states that in the State of North Carolina the colored people enjoy all their rights as far as the highways are concerned; that in the hotels, and in the railroad cars, and in the various public places of resort, they have all the rights and all the immunities accorded to any other class of citizens of the United States. Now, it may not have come under his observation, but it has under mine, that such really is not the case; and the reason why I know and feel it more than he does is because my face is painted black and his is painted white. We who have the color—I may say the objectionable color—know and feel all this. A few days ago, in passing from South Carolina to this city, I entered a place of public resort where hungry men are fed, but I did not dare—I could not without trouble—sit down to the table. I could not sit down at Wilmington or at Weldon without entering into a contest, which I did not desire to do. My colleague, the gentleman who so eloquently spoke on this subject the other day [South Carolina representative Robert Browne Elliott], a few months ago entered a restaurant at Wilmington and sat down to be served, and while there a gentleman stepped up to him and said, "You can not eat here." All the other gentlemen upon the railroad as passengers were eating there; he had only twenty minutes, and was compelled to leave the restaurant or have a fight for it. He showed fight, however, and got his dinner; but he has never been back there since. Coming here last week I felt we did not desire to draw revolvers and present the bold front of warriors, and therefore we ordered our dinners to be brought into the cars, but even there we found the existence of this feeling; for, although we had paid a dollar apiece for our meals, to be brought by the servants into the cars, still there was objection on the part of the railroad people to our eating our meals in the cars, because they said we were putting on airs. They refused us in the restaurant, and then did not desire that we should eat our meals in the cars, although we paid for them. Yet this was in the noble State of North Carolina.

Mr. Speaker, the colored men of the South do not want the adoption of any force measure. No; they do not want anything by force. All they ask is that you will give them, by statutory enactment under the fundamental law, the right to enjoy precisely the same privileges accorded to every other class of citizens.

The gentleman, moreover, has told us that if we pass this civil-rights bill we will thereby rob the colored men of the South of the friendship of the whites. Now, I am at a loss to see how the friendship of our white friends can be lost to us by simply saying we should be permitted to enjoy the rights enjoyed by other citizens. I have a higher opinion of the friendship of the southern men than to suppose any such thing. I know them too well. I know their friendship will not be lost by the passage of this bill. For eight years I have been in South Carolina, and I have found this to be the fact, that the higher class, comprising gentlemen of learning and refinement, are less opposed to this measure than are those who do not occupy so high a position in the social scale.

Sir, I think that there will be no difficulty. But I do think this, that there will be more trouble if we do not have those rights. I regard it important, therefore, that we should make the law so strong that no man can infringe those rights.

But, says the gentleman from North Carolina, some ambitious colored man will, when this law is passed, enter a hotel or railroad car, and thus create disturbance. If it be his right, then there is no vaulting ambition in his enjoying that right. And if he can pay for his seat in a first-class car or his room in a hotel, I see no objection to his enjoying it. But the gentleman says more. He cited, on the school question, the evidence of South Carolina, and says the South Carolina University has been destroyed by virtue of bringing into contact the white students with the colored. I think not. It is true that a small number of students left the institution, but the institution still remains. The buildings are there as erect as ever; the faculty are there as attentive to their duties as ever they were; the students are coming in as they did before. It is true, sir, that there is a mixture of students now; that there are colored and white students of law and medicine sitting side by side; it is true, sir, that the prejudice of some of the professors was so strong that it drove them out of the institution; but the philanthropy and good sense of others were such that they remained; and thus we have still the institution going on, and because some students have left, it cannot be reasonably argued that the usefulness of the institution has been destroyed. The University of South Carolina has not been destroyed.

The Old Ghost of Prejudice

But the gentleman says more. The colored man cannot stand, he says, where this antagonism exists, and he deprecates the idea of antagonizing the races. The gentleman says there is no antagonism on his part. I think there is not antagonism so far as the country is concerned. So far as my observation extends, it goes to prove this: that there is a general acceptance upon the part of the

A Color-Blind Constitution

In 1883 the Supreme Court invalidated the 1875 Civil Rights Act by an 8-1 ruling. The sole dissenter was John Marshall Harlan, an associate justice from 1877 until his death in 1911. Harlan was also the only justice who argued that racial segregation was unconstitutional in the 1896 case of Plessy v. Ferguson, *in which a Louisiana law mandating racial segregation for railroad passengers was upheld. Excerpts from his dissenting opinion in* Plessy *appear here.*

The white race deems itself to be the dominant race in this country. And so it is, in prestige, in achievements, in education, in wealth and in power. So, I doubt not, it will continue to be for all time, if it remains true to its great heritage and holds fast to the principles of constitutional liberty. But in view of the Constitution, in the eye of the law, there is in this country no superior, dominant, ruling class of citizens. There is no caste here. Our Constitution is color-blind, and neither knows nor tolerates classes among citizens. In respect of civil rights, all citizens are equal before the law. The humblest is the peer of the most powerful. The law regards man as man, and takes no account of his surroundings or of his color when his civil rights as guaranteed by the supreme law of the land are involved. It is, therefore, to be regretted that this high tribunal, the final expositor of the fundamental law of the land, has reached the conclusion that it is competent for a State to regulate the enjoyment by citizens of their civil rights solely upon the basis of race. . . .

The present decision, it may well be apprehended, will not only stimulate aggressions, more or less brutal and irritating, upon the admitted rights of colored citizens, but will encourage the belief that it is possible, by means of state enactments, to defeat the beneficent purposes which the people of the United States had in view when they adopted the recent amendments of the Constitution, by one of which the blacks of this country were made citizens of the United States and of the States in which they respectively reside, and whose privileges and immunities, as citizens, the States are forbidden to abridge. Sixty millions of whites are in no danger from the presence here of eight millions of blacks. The destinies of the two races, in this country, are indissolubly linked together, and the interests of both require that the common government of all shall not permit the seeds of race hate to be planted under the sanction of law. What can more certainly arouse race hate, what more certainly create and perpetuate a feeling of distrust between these races, than state enactments, which, in fact, proceed on the ground that colored citizens are so inferior and degraded that they cannot be allowed to sit in public coaches occupied by white citizens? That, as all will admit, is the real meaning of such legislation as was enacted in Louisiana.

larger and better class of the whites of the South of the situation, and that they regard the education and the development of the colored people as essential to their welfare, and the peace, happiness, and prosperity of the whole country. Many of them, including the best minds of the South, are earnestly engaged in seeking to make this great system of education permanent in all the States. I do not believe, therefore, that it is possible there can be such an antagonism. Why, sir, in Massachusetts there is no such antagonism. There the colored and the white children go to school side by side. In Rhode Island there is not that antagonism. There they are educated side by side in the high schools. In New York, in the highest schools, are to be found of late colored men and colored women. Even old democratic New York does not refuse to give the colored people their rights, and there is no antagonism. A few days ago, when in New York, I made it my business to find out what was the position of matters there in this respect. I ascertained that there are, I think, seven colored ladies in the highest school in New York, and I believe they stand No. 1 in their class, side by side with members of the best and most refined families of the citizens of New York, and without any objection to their presence.

I cannot understand how it is that our southern friends, or a certain class of them, always bring back this old ghost of prejudice and of antagonism. There was a time, not very far distant in the past, when this antagonism was not recognized, when a feeling of fraternization between the white and the colored races existed, that made them kindred to each other. But since our emancipation, since liberty has come, and only since—only since we have stood up clothed in our manhood, only since we have proceeded to take hold and help advance the civilization of this nation—it is only since then that this bugbear is brought up against us again. Sir, the progress of the age demands that the colored man of this country shall be lifted by law into the enjoyment of every right, and that every appliance which is accorded to the German, to the Irishman, to the Englishman, and every foreigner, shall be given to him; and I shall give some reasons why I demand this in the name of justice.

For two hundred years the colored men of this nation have assisted in building up its commercial interests. There are in this country nearly five millions of us, and for a space of two hundred and forty-seven years we have been hewers of wood and drawers of water; but we have been with you in promoting all the interests of the country. My distinguished colleague, who defended the civil rights of our race the other day on this floor, set this forth so clearly that I need not dwell upon it at this time.

I propose to state just this: that we have been identified with the interests of this country from its very foundation. The cotton crop of this country has been raised and its rice-fields have been tilled by the hands of our race. All along as the march of progress, as the march of commerce, as the development of your resources has been widening and expanding and spreading, as your vessels have gone on every sea, with the stars and stripes waving over them, and carried your commerce everywhere, there the black man's labor has gone to enrich your country and to augment the grandeur of your nationality. This was done in the time of slavery. And if, for the space of time I have noted, we have been hewers of wood and drawers of water; if we have made your cotton-fields blossom as the rose; if we have made your rice-fields wave with luxuriant harvests; if we have made your corn-fields rejoice; if we have sweated and toiled to build up the prosperity of the whole country by the productions of our labor, I submit, now that the war has made a change, now that we are free—I submit to the nation whether it is not fair and right that we should come in and enjoy to the fullest extent our freedom and liberty.

The Question of Education

A word now as to the question of education. Sir, I know that, indeed, some of our Republican friends are even a little weak on the school clause of this bill; but, sir, the education of the race, the education of the nation, is paramount to all other considerations. I regard it important, therefore, that the colored people should take place in the educational march of this nation, and I would suggest that there should be no discrimination. It is against discrimination in this particular that we complain.

Sir, if you look over the reports of superintendents of schools in the several States, you will find, I think, evidences sufficient to warrant Congress in passing the civil-rights bill as it now stands. The report of the commissioner of education of California shows that, under the operation of law and of prejudice, the colored children of that State are practically excluded from schooling. Here is a case where a large class of children are growing up in our midst in a state of ignorance and semi-barbarism. Take the report of the superintendent of education of Indiana, and you will find that while efforts have been made in some places to educate the colored children, yet the prejudice is so great that it debars the colored children from enjoying all the rights which they ought to enjoy under the law. In Illinois, too, the superintendent of education makes this statement: that, while the law guarantees education to every child, yet such are the operations among the school trustees that they almost ignore, in some places, the education of colored children.

All we ask is that you, the legislators of the nation, shall pass a law so strong and so powerful that no one shall be able to elude it and destroy our rights under the Constitution and laws of our country. That is all we ask.

But, Mr. Speaker, the gentleman from North Carolina asks that the colored man shall place himself in an attitude to receive his rights. I ask, what attitude can we assume? We have tilled your soil, and during the rude shock of war, until our hour came, we were docile during that long, dark night, waiting patiently the coming day. In the Southern States during that war our men and women stood behind their masters; they tilled the soil, and there were no insurrections in all the broad lands of the South; the wives and daughters of the slaveholders were as sacred then as they were before; and the history of the war does not record a single event, a single instance, in which the colored people were unfaithful, even in slavery; nor does the history of the war record the fact that on the other side, on the side of the Union, there were any colored men who were not willing at all times to give their lives for their country. Sir, upon both sides we waited patiently. I was a student at Wilberforce University, in Ohio, when the tocsin of war was sounded, when Fort Sumter was fired upon, and I never shall forget the thrill that ran through my soul when I thought of the coming consequences of that shot. There were one hundred and fifteen of us, students at that university, who, anxious to vindicate the stars and stripes, made up a company, and offered our services to the governor of Ohio; and, sir, we were told that this was a white man's war and that the negro had nothing to do with it. Sir, we returned—docile, patient, waiting, casting our eyes to the heavens whence help always comes. We knew that there would come a period in the history of this nation when our strong black arms would be needed. We waited patiently; we waited until Massachusetts, through her noble governor, sounded the alarm, and we hastened then to hear the summons and obey it.

Sir, as I before remarked, we were peaceful on both sides. When the call was made on the side of the Union, we were ready; when the call was made for us to obey orders on the other side, in the confederacy, we humbly performed our tasks, and waited patiently. But, sir, the time came when we were called for; and, I ask, who can say that when that call was made, the colored men did not respond as readily and as rapidly as did any other class of your citizens? Sir, I need not speak of the history of this bloody war. It will carry down to coming generations the valor of our soldiers on the battle-field. Fort Wagner will stand forever as a monument of that valor, and until Vicksburg shall be wiped from the galaxy of battles in the great contest for human liberty that valor will be recognized.

And for what, Mr. Speaker, and gentlemen, was the great war made? The gentleman from North Carolina announced before he sat down, in answer to an interrogatory by a gentleman on this side of the House, that they went into the war conscientiously before God. So be it. Then we simply come and plead conscientiously before God that these are our rights, and we want them. We plead conscientiously before God, believing that these are our rights by inheritance, and by the inexorable decree of Almighty God.

We believe in the Declaration of Independence, that all men are born free and equal, and are endowed by their Creator with certain inalienable rights, among which are life, liberty, and the pursuit of happiness. And we further believe that to secure those rights governments are instituted. And we further believe that when governments cease to subserve those ends the people should change them. . . .

I think it is proper and just that the civil-rights bill should be passed. Some think it would be better to modify it, to strike out the school clause, or to so modify it that some of the State constitutions should not be infringed. I regard it essential to us and the people of this country that we should be secured in this if in nothing else. I cannot regard that our rights will be secured until the jury-box and the school-room, those great palladiums of our liberty, shall have been opened to us. Then we will be willing to take our chances with other men.

We do not want any discriminations to be made. If discriminations are made in regard to schools, then there will be accomplished just what we are fighting against. If you say that the schools in the State of Georgia, for instance, shall be allowed to discriminate against colored people, then you will have discriminations made against us. We do not want any discriminations. I do not ask any legislation for the colored people of this country that is not applied to the white people. All that we ask is equal laws, equal legislation, and equal rights throughout the length and breadth of this land.

We Are Not Begging

The gentleman from North Carolina also says that the colored men should not come here begging at the doors of Congress for their rights. I agree with him. I want to say that we do not come here begging for our rights. We come here clothed in the garb of American citizenship. We come demanding our rights in the name of justice. We come, with no arrogance on our part, asking, that this great nation, which laid the foundations of civilization and progress more deeply and more securely than any other nation on the face of the earth, guarantee us protection from outrage. We come here, five millions of people—more than composed this

106

whole nation when it had its great tea-party in Boston Harbor, and demanded its rights at the point of the bayonet—asking that unjust discriminations against us be forbidden. We come here in the name of justice, equity, and law, in the name of our children, in the name of our country, petitioning for our rights.

Our rights will yet be accorded to us, I believe, from the feeling that has been exhibited on this floor of the growing sentiment of the country. Rapid as the weaver's shuttle, swift as the lightning's flash, such progress is being made that our rights will be accorded to us ere long. I believe the nation is perfectly willing to accord this measure of justice, if only those who represent the people here would say the word. Let it be proclaimed that henceforth all the children of this land shall be free; that the stars and stripes, waving over all, shall secure to every one equal rights, and the nation will say "amen."

Let the civil-rights bill be passed this day, and five million black men, women, and children, all over the land, will begin a new song of rejoicing, and the thirty-five millions of noble-hearted Anglo-Saxons will join in the shout of joy. Thus will the great mission be fulfilled of giving to all the people equal rights.

Inasmuch as we have toiled with you in building up this nation; inasmuch as we have suffered side by side with you in the war; inasmuch as we have together passed through affliction and pestilence, let there be now a fulfillment of the sublime thought of our fathers—let all men enjoy equal liberty and equal rights. . . .

Our wives and our children have high hopes and aspirations; their longings for manhood and womanhood are equal to those of any other race. The same sentiment of patriotism and of gratitude, the same spirit of national pride that animates the hearts of other citizens animates theirs. In the name of the dead soldiers of our race, whose bodies lie at Petersburgh and on other battle-fields of the South; in the name of the widows and orphans they have left behind; in the name of the widows of the confederate soldiers who fell upon the same fields, I conjure you let this righteous act be done. I appeal to you in the name of God and humanity to give us our rights, for we ask nothing more. [Loud applause.]

"Until the negroes . . . sternly repress the crime of assaulting women and children, . . . the crime of lynching will never be extirpated."

The Fundamental Cause of Lynching Is Black Crime

Thomas Nelson Page (1853–1922)

Most of the gains African Americans had made during Reconstruction towards economic advancement and racial equality were reversed in the 1880s and 1890s, especially in the South. Southern states used violence and fraud to curtail black voting and, beginning with Mississippi in 1890, revised their constitutions in order to disfranchise blacks by using literacy tests, poll taxes, and other indirect methods. State governments passed laws instituting racial segregation in all realms of life. The debt peonage and convict-lease systems left many black farmworkers bound in working conditions that resembled those of slavery. The period also witnessed the rise of lynching—the execution (and sometimes torture) of blacks by white vigilante mobs. An average of one hundred blacks were lynched every year during the 1880s and 1890s, mostly in the South.

The following viewpoint is excerpted from an article on lynching by Thomas Nelson Page that was published in the January 1904 issue of the *North American Review*. Page, a novelist from Virginia who was later appointed U.S. ambassador to Italy, was a noted

From Thomas Nelson Page, "The Lynching of Negroes—Its Cause and Its Prevention," *North American Review*, January 1904.

writer and lecturer on the South and a defender of the region's racially segregated society. He argues that lynching is an understandable, if lamentable, response by whites to black assaults on white women and children. African-American leaders must take responsibility for controlling members of their race, he asserts.

In dealing with this question the writer wishes to be understood as speaking not of the respectable and law-abiding element among the negroes, who unfortunately are so often confounded with the body of the race from which come most of the malefactors. To say that negroes furnish most of the ravishers is not to say that all negroes are rapists.

The crime of lynching in this country has, at one time or another, become so frequent that it has aroused the interest of the whole people, and has even arrested the attention of people in other countries. It has usually been caused by the boldness with which crime was committed by lawbreakers, and the inefficiency of the law in dealing with them through its regular forms. Such, for instance, were the acts of the Vigilantes in California in the old days, and such have been the acts of the Vigilantes in other sections of the country at times. In these cases, there has always been a form of trial, which, however hasty, was conclusive on the essential points, of the commission of the crime, the identification of the prisoner, the sentence of "Judge Lynch"—that is, of the mob—and the orderly execution of that sentence. And, in such cases, most persons cognizant of all the conditions and circumstances have found some justification for this "wild justice."

Lynching, however, has never before been so common, nor has it existed over so extended a region as of late years in the South. And it has aroused more feeling outside of that section than was aroused formerly by the work of the Vigilantes. This feeling has undoubtedly been due mainly to the belief, that the lynching has been directed almost exclusively against the negroes; though a part has, perhaps, come from the supposition that the laws were entirely effective, and that, consequently, the lynching of negroes has been the result of irrational hostility or of wanton cruelty. Thus, the matter is, to some extent, complicated by a latent idea that it has a political complexion.

This is the chief ground of complaint in the utterances of the negroes themselves and also of a considerable part of the outside press. And, indeed, for a good while, the lynching of negroes appeared to be confined to the South, though lynching of whites was by no means the monopoly of that section, as may be recalled by those familiar with the history of Indiana and some of the other Northwestern States.

Of late, however, several revolting instances of lynching of negroes in its most dreadful form, burning at the stake, have occurred in regions where hitherto such forms of barbarous punishment have been unknown; and the time appears to be ripe for some efficient concert of action, to eradicate what is recognized by cool heads as a serious menace to our civilization.

In discussing the means to put an end to this barbarity, the first essential is that the matter shall be clearly and thoroughly understood.

The ignorance shown by much of the discussion that has grown out of these lynchings would appear to justify plain speaking.

All thoughtful men know that respect for law is the basic principle of civilization, and are agreed as to the evil of any over-riding of the law. All reasonable men know that the over-riding of law readily creates a spirit of lawlessness, under which progress is retarded and civilization suffers and dwindles. This is as clearly recognized at the South as at the North. To overcome this conviction and stir up rational men to a pitch where the law is trampled under foot, the officers of the law are attacked, and their prisoner taken from them and executed, there must be some imperative cause.

And yet the record of such over-riding of law in the past has been a terrible one.

The Chicago *Tribune* has for some time been collecting statistics on the subject of lynching, and the following table taken from that paper, showing the number of lynchings [of all races] for a series of years, is assumed to be fairly accurate:

1885	184	1895	171
1886	138	1896	131
1887	122	1897	166
1888	142	1898	127
1889	176	1899	107
1890	127	1900	115
1891	192	1901	135
1892	235	1902	96
1893	200	1903 (to Sept. 14, eight	
1894	190	and a half months)	76

. . . Over 2,700 lynchings in eighteen years are enough to stagger the mind. Either we are relapsing into barbarism, or there is some terrific cause for our reversion to the methods of mediaevalism; and our laws are inefficient to meet it. The only gleam of light is that, of late years, the number appears to have diminished.

To get at the remedy, we must first get at the cause.

Time was when the crime of assault was unknown throughout the South. During the whole period of slavery, it did not exist, nor did it exist to any considerable extent for some years after Emancipation. During the War, the men were away in the army, and the negroes were the loyal guardians of the women and children. On isolated plantations and in lonely neighborhoods, women were as secure as in the streets of Boston or New York.

Then came the period and process of Reconstruction, with its teachings. Among these was the teaching that the negro was the equal of the white, that the white was his enemy, and that he must assert his equality. The growth of the idea was a gradual one in the negro's mind. This was followed by a number of cases where members of the negro militia ravished white women; in some instances in the presence of their families.

The result of the hostility between the Southern whites and Government at that time was to throw the former upon their own acts for their defence or revenge, with a consequent training in lawless punishment of acts which should have been punished by law. And here lynching had its evil origin. . . .

The first instance of rape, outside of these attacks by armed negroes, and of consequent lynching, that attracted the attention of the country was a case which occurred in Mississippi, where the teaching of equality and of violence found one of its most fruitful fields. A negro dragged a woman down into the woods and, tying her, kept her bound there a prisoner for several days, when he butchered her. He was caught and was lynched.

With the resumption of local power by the whites came the temporary and partial ending of the crimes of assault and of lynching.

As the old relation, which had survived even the strain of Reconstruction, dwindled with the passing of the old generation from the stage, and the "New Issue" with the new teaching took its place, the crime broke out again with renewed violence. The idea of equality began to percolate more extensively among the negroes. In evidence of it is the fact that since the assaults began again they have been chiefly directed against the plainer order of people, instances of attacks on women of the upper class, though not unknown, being of rare occurrence.

Conditions in the South render the commission of this crime peculiarly easy. The white population is sparse, the forests are extensive, the officers of the law distant and difficult to reach; but, above all, the negro population has appeared inclined to condone the fact of mere assault.

Twenty-five years ago, women went unaccompanied and unafraid throughout the South, as they still go throughout the North. To-day, no white woman, or girl, or female child, goes alone out of sight of the house except on necessity; and no man leaves his wife alone in his house, if he can help it. Cases have occurred of assault and murder in broad day, within sight and sound of the victim's home. Indeed, an instance occurred not a great while ago in the District of Columbia, within a hundred yards of a fashionable drive, when, about three o'clock of a bright June day, a young girl was attacked within sight and sound of her house, and when she screamed her throat was cut. So near to her home was the spot that her mother and an officer, hearing her cries, reached her before life was extinct.

A Response to Brutal Crimes

For a time, the ordinary course of the law was, in the main, relied on to meet the trouble; but it was found that, notwithstanding the inevitable infliction of the death penalty, several evils resulted therefrom. The chief one was that the ravishing of women, instead of diminishing, steadily increased. The criminal, under the ministrations of his preachers, usually professed to have "gotten religion," and from the shadow of the gallows called on his friends to follow him to glory. So that the punishment lost to these emotional people much of its deterrent force, especially where the real sympathy of the race was mainly with the criminal rather than with his victim. Another evil was the dreadful necessity of calling on the innocent victim, who, if she survived, as she rarely did, was already bowed to the earth by shame, to relate in public the story of the assault—an ordeal which was worse than death. Yet another was the delay in the execution of the law. With these, however, was one other which, perhaps, did more than all the rest together to wrest the trial and punishment from the Courts and carry them out by mob-violence. This was the unnamable brutality with which the causing crime was, in nearly every case, attended. The death of the victim of the ravisher was generally the least of the attendant horrors. In Texas, in Mississippi, in Georgia, in Kentucky, in Colorado, as later in Delaware, the facts in the case were so unspeakable that they have never been put in print. They could not be put in print. It is these unnamable horrors which have outraged the minds of those who live in regions where they have occurred, and where they may at any time occur again, and, upsetting reason, have swept from their bearings cool men and changed them into madmen, drunk with the lust of revenge.

Not unnaturally, such barbarity as burning at the stake has shocked the sense of the rest of the country, and, indeed, of the world. But it is well for the rest of the country, and for the world, to know that it has also shocked the sense of the South, and, in their calmer moments, even the sense of those men who, in their

112

frenzy, have been guilty of it. Only, a deeper shock than even this is at the bottom of their ferocious rage—the shock which comes from the ravishing and butchery of their women and children.

It is not necessary to be an apologist for barbarity because one states with bluntness the cause. The stern underlying principle of the people who commit these barbarities is one that has its root deep in the basic passions of humanity; the determination to put an end to the ravishing of their women by an inferior race, no matter what the consequence.

For a time, a speedy execution by hanging was the only mode of retribution resorted to by the lynchers; then, when this failed of its purpose, a more savage method was essayed, born of a savage fury at the failure of the first, and a stern resolve to strike a deeper terror into those whom the other method had failed to awe. . . .

Spreading to the North

Of late, lynching at the stake has spread beyond the region where it has such reason for existence as may be given by the conditions that prevail in the South. Three frightful instances by burning have occurred recently in Northern States, in communities where some of these conditions were partly wanting. The horror of the main fact of lynching was increased, in two of the cases, by a concerted attack on a large element of the negro population which was wholly innocent. Even the unoffending negroes were driven from their homes, a consequence which has never followed in the South, where it might seem there was more occasion for it.

It thus appears that the original crime, and also the consequent one in its most brutal form, are not confined to the South, and, possibly, are only more frequent there because of the greater number of negroes in that section. The deep racial instincts are not limited by geographical bounds.

These last-mentioned lynchings were so ferocious, and so unwarranted by any such necessity, real or fancied, as may be thought to exist at the South by reason of the frequency of assault and the absence of a strong police force, that they not unnaturally called forth almost universal condemnation. The President felt it proper to write an open letter, commending the action of the Governor of Indiana on the proper and efficient exercise of his authority to uphold the law and restore order in his State. But who has ever thought it necessary to commend the Governors of the Southern States under similar circumstances? The militia of some of the Southern States are almost veterans, so frequently have they been called on to protect wretches whose crimes stank in the nostrils of all decent men. The Governor of Virginia boasted, a few years ago, that no lynching should take place during his incumbency, and he nearly made good his boast; though, to do so, he had to call out at one time or another almost the entire force of the State. . . .

The Case of Samuel Hose

For a time, the assaults by negroes were confined to young women who were caught alone in solitary and secluded places. The company even of a child was sufficient to protect them. Then the ravishers grew bolder, and attacks followed on women when they were in company. And then, not content with this, the ravishers began to attack women in their own homes. Sundry instances of this have occurred within the last few years. As an illustration, may be cited the notorious case of Samuel Hose, who, after making a bet with a negro preacher that he could have access to a white woman, went into a farmer's house while the family, father, mother and child, were at supper; brained the man with his axe; threw the child into a corner with a violence which knocked it senseless, and ravished the wife and mother with unnamable horrors, butchered her and bore away with him the indisputable proof of having won his wager. He was caught and was burnt.

Another instance, only less appalling, occurred two years ago in Lynchburg, Virginia, where the colored janitor of a white female school, who had been brought up and promoted by the Superintendent of Schools, and was regarded as a shining example of what education might accomplish with his race, entered the house of a respectable man one morning, after the husband, who was a foreman in a factory, had gone to his work; ravished the wife, and, then putting his knee on her breast, coolly cut her throat as he might have done a calf's. There was no attempt at lynching; but the Governor, resolved to preserve the good name of the commonwealth, felt it necessary to order out two regiments of soldiers, in which course he was sustained by the entire sentiment of the State.

These cases were neither worse nor better than many of those which have occurred in the South in the last twenty years, and in that period hundreds of women and a number of children have been ravished and slain.

Stopping the Crime of Assault

Now, how is this crime of assault to be stopped? For stopped it must be, and stopped it will be, whatever the cost. One proposition is that separation of the races, complete separation, is the only remedy. The theory appears Utopian. Colonization has been the dream of certain philanthropists for a hundred years. And, meantime, the negroes have increased from less than a million to nine millions. They will never be deported; not because we have not the money, for an amount equal to that spent in pensions during three years would pay the expenses of such deportation, and an amount equal to that paid in six years would set them up in a new country. But the negroes have rights; many of them are estimable citizens; and even the body of them, when well regulated, are valuable laborers. It might, therefore, as well be assumed that this plan will never be carried out, unless the occasion becomes so imperative that all other rights give way to the supreme right of necessity.

It is plain, then, that we must deal with the matter in a more practicable manner, accepting conditions as they are, and applying to them legal methods which will be effective. Lynching does not end ravishing, and that is the prime necessity. . . .

Many expedients have been suggested; some of the most drastic by Northern men. One of them proposed, not long since, that to meet the mob-spirit, a trial somewhat in the nature of a drumhead court-martial might be established by law, by which the accused may be tried and, if found guilty, executed immediately. Others have proposed as a remedy emasculation by law; while a Justice of the Supreme Court has recently given the weight of his personal opinion in favor of prompt trial and the abolishment of appeals in such cases. Even the terrible suggestion has been made that burning at the stake might be legalized!

These suggestions testify how grave the matter is considered to be by those who make them.

But none of these, unless it be the one relating to emasculation, is more than an expedient. The trouble lies deeper. The crime of lynching is not likely to cease until the crime of ravishing and murdering women and children is less frequent than it has been of late. And this crime, which is well-nigh wholly confined to the negro race, will not greatly diminish until the negroes themselves take it in hand and stamp it out.

From recent developments, it may be properly inferred that the absence of this crime during the period of Slavery was due more to the feeling among the negroes themselves than to any repressive measures on the part of the whites. The negro had the same animal instincts in Slavery that he exhibits now; the punishment that follows the crime now is as certain, as terrible, and as swift as it could have been then. So, to what is due the alarming increase of this terrible brutality?

Talk of Social Equality

To the writer it appears plain that it is due to two things: first, to racial antagonism and to the talk of social equality, from which it first sprang, that inflames the ignorant negro, who has grown up unregulated and undisciplined; and, secondly, to the absence of a strong restraining public opinion among the negroes of any class, which alone can extirpate the crime. In the first place, the negro does not generally believe in the virtue of women. It is beyond his experience. He does not generally believe in the existence of actual assault. It is beyond his comprehension. In the next place, his passion, always his controlling force, is now, since the new teaching, for the white woman.

Views on Lynching

Herbert J. Seligmann traveled south in 1919 to investigate lynching for the National Association for the Advancement of Colored People (NAACP). In the following excerpts from his report to the NAACP, he sums up the opinions of several southern whites he interviewed.

Dr. A.R. Quinn in Vicksburg. He believed "the government was responsible" for inducting Negroes into the army, thus putting them on an equality with white men. Negroes, he said, should not have served in the war. He condemned the agitation for equal rights for Negroes. To meet the lynching evil Dr. Quinn predicted the resurrection of the Ku Klux Klan among "the best people" of the South. Dr. Quinn did not know he was talking to an investigator. . . .

Rene Clair, wine merchant of New Orleans. Mr. Clair deplored lynching, though only in half hearted fashion. He represented a point of view typical of certain cultured Southerners, in that he insisted the Negro race was inferior to the white and would never in the South be admitted to political, economic or social equality. The Negro's part in the war, and especially the belief, widely held throughout the South, that Negro soldiers had been received on equal terms by white women in France, contributed to the tensity of the race antagonism.

Rudolf Giefers, candidate for election to the Louisiana state legislature, held that lynching was necessary, that the Negro race should never be enfranchised, that "educating Negroes only makes confidence men of the males and prostitutes of the females." Mr. Giefers gets along with individuals of the race by knocking them down when he considers it necessary.

That there are many negroes who are law-abiding and whose influence is for good, no one who knows the worthy members of the race, those who represent the better element, will deny. But while there are, of course, notable exceptions, they are not often of the "New Issue," nor even generally among the prominent leaders: those who publish papers and control conventions.

As the crime of rape had its baleful origin in the teaching of equality and the placing of power in the ignorant negroes' hands, so its perpetration and increase have undoubtedly been due in large part to the same teaching. The intelligent negro may understand what social equality truly means; but to the ignorant and brutal young negro, it signifies but one thing: the opportunity to enjoy, equally with white men, the privilege of cohabiting with white women. This the whites of the South understand; and if it were understood abroad, it would serve to explain some things which have not been understood hitherto. It will explain, in part, the universal and furious hostility of the South to even the least suggestion of social equality.

The Failure of Negro Leaders

A close following of the instances of rape and lynching, and the public discussion consequent thereon, has led the writer to the painful realization that even the leaders of the negro race—at least, those who are prominent enough to hold conventions and write papers on the subject—have rarely, by act or word, shown a true appreciation of the enormity of the crime of ravishing and murdering women. Their discussion and denunciation have been almost invariably and exclusively devoted to the crime of lynching. Underlying most of their protests is the suggestion, that the victim of the mob is innocent and a martyr. Now and then, there is a mild generalization on the evil of lawbreaking and the violation of women; but, for one stern word of protest against violating women and cutting their throats, the records of negro meetings will show many against the attack of the mob on the criminal. And, as to any serious and determined effort to take hold of and stamp out the crime that is blackening the entire negro race to-day, and arousing against them the fatal and possibly the undying enmity of the stronger race, there is, with the exception of the utterances of a few score individuals like Booker Washington, who always speaks for the right, Hannibal Thomas and Bishop [Henry M.] Turner, hardly a trace of such a thing. A crusade has been preached against lynching, even as far as England; but none has been thought of against the ravishing and tearing to pieces of white women and children.

Happily, there is an element of sound-minded, law-abiding negroes, representative of the old negro, who without parade stand for good order, and do what they can to repress lawlessness among their people. But for this class and the kindly relations which are preserved between them and the whites, the situation in the South would long since have become unbearable. These, however, are not generally among the leaders, and, unfortunately, their influence is not sufficiently extended to counteract the evil influences which are at work with such fatal results.

One who reads the utterances of negro orators and preachers on the subject of lynching, and who knows the negro race, cannot

117

doubt that, at bottom, their sympathy is generally with the "victim" of the mob, and not with his victim.

Until the negroes shall create among themselves a sound public opinion which, instead of fostering, shall reprobate and sternly repress the crime of assaulting women and children, the crime will never be extirpated, and until this crime is stopped the crime of lynching will never be extirpated. Lynching will never be done away with while the sympathy of the whites is with the lynchers, and no more will ravishing be done away with while the sympathy of the negroes is with the ravisher. When the negroes shall stop applying all their energies to harboring and defending negroes, no matter what their crime so it be against the whites, and shall distinguish between the law-abiding negro and the law-breaker, a long step will have been taken.

Should the negroes sturdily and faithfully set themselves to prevent the crime of rape by members of that race, it could be stamped out. Should the whites set themselves against lynching, lynching would be stopped. The remedy then is plain. Let the negroes take charge of the crime of ravishing and firmly put it away from them, and let the whites take charge of the crime of lynching and put it away from them. It is time that the races should address themselves to the task; for it is with nations as with individual men; whatsoever they sow that shall they also reap.

It is the writer's belief that the arrest and the prompt handing over to the law of negroes by negroes, for assault on white women, would do more to break up ravishing, and to restore amicable relations between the two races, than all the resolutions of all the Conventions and all the harangues of all the politicians. . . .

Few ravishings by negroes would occur if the more influential members of the race were held accountable for the good order of their race in every community; and few lynchings would occur, at least after the prisoners were in the hands of the officers of the law, if those officers, by the mere fact of relinquishing their prisoners should be disqualified from ever holding office again.

These suggestions may be as Utopian as others which have been made; but if they cannot be carried out, it is because the ravishings by negroes and the murders by mobs have their roots so deep in racial instincts that nothing can eradicate them, and in such case the ultimate issue will be a resort to the final test of might, which in the last analysis underlies everything.

"Lynching cannot be suppressed in the South until all classes of white people who dwell there . . . respect the rights of other human beings, no matter what may be the color of their skin."

The Fundamental Cause of Lynching Is White Racism

Mary Church Terrell (1863–1954)

From the 1890s until her death in 1954, Mary Church Terrell was an activist for equal rights for African Americans and for women. The child of former slaves who had amassed a fortune in real estate, she was educated at Oberlin College in Ohio. In 1895 she became the first black woman to be appointed to the school board of Washington, D.C. She helped start the National Association of Colored Women in 1896, and later was a founding member of the National Association for the Advancement of Colored People (NAACP).

The following viewpoint by Terrell is excerpted from a 1904 article in the *North American Review*. The subject of the article—lynching—had become a critical concern of African Americans. In 1892 alone 161 black men and women were killed by white vigilante mobs acting outside the law. Responding in part to arguments presented by Thomas Nelson Page in a prior issue of the *North American Review*, Terrell argues that the underlying cause of such acts is not black crime, but the racial hatred and lawlessness

From Mary Church Terrell, "Lynching from a Negro's Point of View," *North American Review*, June 1904.

of the white population. Lynching, she asserts, is but the most extreme manifestation of racial injustice endemic in the South, a region where blacks also faced limited suffrage, the peonage system (in which black farmworkers were bound by debt to work for their creditors), and segregation laws.

Before 1904 was three months old, thirty-one negroes had been lynched. Of this number, fifteen were murdered within one week in Arkansas, and one was shot to death in Springfield, Ohio, by a mob composed of men who did not take the trouble to wear masks. Hanging, shooting and burning black men, women and children in the United States have become so common that such occurrences create but little sensation and evoke but slight comment now. Those who are jealous of their country's fair name feel keenly the necessity of extirpating this lawlessness, which is so widespread and has taken such deep root. But means of prevention can never be devised, until the cause of lynching is more generally understood.

The reasons why the whole subject is deeply and seriously involved in error are obvious. Those who live in the section where nine-tenths of the lynchings occur do not dare to tell the truth, even if they perceive it. When men know that the death-knell of their aspirations and hopes will be sounded as soon as they express views to which the majority in their immediate vicinage are opposed, they either suppress their views or trim them to fit the popular mind. Only martyrs are brave and bold enough to defy the public will, and the manufacture of martyrs in the negro's behalf is not very brisk just now. Those who do not live in the section where most of the lynchings occur borrow their views from their brothers who do, and so the errors are continually repeated and inevitably perpetuated.

In the discussion of this subject, four mistakes are commonly made.

Rape Is Not the Cause of Lynching

In the first place, it is a great mistake to suppose that rape is the real cause of lynching in the South. Beginning with the Ku-Klux Klan, the negro has been constantly subjected to some form of organized violence ever since he became free. It is easy to prove that rape is simply the pretext and not the cause of lynching. Statistics show that, out of every hundred negroes who are lynched, from seventy-five to eighty-five are not even accused of this crime, and many who are accused of it are innocent. And, yet, men who admit the accuracy of these figures gravely tell the country that lynching can never be suppressed, until negroes cease to commit a crime with which less than one-fourth of those murdered by mobs are charged.

The prevailing belief that negroes are not tortured by mobs unless they are charged with the "usual" crime, does not tally with the facts. The savagery which attended the lynching of a man and his wife the first week in March of the present year [1904] was probably never exceeded in this country or anywhere else in the civilized world. A white planter was murdered at Doddsville, Miss., and a negro was charged with the crime. The negro fled, and his wife, who was known to be innocent, fled with him to escape the fate which she knew awaited her, if she remained. The two negroes were pursued and captured, and the following account of the tragedy by an eye-witness appeared in the "Evening Post," a Democratic daily of Vicksburg, Miss.

> When the two negroes were captured, they were tied to trees, and while the funeral pyres were being prepared they were forced to suffer the most fiendish tortures. The blacks were forced to hold out their hands while one finger at a time was chopped off. The fingers were distributed as souvenirs. The ears of the murderers were cut off. Holbert was beaten severely, his skull was fractured, and one of his eyes, knocked out with a stick, hung by a shred from the socket. Neither the man nor the woman begged for mercy, nor made a groan or plea. When the executioner came forward to lop off fingers, Holbert extended his hand without being asked. The most excruciating form of punishment consisted in the use of a large corkscrew in the hands of some of the mob. This instrument was bored into the flesh of the man and the woman, in the arms, legs and body, and then pulled out, the spirals tearing out big pieces of raw, quivering flesh every time it was withdrawn. Even this devilish torture did not make the poor brutes cry out. When finally they were thrown on the fire and allowed to be burned to death, this came as a relief to the maimed and suffering victims.

The North frequently sympathizes with the Southern mob, because it has been led to believe the negro's diabolical assaults upon white women are the chief cause of lynching. In spite of the facts, distinguished representatives from the South are still insisting, in Congress and elsewhere, that "whenever negroes, cease committing the crime of rape, the lynchings and burnings will cease with it." But since three-fourths of the negroes who have met a violent death at the hands of Southern mobs have not been accused of this crime, it is evident that, instead of being the "usual" crime, rape is the most unusual of all the crimes for which negroes are shot, hanged and burned.

Although Southern men of prominence still insist that "this

crime is more responsible for mob violence than all other crimes combined," it is gratifying to observe that a few of them, at least, are beginning to feel ashamed to pervert the facts. During the past few years, several Southern gentlemen, of unquestioned ability and integrity, have publicly exposed the falsity of this plea. Two years ago, in a masterful article on the race problem, Professor Andrew Sledd, at that time an instructor in a Southern college, admitted that only a small number of the negroes who are lynched are even accused of assaulting white women. Said he:

> On the contrary, a frank consideration of all the facts, with no other desire than to find the truth, the whole truth and nothing but the truth, however contrary to our wishes and humiliating to our section the truth may be, will show that by far the most of our Southern lynchings are carried through in *sheer, unqualified and increasing brutality*.

But a heavy penalty was paid by this man who dared to make such a frank and fearless statement of facts. He was forced to resign his position as professor, and lost prestige in his section in various ways. . . .

The Demand for Social Equality

In the second place, it is a mistake to suppose that the negro's desire for social equality sustains any relation whatsoever to the crime of rape. According to the testimony of eye-witnesses, as well as the reports of Southern newspapers, the negroes who are known to have been guilty of assault have, as a rule, been ignorant, repulsive in appearance and as near the brute creation as it is possible for a human being to be. It is safe to assert that, among the negroes who have been guilty of ravishing white women, not one had been taught that he was the equal of white people or had ever heard of social equality. And if by chance he had heard of it, he had no clearer conception of its meaning than he had of the principle of the binomial theorem. In conversing with a large number of ignorant negroes, the writer has never found one who seemed to have any idea of what social equality means, or who expressed a desire to put this theory into practice when it was explained to him.

Negroes who have been educated in Northern institutions of learning with white men and women, and who for that reason might have learned the meaning of social equality and have acquired a taste for the same, neither assault white women nor commit other crimes, as a rule. A careful review of the facts will show that negroes who have the "convention habit" developed to a high degree, or who are able to earn their living by editing newspapers, do not belong to the criminal class, although such negroes are always held up by Southern gentlemen as objects of ridicule, contempt and scorn. Strange as it may appear, illiterate negroes, who are the only ones contributing largely to the criminal class, are coddled and caressed by the South. To the educated, cultivated members of the race, they are held up as bright and shining examples of what a really good negro should be. The dictionary is searched in vain by Southern gentlemen and gentlewomen for words sufficiently ornate and strong to express their admiration for a dear old "mammy" or a faithful old "uncle," who can neither read nor write, and who assure their white friends they would not, if they could.

A photograph of a Louisiana lynching in 1938. The House of Representatives voted to make lynching a federal crime in 1922, 1937, and 1940, but the Senate each time refused to pass the measure.

On the other hand, no language is sufficiently caustic, bitter and severe, to express the disgust, hatred and scorn which Southern gentlemen feel for what is called the "New Issue," which, being interpreted, means, negroes who aspire to knowledge and culture, and who have acquired a taste for the highest and best things in life. At the door of this "New Issue," the sins and shortcomings of the whole race are laid. This "New Issue" is beyond hope of redemption, we are told, because somebody, nobody knows who, has taught it to believe in social equality, something, nobody knows what. The alleged fear of social equality has always been used by the South to explain its unchristian treatment of the negro and to excuse its many crimes. How many crimes have been committed, and how many falsehoods have been uttered, in the name of social equality by the South! Of all these, the greatest is the determination to lay lynching at its door. In the North, which is the only section that accords the negro the scrap of social equality enjoyed by him in the United States, he is rarely accused of rape. The only form of social equality ever attempted between the two races, and practised to any considerable extent, is that which was originated by the white masters of slave women, and which has been perpetuated by them and their descendants even unto the present day. Of whatever other crime we may accuse the big, black burly brute, who is so familiar a figure in the reports of rape and lynching-bees sent out by the Southern press, surely we cannot truthfully charge him with an attempt to introduce social equality into this republican form of government, or to foist it upon a democratic land. There is no more connection between social equality and lynching to-day than there was between social equality and slavery before the war, or than there is between social equality and the convict-lease system, or any other form of oppression to which the negro has uniformly been subjected in the South.

Victims of Lynching Are Often Innocent

The third error on the subject of lynching consists of the widely circulated statement that the moral sensibilities of the best negroes in the United States are so stunted and dull, and the standard of morality among even the leaders of the race is so low, that they do not appreciate the enormity and heinousness of rape. Those who claim to know the negro best and to be his best friends declare, that he usually sympathizes with the black victim of mob violence rather than with the white victim of the black fiend's lust, even when he does not go so far as to condone the crime of rape. Only those who are densely ignorant of the standards and sentiments of the best negroes, or who wish wilfully to misrepresent and maliciously to slander a race already resting under burdens greater than it can bear, would accuse its thousands of reputable men and women of sympathizing with rapists, either black or white, or of condoning their crime. The negro preachers and teachers who have had the advantage of education and moral training, together with others occupying positions of honor and trust, are continually expressing their horror of this one particular crime, and exhorting all whom they can reach by voice or pen to do everything in their power to wash the ugly stain of rape from the race's good name. And whenever the slightest pity for the victim of mob violence is expressed by a negro who represents the intelligence and decency of his race, it is invariably because there is a reasonable doubt of his innocence, rather than because there is condonation of the alleged crime.

Everybody who is well informed on the subject of lynching knows that many a negro who has been accused of assault or murder, or other violation of the law, and has been tortured to death by a mob, has afterward been proved innocent of the crime with which he was charged. So great is the thirst for the negro's blood in the South, that but a single breath of suspicion is sufficient to kindle into an all-consuming flame the embers of hatred ever smouldering in the breasts of the fiends who compose a typical mob. When once such a bloodthirsty company starts on a negro's trail, and the right one cannot be found, the first available specimen is sacrificed to their rage, no matter whether he is guilty or not.

A white man who died near Charleston, South Carolina, in March of the present year, confessed on his death-bed that he had murdered his wife, although three negroes were lynched for this crime at Ravenel, South Carolina, in May, 1902. This murder was one of the most brutal ever committed in the State, and the horrible tortures to which the three innocent negroes were subjected indicated plainly that the mob intended the punishment to fit the crime. In August, 1901, three negroes, a mother, her daughter and her son, were lynched in Carrollton, Miss., because it was rumored that they had heard of a murder before it was committed, and had not reported it. A negro was accused of murdering a woman, and was lynched in Shreveport, Louisiana, in April, 1902, who was afterward proved innocent. The woman who was lynched in Mississippi this year was not even accused of a crime. The charge of murder had not been proved against her husband, and, as the white man who was murdered had engaged in an altercation with him, it is quite likely that, if the negro had been tried in a court of law, it would have been shown to be a case of justifiable homicide. And so other cases might easily be cited to prove that the charge that innocent negroes are sometimes lynched is by no means without foundation. It is not strange, therefore, that even reputable, law-abiding negroes should protest against the tortures and cruelties inflicted by mobs which wreak vengeance upon the guilty and innocent and upon the just and unjust of their race alike. It is to the credit and not to the shame of the negro that he tries to uphold the sacred majesty of the law, which is so often trailed in the dust and trampled under foot by white mobs.

The Case of Sam Hose

In the fourth place, it is well to remember, in discussing the subject of lynching, that it is not always possible to ascertain the facts from the accounts in the newspapers. The facts are often suppressed, intentionally or unintentionally, or distorted by the press. The case of Sam Hose, to which reference has so often been made, is a good illustration of the unreliability of the press in reporting the lynching of negroes. Sam Hose, a negro, murdered Alfred Cranford, a white man, in a dispute over wages which the white employer refused to pay the colored workman. It was decided to make an example of a negro who dared to kill a white man. A well-known, influential newspaper immediately offered a reward of $500 for the capture of Sam Hose. This same newspaper predicted a lynching, and stated that, though several modes of punishment had been suggested, it was the consensus of opinion that the negro should be burned at the stake and tortured before being burned. A rumor was started, and circulated far and wide by the press, that Sam Hose had assaulted the wife of Alfred Cranford, after the latter had been killed. One of the best detectives in Chicago was sent to Atlanta to investigate the affair. After securing all the information it was possible to obtain from black and white alike, and carefully weighing the evidence, this white detective declared it would have been a physical impossibility for the negro to assault the murdered man's wife, and expressed it as his opinion that the charge of assault was an invention intended to make the burning a certainty.

The Sunday on which Sam Hose was burned was converted into a holiday. Special trains were made up to take the Christian people of Atlanta to the scene of the burning, a short distance from the city. After the first train moved out with every inch of available space inside and out filled to overflowing, a second had to be made up, so as to accommodate those who had just come from church. After Sam Hose had been tortured and burned to death, the great concourse of Christians who had witnessed the tragedy scraped for hours among his ashes in the hope of finding a sufficient number of his bones to take to their friends as souvenirs. The charge has been made that Sam Hose boasted to another negro that he intended to assault Alfred Cranford's wife. It would be difficult for anybody who understands conditions in the South to believe that a sane negro would announce his purpose to violate a white woman there, then deliberately enter her husband's house, while all the family were present, to carry out his threat.

Two years ago a riot occurred in Atlanta, Georgia, in which four white policemen were killed and several wounded by a colored man named Richardson, who was himself finally burned to death. Through the press the public was informed that the negro was a desperado. As a matter of fact, Richardson was a merchant, well to do and law-abiding. The head and front of his offending

126

was that he dared to reprimand an ex-policeman for living in open adultery with a colored woman. When it was learned that this negro had been so impudent to a white man, the sheriff led out a posse, consisting of the city police, to arrest Richardson. Seeing the large number of officers surrounding his house, and knowing what would be his fate, if caught, the negro determined to sell his life dear, and he did. With the exception of the Macon "Telegraph," but few white newspapers ever gave the real cause of the riot, and so Richardson has gone down to history as a black desperado, who shot to death four officers of the law and wounded as many more. Several years ago, near New Orleans, a negro was at work in a corn-field. In working through the corn he made considerable noise, which frightened a young white woman, who happened to be passing by. She ran to the nearest house, and reported that a negro had jumped at her. A large crowd of white men immediately shouldered guns and seized the negro, who had no idea what it meant. When told why he was taken, the negro protested that he had not even seen the girl whom he was accused of frightening, but his protest was of no avail and he was hanged to the nearest tree. The press informed the country that this negro was lynched for attempted rape. Instance after instance might be cited to prove that facts bearing upon lynching, as well as upon other phases of the race problem, are often garbled—without intention, perhaps—by the press.

Two Causes of Lynching

What, then, is the cause of lynching? At the last analysis, it will be discovered that there are just two causes of lynching. In the first place, it is due to race hatred, the hatred of a stronger people toward a weaker who were once held as slaves. In the second place, it is due to the lawlessness so prevalent in the section where nine-tenths of the lynchings occur. View the question of lynching from any point of view one may, and it is evident that it is just as impossible for the negroes of this country to prevent mob violence by any attitude of mind which they may assume, or any course of conduct which they may pursue, as it is for a straw dam to stop Niagara's flow. Upon the same spirit of intolerance and of hatred the crime of lynching must be fastened as that which called into being the Ku-Klux Klan, and which has prompted more recent exhibitions of hostility toward the negro, such as the disfranchisement acts, the Jim Crow Car Laws, and the new slavery called "peonage," together with other acts of oppression which make the negro's lot so hard.

Lynching is the aftermath of slavery. The white men who shoot negroes to death and flay them alive, and the white women who apply flaming torches to their oil-soaked bodies to-day, are the sons and daughters of women who had but little, if any, compassion on the race when it was enslaved. . . . It is as impossible to comprehend the cause of the ferocity and barbarity which attend the average lynching-bee without taking into account the brutalizing effect of slavery upon the people of the section where most of the lynchings occur, as it is to investigate the essence and nature of fire without considering the gases which cause the flame to ignite. It is too much to expect, perhaps, that the children of women who for generations looked upon the hardships and the degradation of their sisters of a darker hue with few if any protests, should have mercy and compassion upon the children of that oppressed race now. But what a tremendous influence for law and order, and what a mighty foe to mob violence Southern

---

The True Cause of Lynching

Ida B. Wells-Barnett, a black female journalist and social reformer, is best remembered for her campaign against lynching. Her editorials on lynching in her newspaper Free Speech, *which she cofounded in Memphis, Tennessee, in 1891, caused her to be forcibly exiled from the South. She used newspaper records and other sources to refute the argument that lynching was a response by whites to the threat of rape. The following passage is excerpted from an article in the magazine* Independent *published on May 16, 1901.*

Among many thousand editorial clippings I have received in the past five years, 99 percent discuss the question upon the presumption that lynchings are the desperate effort of the Southern people to protect their women from black monsters, and, while the large majority condemn lynching, the condemnation is tempered with a plea for the lyncher—that human nature gives way under such awful provocation and that the mob, insane for the moment, must be pitied as well as condemned. . . .

This almost universal tendency to accept as true the slander which the lynchers offer to civilization as an excuse for their crime might be explained if the true facts were difficult to obtain; but not the slightest difficulty intervenes. The Associated Press dispatches, the press clipping bureau, frequent book publications, and the annual summary of a number of influential journals give the lynching record every year. This record, easily within the reach of everyone who wants it, makes inexcusable the statement and cruelly unwarranted the assumption that Negroes are lynched only because of their assaults upon womanhood. . . .

In 1896 less than 39 percent of the Negroes lynched were charged with this crime; in 1897, less than 18 percent; in 1898, less than 16 percent; in 1899, less than 14 percent; and in 1900, less than 15 percent were so charged.

white women might be, if they would arise in the purity and power of their womanhood to implore their fathers, husbands and sons no longer to stain their hands with the black man's blood! . . .

If there were one particularly heinous crime for which an infuriated people took vengeance upon the negro, or if there were a genuine fear that a guilty negro might escape the penalty of the law in the South, then it might be possible to explain the cause of lynching on some other hypothesis than that of race hatred. It has already been shown that the first supposition has no foundation in fact. It is easy to prove that the second is false. Even those who condone lynching do not pretend to fear the delay or the uncertainty of the law, when a guilty negro is concerned. With the courts of law entirely in the hands of the white man, with judge and jury belonging to the superior race, a guilty negro could no more extricate himself from the meshes of the law in the South than he could slide from the devil-fish's embrace or slip from the anaconda's coils. Miscarriage of justice in the South is possible only when white men transgress the law.

Manifestations of Racial Hate

In addition to lynching, the South is continually furnishing proof of its determination to wreak terrible vengeance upon the negro. The recent shocking revelations of the extent to which the actual enslavement of negroes has been carried under the peonage system of Alabama and Mississippi, and the unspeakable cruelties to which men, women and children are alike subjected, all bear witness to this fact. In January of the present year, a government detective found six negro children ranging in age from six to sixteen years working on a Georgia plantation in bare feet, scantily clad in rags, although the ground was covered with snow. The owner of the plantation is one of the wealthiest men in northeast Georgia, and is said to have made his fortune by holding negroes in slavery. When he was tried it was shown that the white planter had killed the father of the six children a few years before, but was acquitted of the murder, as almost invariably happens, when a white man takes a negro's life. After the death of their father, the children were treated with incredible cruelty. They were often chained in a room without fire and were beaten until the blood streamed from their backs, when they were unable to do their stint of work. The planter was placed under $5,000 bail, but it is doubtful whether he will ever pay the penalty of his crime. Like the children just mentioned hundreds of negroes are to-day groaning under a bondage more crushing and more cruel than that abolished forty years ago.

This same spirit manifests itself in a variety of ways. Efforts are constantly making to curtail the educational opportunities of colored children. Already one State has enacted a law by which colored children in the public schools are prohibited from receiving instruction higher than the sixth grade, and other States will, doubtless, soon follow this lead. It is a well-known fact that a Governor recently elected in one of the Southern States owes his popularity and his votes to his open and avowed opposition to the education of negroes. Instance after instance might be cited to prove that the hostility toward the negro in the South is bitter and pronounced, and that lynching is but a manifestation of this spirit of vengeance and intolerance in its ugliest and most brutal form.

To the widespread lawlessness among the white people of the South lynching is also due. In commenting upon the blood-guiltiness of South Carolina, the Nashville "American" declared some time ago that, if the killings in the other States had been in the same ratio to population as in South Carolina, a larger number of people would have been murdered in the United States during 1902 than fell on the American side in the Spanish and Philippine wars.

Slandering the Negro Race

Whenever Southern white people discuss lynching, they are prone to slander the whole negro race. Not long ago, a Southern writer of great repute [Thomas Nelson Page] declared without qualification or reservation that "the crime of rape is well-nigh wholly confined to the negro race," and insisted that "negroes furnish most of the ravishers." These assertions are as unjust to the negro as they are unfounded in fact. According to statistics recently published, only one colored male in 100,000 over five years of age was accused of assault upon a white woman in the South in 1902, whereas one male out of every 20,000 over five years of age was charged with rape in Chicago during the same year. If these figures prove anything at all, they show that the [white] men and boys in Chicago are many times more addicted to rape than are the negroes in the South. Already in the present year two white men have been arrested in the national capital for attempted assault upon little children. One was convicted and sentenced to six years in the penitentiary. The crime of which the other was accused was of the most infamous character. A short account of the trial of the convicted man appeared in the Washington dailies, as any other criminal suit would have been reported; but if a colored man had committed the same crime, the newspapers from one end of the United States to the other would have published it broadcast. Editorials upon the total depravity and the hopeless immorality of the negro would have been written, based upon this particular case as a text. With such facts to prove the falsity of the charge that "the crime of rape is well-nigh wholly confined to the negro race," it is amazing that any writer of repute should affix his signature to such a slander.

But even if the negro's morals were as loose and as lax as some claim them to be, and if his belief in the virtue of women were as slight as we are told, the South has nobody to blame but itself. The only object lesson in virtue and morality which the negro received for 250 years came through the medium of slavery, and that peculiar institution was not calculated to set his standards of correct living very high. Men do not gather grapes of thorns nor figs of thistles. Throughout their entire period of bondage colored women were debauched by their masters. From the day they were liberated to the present time, prepossessing young colored girls have been considered the rightful prey of white gentlemen in the South, and they have been protected neither by public sentiment nor by law. In the South, the negro's home is not considered sacred by the superior race. White men are neither punished for invading it, nor lynched for violating colored women and girls. . . . In demanding so much of the negro, the South places itself in the anomalous position of insisting that the conduct of the inferior race shall be better, and its standards higher, than those of the people who claim to be superior. . . .

How Lynching Can Be Stopped

How can lynching be extirpated in the United States? There are just two ways in which this can be accomplished. In the first place, lynching can never be suppressed in the South, until the masses of ignorant white people in that section are educated and lifted to a higher moral plane. It is difficult for one who has not seen these people to comprehend the density of their ignorance and the depth of their degradation. A well-known white author who lives in the South describes them as follows:

> Wholly ignorant, absolutely without culture, apparently without even the capacity to appreciate the nicer feelings or higher sense, yet conceited on account of their white skin which they constantly dishonor, they make, when aroused, as wild and brutal a mob as ever disgraced the face of the earth.

In lamenting the mental backwardness of the white people of the South, the Atlanta "Constitution" expressed itself as follows two years ago: "We have as many illiterate white men over the age of twenty-one years in the South to-day as there were fifty-two years ago, when the census of 1850 was taken." Over against these statistics stands the record of the negro, who has reduced his illiteracy 44.5 per cent. in forty years. The hostility which has always existed between the poor whites and the negroes of the

South has been greatly intensified in these latter days, by the material and intellectual advancement of the negro. The wrath of a Spanish bull, before whose maddened eyes a red flag is flaunted, is but a feeble attempt at temper compared with the seething, boiling rage of the average white man in the South who beholds a well-educated negro dressed in fine or becoming clothes. In the second place, lynching cannot be suppressed in the South until all classes of white people who dwell there, those of high as well as middle and low degree, respect the rights of other human beings, no matter what may be the color of their skin, become merciful and just enough to cease their persecution of a weaker race and learn a holy reverence for the law.

It is not because the American people are cruel, as a whole, or indifferent on general principles to the suffering of the wronged or oppressed, that outrages against the negro are permitted to occur and go unpunished, but because many are ignorant of the extent to which they are carried, while others despair of eradicating them. The South has so industriously, persistently and eloquently preached the inferiority of the negro, that the North has apparently been converted to this view—the thousands of negroes of sterling qualities, moral worth and lofty patriotism to the contrary notwithstanding. The South has insisted so continuously and belligerently that it is the negro's best friend, that it understands him better than other people on the face of the earth and that it will brook interference from nobody in its method of dealing with him, that the North has been persuaded or intimidated into bowing to this decree.

Then, too, there seems to be a decline of the great convictions in which this government was conceived and into which it was born. Until there is a renaissance of popular belief in the principles of liberty and equality upon which this government was founded, lynching, the Convict Lease System, the Disfranchisement Acts, the Jim Crow Car Laws, unjust discriminations in the professions and trades and similar atrocities will continue to dishearten and degrade the negro, and stain the fair name of the United States. For there can be no doubt that the greatest obstacle in the way of extirpating lynching is the general attitude of the public mind toward this unspeakable crime. The whole country seems tired of hearing about the black man's woes. The wrongs of the Irish, of the Armenians, of the Roumanian and Russian Jews, of the exiles of Russia and of every other oppressed people upon the face of the globe, can arouse the sympathy and fire the indignation of the American public, while they seem to be all but indifferent to the murderous assaults upon the negroes in the South.

CHAPTER 4

Booker T. Washington and His Critics

Chapter Preface

In September 1895 a former slave became a national figure after delivering a speech at the Atlanta Exposition. The speaker, Booker T. Washington, was the founder and president of the Tuskegee Institute, an industrial school for blacks in Alabama. His address on black/white relations in the South was favorably received by many whites because of its conciliatory message and tone. The widespread acclamation his speech received, combined with his own talents, energy, and self-promotion, established Washington as the nation's preeminent African-American leader from 1895 until his death in 1915.

In many respects, the years surrounding the start of the twentieth century were dark ones for African Americans. Most still lived in the South, where many states had passed laws instituting racial segregation and black disfranchisement. In 1896, the Supreme Court ruled in the case of *Plessy v. Ferguson* that a Louisiana law requiring racial segregation of railroad passengers was constitutional as long as the facilities provided to blacks were of a quality equal to those available to whites. The "separate but equal" doctrine became the legal basis for a myriad of laws establishing racial separation in schools, parks, and other public facilities throughout the South and other parts of the country. In addition, African Americans had little hope for fair treatment by the all-white courts and criminal justice system. Hundreds of African Americans became the victims of lynch mobs and race riots during these years.

Washington's prescription for black progress during this troubled period stressed economic advancement rather than political or social equality. He argued that through vocational training and education emphasizing the values of thrift, hard work, and personal morality, blacks could attain economic security as well as respect and acceptance from America's white majority.

Washington's ideas, expressed in numerous speeches and writings following the 1895 Atlanta Exposition address, helped attract a flow of philanthropic funds to his Tuskegee Institute and other projects. Over the next two decades Washington would write an autobiography (*Up from Slavery*), advise Theodore Roosevelt and other U.S. presidents on racial matters, and establish a national political network of schools, newspapers, and various national organizations and umbrella groups such as the National Negro Business League.

Washington's ideas and influence, however, were criticized by some within the black community. Critics opposed his seeming abandonment of the quest for civil rights and political and social equality, and they objected to his emphasis on industrial education. W.E.B. Du Bois, a Harvard University–trained scholar, emerged as one of the most prominent of Washington's detractors. In his book *The Souls of Black Folk* and in other writings, Du Bois questioned Washington's assumption that economic advancement and industrial training alone would secure blacks' acceptance in American society. In 1905 Du Bois and like-minded African Americans met at Niagara Falls to plan a direct campaign against racial segregation, which they argued simply entrenched racial prejudice and discrimination against blacks.

Recent studies by historians have revealed a hidden side to Booker T. Washington and his work. In building what was essentially a political machine, he sometimes used ruthless methods that included spying on and sabotaging leading black critics and secretly financing and controlling black newspapers. On the other hand, despite his public disparagement of political and civil rights activism, Washington engaged in unpublicized efforts against segregation laws, voting discrimination, and racially motivated lynching. Most scholars, taking these factors as well as Washington's public prominence into account, have given Washington a mixed assessment as a black leader. The viewpoints in the following chapter present some of the controversies surrounding Booker T. Washington and his ideas.

VIEWPOINT 1

"The wisest among my race understand that the agitation of questions of social equality is the extremest folly."

Blacks Should Not Agitate for Political Equality

Booker T. Washington (1856–1915)

Booker T. Washington first gained national prominence in 1895 with his speech at the Atlanta Exposition. Prior to that event Washington had served as president of the Tuskegee Institute, a black vocational school in Alabama that he founded in 1881 and built virtually from scratch into a thriving institution. In his 1895 address, reprinted here, Washington advocates a policy of accommodation on civil rights issues, arguing that blacks can better their future by concentrating on self-improvement through vocational education, agriculture, and industry, rather than by trying to change discriminatory laws and customs. Washington's speech was hailed by many and helped propel him to become a national black leader and head of a network of black newspapers, schools, and organizations. However, the "Atlanta Compromise" (as W.E.B. Du Bois called this address) was later criticized by some black leaders and intellectuals, including Du Bois, as being too amenable to the deprivation of blacks' political and civil rights.

From Booker T. Washington, speech at the Atlanta Exposition, September 18, 1895.

Mr. President and Gentlemen of the Board of Directors and Citizens:

One-third of the population of the South is of the Negro race. No enterprise seeking the material, civil, or moral welfare of this section can disregard this element of our population and reach the highest success. I but convey to you, Mr. President and Directors, the sentiment of the masses of my race when I say that in no way have the value and manhood of the American Negro been more fittingly and generously recognized than by the managers of this magnificent exposition at every stage of its progress. It is a recognition that will do more to cement the friendship of the two races than any occurrence since the dawn of our freedom.

Not only this, but the opportunity here afforded will awaken among us a new era of industrial progress. Ignorant and inexperienced, it is not strange that in the first years of our new life we began at the top instead of at the bottom; that a seat in Congress or the state legislature was more sought than real estate or industrial skill; that the political convention or stump speaking had more attractions than starting a dairy farm or truck garden.

Cast Down Your Bucket

A ship lost at sea for many days suddenly sighted a friendly vessel. From the mast of the unfortunate vessel was seen a signal: "Water, water; we die of thirst!" The answer from the friendly vessel at once came back: "Cast down your bucket where you are." A second time the signal, "Water, water, send us water!" ran up from the distressed vessel, and was answered: "Cast down your bucket where you are." And a third and fourth signal for water was answered: "Cast down your bucket where you are." The captain of the distressed vessel, at last heeding the injunction, cast down his bucket, and it came up full of fresh, sparkling water from the mouth of the Amazon River.

To those of my race who depend on bettering their condition in a foreign land or who underestimate the importance of cultivating friendly relations with the Southern white man, who is their next-door neighbor, I would say: Cast down your bucket where you are; cast it down in making friends, in every manly way, of the people of all races by whom we are surrounded. Cast it down in agriculture, mechanics, in commerce, in domestic service, and in the professions. And in this connection it is well to bear in mind that whatever other sins the South may be called to bear, when it comes to business, pure and simple, it is in the South that the Negro is given a man's chance in the commercial world, and in nothing is this exposition more eloquent than in emphasizing this chance.

Our greatest danger is that, in the great leap from slavery to freedom, we may overlook the fact that the masses of us are to live by the productions of our hands and fail to keep in mind that we shall prosper in proportion as we learn to dignify and glorify common labor, and put brains and skill into the common occupations of life; shall prosper in proportion as we learn to draw the line between the superficial and the substantial, the ornamental gewgaws of life and the useful. No race can prosper till it learns that there is as much dignity in tilling a field as in writing a poem. It is at the bottom of life we must begin, and not at the top. Nor should we permit our grievances to overshadow our opportunities.

For two decades, Booker T. Washington was the most influential black voice in the United States.

To those of the white race who look to the incoming of those of foreign birth and strange tongue and habits for the prosperity of the South, were I permitted I would repeat what I say to my own race, "Cast down your bucket where you are." Cast it down among the 8 million Negroes whose habits you know, whose fidelity and love you have tested in days when to have proved treacherous meant the ruin of your firesides. Cast down your bucket among these people who have, without strikes and labor wars, tilled your fields, cleared your forests, builded your rail-roads and cities, and brought forth treasures from the bowels of the earth and helped make possible this magnificent representation of the progress of the South. Casting down your bucket among my people, helping and encouraging them as you are doing on these grounds, and, with education of head, hand, and heart, you will find that they will buy your surplus land, make blossom the waste places in your fields, and run your factories.

While doing this, you can be sure in the future, as in the past, that you and your families will be surrounded by the most patient, faithful, law-abiding, and unresentful people that the world has seen. As we have proved our loyalty to you in the past, in nursing your children, watching by the sickbed of your mothers and fathers, and often following them with tear-dimmed eyes to their graves, so in the future, in our humble way, we shall stand by you with a devotion that no foreigner can approach, ready to lay down our lives, if need be, in defense of yours; interlacing our industrial, commercial, civil, and religious life with yours in a way that shall make the interests of both races one. In all things that are purely social we can be as separate as the fingers, yet one as the hand in all things essential to mutual progress.

Development for All

There is no defense or security for any of us except in the highest intelligence and development of all. If anywhere there are efforts tending to curtail the fullest growth of the Negro, let these efforts be turned into stimulating, encouraging, and making him the most useful and intelligent citizen. Effort or means so invested will pay a thousand percent interest. These efforts will be twice blessed—"blessing him that gives and him that takes."

There is no escape, through law of man or God, from the inevitable:

The laws of changeless justice bind
Oppressor with oppressed;
And close as sin and suffering joined
We march to fate abreast

Nearly 16 millions of hands will aid you in pulling the load upward, or they will pull against you the load downward. We shall constitute one-third and more of the ignorance and crime of the South, or one-third its intelligence and progress; we shall contribute one-third to the business and industrial prosperity of the South, or we shall prove a veritable body of death, stagnating, depressing, retarding every effort to advance the body politic.

Gentlemen of the exposition, as we present to you our humble effort at an exhibition of our progress, you must not expect overmuch. Starting thirty years ago with ownership here and there in a few quilts and pumpkins and chickens (gathered from miscellaneous sources), remember: the path that has led from these to the invention and production of agricultural implements, buggies, steam engines, newspapers, books, statuary, carving, paintings, the management of drugstores and banks, has not been trodden without contact with thorns and thistles. While we take pride in what we exhibit as a result of our independent efforts, we do not for a moment forget that our part in this exhibition would fall far short of your expectations but for the constant help that has come to our educational life, not only from the Southern states but especially from Northern philanthropists who have made their gifts a constant stream of blessing and encouragement.

Political Rights Will Not Come from Artificial Forcing

In this passage from his 1901 autobiography, Up From Slavery, *Booker T. Washington expresses his opinions on the political rights and responsibilities of blacks.*

My own belief is, although I have never before said so in so many words, that the time will come when the Negro in the South will be accorded all the political rights which his ability, character, and material possessions entitle him to. I think, though, that the opportunity to freely exercise such political rights will not come in any large degree through outside or artificial forcing, but will be accorded to the Negro by the Southern white people themselves, and that they will protect him in the exercise of those rights. . . .

I believe it is the duty of the Negro—as the greater part of the race is already doing—to deport himself modestly in regard to political claims, depending upon the slow but sure influences that proceed from the possession of property, intelligence, and high character for the full recognition of his political rights. I think that the according of the full exercise of political rights is going to be a matter of natural, slow growth, not an over-night, gourd-vine affair.

The wisest among my race understand that the agitation of questions of social equality is the extremest folly, and that progress in the enjoyment of all the privileges that will come to us must be the result of severe and constant struggle rather than of artificial forcing. No race that has anything to contribute to the markets of the world is long in any degree ostracized. It is important and right that all privileges of the law be ours, but it is vastly more important that we be prepared for the exercise of these privileges. The opportunity to earn a dollar in a factory just now is worth infinitely more than the opportunity to spend a dollar in an opera house.

A Pledge to Cooperate

In conclusion, may I repeat that nothing in thirty years has given us more hope and encouragement and drawn us so near to you of the white race as this opportunity offered by the exposition; and here bending, as it were, over the altar that represents the results of the struggles of your race and mine, both starting practically empty-handed three decades ago, I pledge that, in your effort to work out the great and intricate problem which God has laid at the doors of the South, you shall have at all times the patient, sympathetic help of my race; only let this be constantly in mind that, while from representations in these buildings of the product of field, of forest, of mine, of factory, letters, and art, much good will come—yet far above and beyond material benefits will be that higher good, that let us pray God will come, in a blotting out of sectional differences and racial animosities and suspicions, in a determination to administer absolute justice, in a willing obedience among all classes to the mandates of law. This, coupled with our material prosperity, will bring into our beloved South a new heaven and a new earth.

"By every civilized and peaceful method we must strive for the rights which the world accords to men."

Blacks Should Strive for Political Equality

W.E.B. Du Bois (1868–1963)

Booker T. Washington reached the height of his national influence in the first years of the twentieth century, serving as the leader of a national network of organizations and as an unofficial adviser to Presidents Theodore Roosevelt and William Howard Taft. However, not all blacks agreed with his ideas on political activism and other issues. Perhaps the most prominent of his critics was W.E.B. Du Bois, whose long public career as a writer, scholar, and civil rights activist spanned from the end of the nineteenth century to the height of the civil rights movement in the early 1960s. Du Bois gained acclaim for his 1903 book *The Souls of Black Folk*, a collection of essays on African-American life. In the part of the book excerpted here, Du Bois criticizes Washington for abandoning the political struggle against racial segregation. Du Bois was the most notable black public figure of his time to question Washington's ideas. Shortly thereafter Du Bois and other blacks who shared his opinions met at Niagara Falls in 1905 and drafted a list of demands, including an end to segregation in courts and public accommodations. The Niagara Movement disbanded after a few years due to lack of financial support, but its work was continued by the National Association for the Advancement of Colored People, an interracial organization founded by Du Bois and others in 1909.

From W.E.B. Du Bois, *The Souls of Black Folk* (Chicago: A.C. McClurg, 1903).

Easily the most striking thing in the history of the American Negro since 1876 is the ascendancy of Mr. Booker T. Washington. It began at the time when war memories and ideals were rapidly passing; a day of astonishing commercial development was dawning; a sense of doubt and hesitation overtook the freedmen's sons,—then it was that his leading began. Mr. Washington came, with a single definite programme, at the psychological moment when the nation was a little ashamed of having bestowed so much sentiment on Negroes, and was concentrating its energies on Dollars. His programme of industrial education, conciliation of the South, and submission and silence as to civil and political rights, was not wholly original; the Free Negroes from 1830 up to wartime had striven to build industrial schools, and the American Missionary Association had from the first taught various trades; and [Joseph C.] Price and others had sought a way of honorable alliance with the best of the Southerners. But Mr. Washington first indissolubly linked these things; he put enthusiasm, unlimited energy, and perfect faith into this programme, and changed it from a by-path into a veritable Way of Life. And the tale of the methods by which he did this is a fascinating study of human life.

It startled the nation to hear a Negro advocating such a programme after many decades of bitter complaint: it startled and won the applause of the South, it interested and won the admiration of the North; and after a confused murmur of protest, it silenced if it did not convert the Negroes themselves.

To gain the sympathy and coöperation of the various elements comprising the white South was Mr. Washington's first task; and this, at the time Tuskegee was founded, seemed, for a black man, well-nigh impossible. And yet ten years later it was done in the word spoken at Atlanta: "In all things purely social we can be as separate as the five fingers, and yet one as the hand in all things essential to mutual progress." This "Atlanta Compromise" is by all odds the most notable thing in Mr. Washington's career. The South interpreted it in different ways: the radicals received it as a complete surrender of the demand for civil and political equality; the conservatives, as a generously conceived working basis for mutual understanding. So both approved it, and to-day its author is certainly the most distinguished Southerner since Jefferson Davis, and the one with the largest personal following.

Next to this achievement comes Mr. Washington's work in gaining place and consideration in the North. Others less shrewd and tactful had formerly essayed to sit on these two stools and had fallen between them; but as Mr. Washington knew the heart of the

South from birth and training, so by singular insight he intuitively grasped the spirit of the age which was dominating the North. And so thoroughly did he learn the speech and thought of triumphant commercialism, and the ideals of material prosperity, that the picture of a lone black boy poring over a French grammar amid the weeds and dirt of a neglected home soon seemed to him the acme of absurdities. One wonders what Socrates and St. Francis of Assisi would say to this.

And yet this very singleness of vision and thorough oneness with his age is a mark of the successful man. It is as though Nature must needs make men narrow in order to give them force. So Mr. Washington's cult has gained unquestioning followers, his work has wonderfully prospered, his friends are legion, and his enemies are confounded. To-day he stands as the one recognized spokesman of his ten million fellows, and one of the most notable figures in a nation of seventy millions. One hesitates, therefore, to criticise a life which, beginning with so little, has done so much. And yet the time is come when one may speak in all sincerity and utter courtesy of the mistakes and shortcomings of Mr. Washington's career, as well as of his triumphs, without being thought captious or envious, and without forgetting that it is easier to do ill than well in the world. . . .

The Old Attitude of Submission

Mr. Washington represents in Negro thought the old attitude of adjustment and submission; but adjustment at such a peculiar time as to make his programme unique. This is an age of unusual economic development, and Mr. Washington's programme naturally takes an economic cast, becoming a gospel of Work and Money to such an extent as apparently almost completely to overshadow the higher aims of life. Moreover, this is an age when the more advanced races are coming in closer contact with the less developed races, and the race-feeling is therefore intensified; and Mr. Washington's programme practically accepts the alleged inferiority of the Negro races. In our own land, the reaction from the sentiment of war time has given impetus to race-prejudice against Negroes, and Mr. Washington withdraws many of the high demands of Negroes as men and American citizens. In other periods of intensified prejudice all the Negro's tendency to self-assertion has been called forth; at this period a policy of submission is advocated. In the history of nearly all other races and peoples the doctrine preached at such crises has been that manly self-respect is worth more than lands and houses, and that a people who voluntarily surrender such respect, or cease striving for it, are not worth civilizing.

In answer to this, it has been claimed that the Negro can survive only through submission. Mr. Washington distinctly asks that black people give up, at least for the present, three things,—

First, political power,

Second, insistence on civil rights,

Third, higher education of Negro youth,—

and concentrate all their energies on industrial education, the accumulation of wealth, and the conciliation of the South. This policy has been courageously and insistently advocated for over fifteen years, and has been triumphant for perhaps ten years. As a result of this tender of the palm-branch, what has been the return? In these years there have occurred:

1. The disfranchisement of the Negro
2. The legal creation of a distinct status of civil inferiority for the Negro
3. The steady withdrawal of aid from institutions for the higher training of the Negro

These movements are not, to be sure, direct results of Mr. Washington's teachings; but his propaganda has, without a shadow of doubt, helped their speedier accomplishment. The question then comes: Is it possible, and probable, that nine millions of men can make effective progress in economic lines if they are deprived of political rights, made a servile caste, and allowed only the most meager chance for developing their exceptional men? If history and reason give any distinct answer to these questions, it is an emphatic *No*. And Mr. Washington thus faces the triple paradox of his career:

1. He is striving nobly to make Negro artisans business men and property-owners; but it is utterly impossible, under modern competitive methods, for workingmen and property-owners to defend their rights and exist without the right of suffrage.
2. He insists on thrift and self-respect, but at the same time counsels a silent submission to civic inferiority such as is bound to sap the manhood of any race in the long run.
3. He advocates common-school and industrial training, and depreciates institutions of higher learning; but neither the Negro common-schools, nor Tuskegee itself, could remain open a day were it not for teachers trained in Negro colleges, or trained by their graduates.

This triple paradox in Mr. Washington's position is the object of criticism by two classes of colored Americans. One class is spiritually descended from Toussaint the Savior [Haitian rebellion leader Toussaint L'Ouverture], through Gabriel, Vesey, and Turner [Gabriel Prosser, Denmark Vesey, Nat Turner], and they represent the attitude of revolt and revenge; they hate the white South blindly and distrust the white race generally, and so far as

145

they agree on definite action, think that the Negro's only hope lies in emigration beyond the borders of the United States. And yet, by the irony of fate, nothing has more effectually made this programme seem hopeless than the recent course of the United States toward weaker and darker peoples in the West Indies, Hawaii, and the Philippines,—for where in the world may we go and be safe from lying and brute force?

A Favorite of Whites

One of the most vocal critics of Booker T. Washington was William Monroe Trotter, founder and editor of the Boston Guardian. *The following passage is taken from the January 9, 1904, edition of the* Guardian.

If Mr. Booker Washington is in any sense the leader of the Colored American people he certainly has been chosen for that position by the white American race. Everyone will admit that the Colored people never have chosen or indeed acclaimed him leader. Even Washington's friends will admit that his start for leadership came after his Atlanta speech in 1895, and that speech certainly was not popular with the Colored race.

He has been kept in a position as leader by the active work of the white race, with whom he has been extraordinarily popular, North and South. Their churches, their clubs, their pulpits, their press have boomed him and insisted he was the leader of his race. Mr. Washington has evidently realized this for he has always gone out of his way to say things that would suit prejudiced or race-proud white people, and he has been perfectly reckless as to the favor of his own race. In fact, at first he utterly ignored his own race, and only when told that he was valuable to the whites in so far as he induced his own people to follow his advice, did he begin to speak before them, and seek their favor, and endorsement. His sayings have been so hostile to his own race's wishes that his endeavor to get their endorsement has appeared to many to be unreasonable, in fact, a piece of effrontery. And it is no wonder that a man who talks as he does finds himself compelled to use money and school and political patronage, threats and persecution, abetted by his white supporters in order to get Negro endorsement, or stop Negro opposition.

The other class of Negroes who cannot agree with Mr. Washington has hitherto said little aloud. They deprecate the sight of scattered counsels, of internal disagreement; and especially they dislike making their just criticism of a useful and earnest man an excuse for a general discharge of venom from small-minded opponents. Nevertheless, the questions involved are so fundamental and serious that it is difficult to see how men like . . . Kelly

Miller, J.W.E. Bowen, and other representatives of this group, can much longer be silent. Such men feel in conscience bound to ask of this nation three things:

1. The right to vote
2. Civic equality
3. The education of youth according to ability

They acknowledge Mr. Washington's invaluable service in counselling patience and courtesy in such demands; they do not ask that ignorant black men vote when ignorant whites are debarred, or that any reasonable restrictions in the suffrage should not be applied; they know that the low social level of the mass of the race is responsible for much discrimination against it, but they also know, and the nation knows, that relentless color-prejudice is more often a cause than a result of the Negro's degradation; they seek the abatement of this relic of barbarism, and not its systematic encouragement and pampering by all agencies of social power from the Associated Press to the Church of Christ. They advocate, with Mr. Washington, a broad system of Negro common schools supplemented by thorough industrial training; but they are surprised that a man of Mr. Washington's insight cannot see that no such educational system ever has rested or can rest on any other basis than that of the well-equipped college and university, and they insist that there is a demand for a few such institutions throughout the South to train the best of the Negro youth as teachers, professional men, and leaders.

This group of men honor Mr. Washington for his attitude of conciliation toward the white South; they accept the "Atlanta Compromise" in its broadest interpretation; they recognize, with him, many signs of promise, many men of high purpose and fair judgment, in this section; they know that no easy task has been laid upon a region already tottering under heavy burdens. But, nevertheless, they insist that the way to truth and right lies in straightforward honesty, not in indiscriminate flattery; in praising those of the South who do well and criticising uncompromisingly those who do ill; in taking advantage of the opportunities at hand and urging their fellows to do the same, but at the same time in remembering that only a firm adherence to their higher ideals and aspirations will ever keep those ideals within the realm of possibility. They do not expect that the free right to vote, to enjoy civic rights, and to be educated, will come in a moment; they do not expect to see the bias and prejudices of years disappear at the blast of a trumpet; but they are absolutely certain that the way for a people to gain their reasonable rights is not by voluntarily throwing them away and insisting that they do not want them; that the way for a people to gain respect is not by continually belittling and ridiculing themselves; that, on the contrary, Negroes must insist continually, in season and out of season, that voting is necessary to modern manhood, that color discrimination is barbarism, and that black boys need education as well as white boys.

Legitimate Demands

In failing thus to state plainly and unequivocally the legitimate demands of their people, even at the cost of opposing an honored leader, the thinking classes of American Negroes would shirk a heavy responsibility,—a responsibility to themselves, a responsibility to the struggling masses, a responsibility to the darker races of men whose future depends so largely on this American experiment, but especially a responsibility to this nation,—this common Fatherland. It is wrong to encourage a man or a people in evildoing; it is wrong to aid and abet a national crime simply because it is unpopular not to do so. The growing spirit of kindliness and reconciliation between the North and South after the frightful difference of a generation ago ought to be a source of deep congratulation to all, and especially to those whose mistreatment caused the war; but if that reconciliation is to be marked by the industrial slavery and civic death of those same black men, with permanent legislation into a position of inferiority, then those black men, if they are really men, are called upon by every consideration of patriotism and loyalty to oppose such a course by all civilized methods, even though such opposition involves disagreement with Mr. Booker T. Washington. We have no right to sit silently by while the inevitable seeds are sown for a harvest of disaster to our children, black and white.

First, it is the duty of black men to judge the South discriminatingly. The present generation of Southerners are not responsible for the past, and they should not be blindly hated or blamed for it. Furthermore, to no class is the indiscriminate endorsement of the recent course of the South toward Negroes more nauseating than to the best thought of the South. The South is not "solid"; it is a land in the ferment of social change, wherein forces of all kinds are fighting for supremacy; and to praise the ill the South is to-day perpetrating is just as wrong as to condemn the good. Discriminating and broad-minded criticism is what the South needs,—needs it for the sake of her own white sons and daughters, and for the insurance of robust, healthy mental and moral development.

To-day even the attitude of the Southern whites toward the blacks is not, as so many assume, in all cases the same; the ignorant Southerner hates the Negro, the workingmen fear his competition, the money-makers wish to use him as a laborer, some of the educated see a menace in his upward development, while others—usually the sons of the masters—wish to help him to rise.

National opinion has enabled this last class to maintain the Negro common schools, and to protect the Negro partially in property, life, and limb. Through the pressure of the money-makers, the Negro is in danger of being reduced to semi-slavery, especially in the country districts; the workingmen, and those of the educated who fear the Negro, have united to disfranchise him, and some have urged his deportation; while the passions of the ignorant are easily aroused to lynch and abuse any black man. To praise this intricate whirl of thought and prejudice is nonsense; to inveigh indiscriminately against "the South" is unjust; but to use the same breath in praising Governor [Charles B.] Aycock, exposing Senator [John T.] Morgan, arguing with Mr. Thomas Nelson Page, and denouncing Senator Ben Tillman, is not only sane, but the imperative duty of thinking black men.

Half-Truths

It would be unjust to Mr. Washington not to acknowledge that in several instances he has opposed movements in the South which were unjust to the Negro; he sent memorials to the Louisiana and Alabama constitutional conventions, he has spoken against lynching, and in other ways has openly or silently set his influence against sinister schemes and unfortunate happenings. Notwithstanding this, it is equally true to assert that on the whole the distinct impression left by Mr. Washington's propaganda is, first, that the South is justified in its present attitude toward the Negro because of the Negro's degradation; secondly, that the prime cause of the Negro's failure to rise more quickly is his wrong education in the past; and, thirdly, that his future rise depends primarily on his own efforts. Each of these propositions is a dangerous half-truth. The supplementary truths must never be lost sight of first, slavery and race-prejudice are potent if not sufficient causes of the Negro's position; second, industrial and common-school training were necessarily slow in planting because they had to await the black teachers trained by higher institutions,—it being extremely doubtful if any essentially different development was possible, and certainly a Tuskegee was unthinkable before 1880; and, third, while it is a great truth to say that the Negro must strive and strive mightily to help himself, it is equally true that unless his striving be not simply seconded, but rather aroused and encouraged, by the initiative of the richer and wiser environing group, he cannot hope for great success.

In his failure to realize and impress this last point, Mr. Washington is especially to be criticised. His doctrine has tended to make the whites, North and South, shift the burden of the Negro problem to the Negro's shoulders and stand aside as critical and rather pessimistic spectators; when in fact the burden belongs to the nation, and the hands of none of us are clean if we bend not our energies to righting these great wrongs.

The South ought to be led, by candid and honest criticism, to assert her better self and do her full duty to the race she has cruelly wronged and is still wronging. The North—her co-partner in guilt—cannot salve her conscience by plastering it with gold. We cannot settle this problem by diplomacy and suaveness, by "policy" alone. If worse comes to worst, can the moral fibre of this country survive the slow throttling and murder of nine millions of men?

The black men of America have a duty to perform, a duty stern and delicate,—a forward movement to oppose a part of the work of their greatest leader. So far as Mr. Washington preaches Thrift, Patience, and Industrial Training for the masses, we must hold up his hands and strive with him, rejoicing in his honors and glorying in the strength of this Joshua called of God and of man to lead the headless host. But so far as Mr. Washington apologizes for injustice, North or South, does not rightly value the privilege and duty of voting, belittles the emasculating effects of caste distinctions, and opposes the higher training and ambition of our brighter minds,—so far as he, the South, or the Nation, does this,—we must unceasingly and firmly oppose them. By every civilized and peaceful method we must strive for the rights which the world accords to men, clinging unwaveringly to those great words which the sons of the Fathers would fain forget: "We hold these truths to be self-evident: That all men are created equal; that they are endowed by their Creator with certain unalienable rights; that among these are life, liberty, and the pursuit of happiness."

"I plead for industrial education and development for the Negro not because I want to cramp him, but because I want to free him."

The Industrial Training of the Masses Should Be Emphasized

Booker T. Washington (1856–1915)

One of the areas of dispute between Booker T. Washington and his critics concerned how black Americans should be educated. Washington was a lifelong advocate of "industrial" training for blacks as the best and most practical method of assuring their economic livelihood and improving their standing in American society. Washington, born a slave, received most of his education from the Hampton Institute, an industrial college for blacks founded in 1868 by Samuel C. Armstrong, who had been a Union general during the Civil War. In 1881 Washington founded the Tuskegee Institute, which was modeled largely after the Hampton Institute and which stressed agricultural, vocational, and moral learning for its students, who were often put to work constructing and maintaining the school's facilities.

In the following viewpoint, excerpted from a 1903 essay, Washington criticizes some of the colleges established for blacks following the Civil War for teaching impractical subjects, such as Latin and theology, instead of practical training. He holds up the program at Tuskegee as a model for black education and argues that such training for economic self-improvement provides a long-range solution for the problems African Americans face in the United States.

From Booker T. Washington, "Industrial Education," in *The Negro Problem* (New York: James Patt, 1903).

One of the most fundamental and far-reaching deeds that has been accomplished during the last quarter of a century has been that by which the Negro has been helped to find himself and to learn the secrets of civilization—to learn that there are a few simple, cardinal principles upon which a race must start its upward course, unless it would fail, and its last estate be worse than its first.

It has been necessary for the Negro to learn the difference between being worked and working—to learn that being worked meant degradation, while working means civilization; that all forms of labor are honorable, and all forms of idleness disgraceful. It has been necessary for him to learn that all races that have got upon their feet have done so largely by laying an economic foundation, and, in general, by beginning in a proper cultivation and ownership of the soil.

Forty years ago my race emerged from slavery into freedom. If, in too many cases, the Negro race began development at the wrong end, it was largely because neither white nor black properly understood the case. Nor is it any wonder that this was so, for never before in the history of the world had just such a problem been presented as that of the two races at the coming of freedom in this country.

Slavery and Industrial Development

For two hundred and fifty years, I believe the way for the redemption of the Negro was being prepared through industrial development. Through all those years the Southern white man did business with the Negro in a way that no one else has done business with him. In most cases if a Southern white man wanted a house built he consulted a Negro mechanic about the plan and about the actual building of the structure. If he wanted a suit of clothes made he went to a Negro tailor, and for shoes he went to a shoemaker of the same race. In a certain way every slave plantation in the South was an industrial school. On these plantations young colored men and women were constantly being trained not only as farmers but as carpenters, blacksmiths, wheelwrights, brick masons, engineers, cooks, laundresses, sewing women and housekeepers.

I do not mean in any way to apologize for the curse of slavery, which was a curse to both races, but in what I say about industrial training in slavery I am simply stating facts. This training was crude, and was given for selfish purposes. It did not answer the highest ends, because there was an absence of mental training in connection with the training of the hand. To a large degree, though, this business contact with the Southern white man, and the industrial training on the plantations, left the Negro at the close of the war in possession of nearly all the common and skilled labor in the South. The industries that gave the South its power, prominence and wealth prior to the Civil War were mainly the raising of cotton, sugar cane, rice and tobacco. Before the way could be prepared for the proper growing and marketing of these crops forests had to be cleared, houses to be built, public roads and railroads constructed. In all these works the Negro did most of the heavy work. In the planting, cultivating and marketing of the crops, not only was the Negro the chief dependence, but in the manufacture of tobacco he became a skilled and proficient workman, and in this, up to the present time, in the South, holds the lead in the large tobacco manufactories.

In most of the industries, though, what happened? For nearly twenty years after the war, except in a few instances, the value of the industrial training given by the plantations, was overlooked. Negro men and women were educated in literature, in mathematics and in the sciences, with little thought of what had been taking place during the preceding two hundred and fifty years, except, perhaps, as something to be escaped, to be got as far away from as possible. As a generation began to pass, those who had been trained as mechanics in slavery began to disappear by death, and gradually it began to be realized that there were few to take their places. There were young men educated in foreign tongues, but few in carpentry or in mechanical or architectural drawing. Many were trained in Latin, but few as engineers and blacksmiths. Too many were taken from the farm and educated, but educated in everything but farming. For this reason they had no interest in farming and did not return to it. And yet eighty-five per cent. of the Negro population of the Southern states lives and for a considerable time will continue to live in the country districts: The charge is often brought against the members of my race—and too often justly, I confess—that they are found leaving the country districts and flocking into the great cities where temptations are more frequent and harder to resist, and where the Negro people too often become demoralized. Think, though, how frequently it is the case that from the first day that a pupil begins to go to school his books teach him much about the cities of the world and city life, and almost nothing about the country. How natural it is, then, that when he has the ordering of his life he wants to live it in the city.

Only a short time before his death the late Mr. C. P. Huntington, to whose memory a magnificent library has just been given by his widow to the Hampton Institute for Negroes, in Virginia, said in a public address some words which seem to me so wise that I

Opponents of Industrial Education Won Over

In his 1907 book The Negro in Business, *Booker T. Washington recounts how opponents of his educational philosophy changed their minds upon seeing the results of his Tuskegee Institute.*

It ought to be stated frankly here that at first, and for several years after the introduction of industrial training at such educational centers as Hampton and Tuskegee, there was opposition from colored people and from portions of those Northern white people engaged in educational and missionary work among the colored people in the South. Most of those who manifested such opposition were, I believe, actuated by the highest and most honest motives. From the first the rank and file of the blacks were quick to see the advantages of industrial training, as is shown by the fact that industrial schools have always been overcrowded. Opposition to industrial training was based largely on the old and narrow ground that it was something that the Southern white people favored, and therefore must be against the interests of the Negro. Again, others opposed it because they feared that it meant the abandonment of all political privileges, and the higher or classical education of the race. They feared that the final outcome would be the "materialization" of the Negro and the smothering of his spiritual and aesthetic nature. Others felt that industrial education had for its object the limitation of the Negro's development, and the branding him for all time as a special hand-working class.

Now that enough time has elapsed for those who opposed it to see that it meant none of these things, opposition, except from a very few of the colored people living in one or two Northern cities away from the problem, has ceased, and this system has the enthusiastic support of the Negroes and of most of the whites who formerly opposed it. All are beginning to see that it was never meant that all Negro youths should secure industrial education, any more than it is meant that all white youths should pass through the Massachusetts Institute of Technology, or the Amherst Agricultural College, to the exclusion of such training as is given at Harvard, Yale or Dartmouth; but that in a peculiar sense a large proportion of the Negro youths needed to have that education which would enable them to secure an economic foundation, without which no people can succeed in any of the higher walks of life.

want to quote them here:

"Our schools teach everybody a little of almost everything, but, in my opinion, they teach very few children just what they ought to know in order to make their way successfully in life. They do not put into their hands the tools they are best fitted to use, and hence so many failures. Many a mother and sister have worked and slaved, living upon scanty food, in order to give a son and brother a 'liberal education,' and in doing this have built up a barrier between the boy and the work he was fitted to do. Let me say to you that all honest work is honorable work. If the labor is manual, and seems common, you will have all the more chance to be thinking of other things, or of work that is higher and brings better pay, and to work out in your minds better and higher duties and responsibilities for yourselves, and for thinking of ways by which you can help others as well as yourselves, and bring them up to your own higher level."

Some years ago, when we decided to make tailoring a part of our training at the Tuskegee Institute, I was amazed to find that it was almost impossible to find in the whole country an educated colored man who could teach the making of clothing. We could find numbers of them who could teach astronomy, theology, Latin or grammar, but almost none who could instruct in the making of clothing, something that has to be used by every one of us every day in the year. How often have I been discouraged as I have gone through the South, and into the homes of the people of my race, and have found women who could converse intelligently upon abstruse subjects, and yet could not tell how to improve the condition of the poorly cooked and still more poorly served bread and meat which they and their families were eating three times a day. It is discouraging to find a girl who can tell you the geographical location of any country on the globe and who does not know where to place the dishes upon a common dinner table. It is discouraging to find a woman who knows much about theoretical chemistry, and who cannot properly wash and iron a shirt.

Knowledge for Real Life

In what I say here I would not by any means have it understood that I would limit or circumscribe the mental development of the Negro student. No race can be lifted until its mind is awakened and strengthened. By the side of industrial training should always go mental and moral training, but the pushing of mere abstract knowledge into the head means little. We want more than the mere performance of mental gymnastics. Our knowledge must be harnessed to the things of real life. I would encourage the Negro to secure all the mental strength, all the mental culture—whether gleaned from science, mathematics, history, language or literature that his circumstances will allow, but I believe most earnestly that for years to come the education of the people of my race should be so directed that the greatest proportion of the mental strength of the masses will be brought to bear upon the every-day practical things of life, upon something that is needed to be done, and something which they will be permitted to do in the community in which they reside. And just the same with the professional class which the race needs and must have, I would say give the men and women of that class, too, the training which will best fit them to perform in the most successful manner the service which the race demands.

I would not confine the race to industrial life, not even to agriculture, for example, although I believe that by far the greater part of the Negro race is best off in the country districts and must and should continue to live there, but I would teach the race that in industry the foundation must be laid—that the very best service which any one can render to what is called the higher education is to teach the present generation to provide a material or industrial foundation. On such a foundation as this will grow habits of thrift, a love of work, economy, ownership of property, bank accounts. Out of it in the future will grow practical education, professional education, positions of public responsibility. Out of it will grow moral and religious strength. Out of it will grow wealth from which alone can come leisure and the opportunity for the enjoyment of literature and the fine arts.

In the words of the late beloved Frederick Douglass: "Every blow of the sledge hammer wielded by a sable arm is a powerful blow in support of our cause. Every colored mechanic is by virtue of circumstances an elevator of his race. Every house built by a black man is a strong tower against the allied hosts of prejudice. It is impossible for us to attach too much importance to this aspect of the subject. Without industrial development there can be no wealth; without wealth there can be no leisure; without leisure no opportunity for thoughtful reflection and the cultivation of the higher arts."

I would set no limits to the attainments of the Negro in arts, in letters or statesmanship, but I believe the surest way to reach those ends is by laying the foundation in the little things of life that lie immediately about one's door. I plead for industrial education and development for the Negro not because I want to cramp him, but because I want to free him. I want to see him enter the all-powerful business and commercial world.

It was such combined mental, moral and industrial education which the late General Armstrong set out to give at the Hampton Institute when he established that school thirty years ago. The Hampton Institute has continued along the lines laid down by its great founder, and now each year an increasing number of similar schools are being established in the South, for the people of both races.

Experiences at Tuskegee

Early in the history of the Tuskegee Institute we began to combine industrial training with mental and moral culture. Our first efforts were in the direction of agriculture, and we began teaching this with no appliances except one hoe and a blind mule. From this small beginning we have grown until now the Institute owns two thousand acres of land, eight hundred of which are cultivated each year by the young men of the school. We began teaching wheelwrighting and blacksmithing in a small way to the men, and laundry work, cooking and sewing and housekeeping to the young women. The fourteen hundred and over young men and women who attended the school during the last school year received instruction—in addition to academic and religious training—in thirty-three trades and industries, including carpentry, blacksmithing, printing, wheelwrighting, harnessmaking, painting, machinery, founding, shoemaking, brickmasonry and brickmaking, plastering, sawmilling, tinsmithing, tailoring, mechanical and architectural drawing, electrical and steam engineering, canning, sewing, dressmaking, millinery, cooking, laundering, housekeeping, mattress making, basketry, nursing, agriculture, dairying and stock raising, horticulture.

Not only do the students receive instruction in these trades, but they do actual work, by means of which more than half of them pay some part or all of their expenses while remaining at the school. Of the sixty buildings belonging to the school all but four were almost wholly erected by the students as a part of their industrial education. Even the bricks which go into the walls are made by students in the school's brick yard, in which, last year, they manufactured two million bricks.

When we first began this work at Tuskegee, and the idea got spread among the people of my race that the students who came to the Tuskegee school were to be taught industries in connection with their academic studies, were, in other words, to be taught to work, I received a great many verbal messages and letters from parents informing me that they wanted their children taught books, but not how to work. This protest went on for three or four years, but I am glad to be able to say now that our people have very generally been educated to a point where they see their own needs and conditions so clearly that it has been several years since we have had a single protest from parents against the teaching of industries, and there is now a positive enthusiasm for it. In fact, public sentiment among the students at Tuskegee is now so strong for industrial training that it would hardly permit a student to remain on the grounds who was unwilling to labor.

The Limits of Book Education

It seems to me that too often mere book education leaves the Negro young man or woman in a weak position. For example, I have seen a Negro girl taught by her mother to help her in doing laundry work at home. Later, when this same girl was graduated from the public schools or a high school and returned home she finds herself educated out of sympathy with laundry work, and yet not able to find anything to do which seems in keeping with the cost and character of her education. Under these circumstances we cannot be surprised if she does not fulfill the expectations made for her. What should have been done for her, it seems to me, was to give her along with her academic education thorough training in the latest and best methods of laundry work, so that she could have put so much skill and intelligence into it that the work would have been lifted out from the plane of drudgery. The home which she would then have been able to found by the results of her work would have enabled her to help her children to take a still more responsible position in life.

Fitting Students for Occupations

Almost from the first Tuskegee has kept in mind—and this I think should be the policy of all industrial schools—fitting students for occupations which would be open to them in their home communities. Some years ago we noted the fact that there was beginning to be a demand in the South for men to operate dairies in a skillful, modern manner. We opened a dairy department in connection with the school, where a number of young men could have instruction in the latest and most scientific methods of dairy work. At present we have calls—mainly from Southern white men—for twice as many dairymen as we are able to supply. What is equally satisfactory, the reports which come to us indicate that our young men are giving the highest satisfaction and are fast changing and improving the dairy product in the communities into which they go. I use the dairy here as an example. What I have said of this is equally true of many of the other industries which we teach. Aside from the economic value of this work I cannot but believe, and my observation confirms me in my belief, that as we continue to place Negro men and women of intelligence, religion, modesty, conscience and skill in every community in the South, who will prove by actual results their value to the community, I cannot but believe, I say, that this will constitute a solution to many of the present political and social difficulties.

Many seem to think that industrial education is meant to make the Negro work as he worked in the days of slavery. This is far from my conception of industrial education. If this training is worth anything to the Negro, it consists in teaching him how not to work, but how to make the forces of nature—air, steam, water, horse-power and electricity—work for him. If it has any value it is in lifting labor up out of toil and drudgery into the plane of the dignified and the beautiful. The Negro in the South works and works hard; but too often his ignorance and lack of skill causes him to do his work in the most costly and shiftless manner, and this keeps him near the bottom of the ladder in the economic world. . . .

Our Pathway

I close, then, as I began, by saying that as a slave the Negro was worked, and that as a freeman he must learn to work. There is still doubt in many quarters as to the ability of the Negro unguided, unsupported, to hew his own path and put into visible, tangible, indisputable form, products and signs of civilization. This doubt cannot be much affected by abstract arguments, no matter how delicately and convincingly woven together. Patiently, quietly, doggedly, persistently, through summer and winter, sunshine and shadow, by self-sacrifice, by foresight, by honesty and industry, we must re-enforce argument with results. One farm bought, one house built, one home sweetly and intelligently kept, one man who is the largest tax payer or has the largest bank account, one school or church maintained, one factory running successfully, one truck garden profitably cultivated, one patient cured by a Negro doctor, one sermon well preached, one office well filled, one life cleanly lived—these will tell more in our favor than all the abstract eloquence that can be summoned to plead our cause. Our pathway must be up through the soil, up through swamps, up through forests, up through the streams, the rocks, up through commerce, education and religion!

Viewpoint 4

"Education must not simply teach work—it must teach Life. The Talented Tenth of the Negro race must be made leaders of thought and missionaries of culture among their people."

The Higher Education of a Leadership Elite Should Be Emphasized

W.E.B. Du Bois (1868–1963)

Noted civil rights activist W.E.B. Du Bois first gained prominence as an academic scholar who was the first African American to receive a Ph.D. from Harvard University. In the early twentieth century, Du Bois emerged as a leading black critic of Booker T. Washington. He questioned not only Washington's disparagement of political activism for civil rights, but also his emphasis on industrial and vocational education, arguing that such a focus was too narrow and limiting for gifted blacks. In the following viewpoint, excerpted from a 1903 essay titled "The Talented Tenth," Du Bois expresses his belief that the uplifting of African Americans requires an educated elite of black leaders, and that the higher education of "the Talented Tenth" of American blacks must be given greater priority.

The Negro race, like all races, is going to be saved by its exceptional men. The problem of education, then, among Negroes must first of all deal with the Talented Tenth; it is the problem of

From W.E.B. Du Bois, "The Talented Tenth," in *The Negro Problem* (New York: James Patt, 1903).

160

developing the Best of this race that they may guide the Mass away from the contamination and death of the Worst, in their own and other races. Now the training of men is a difficult and intricate task. Its technique is a matter for educational experts, but its object is for the vision of seers. If we make money the object of man-training, we shall develop money-makers but not necessarily men; if we make technical skill the object of education, we may possess artisans but not, in nature, men. Men we shall have only as we make manhood the object of the work of the schools—intelligence, broad sympathy, knowledge of the world that was and is, and of the relation of men to it—this is the curriculum of that Higher Education which must underlie true life. On this foundation we may build bread winning, skill of hand and quickness of brain, with never a fear lest the child and man mistake the means of living for the object of life.

If this be true—and who can deny it—three tasks lay before me; first to show from the past that the Talented Tenth as they have risen among American Negroes have been worthy of leadership; secondly, to show how these men may be educated and developed; and thirdly, to show their relation to the Negro problem.

You misjudge us because you do not know us. From the very first it been the educated and intelligent of the Negro people that have led and elevated the mass, and the sole obstacles that nullified and retarded their efforts were slavery and race prejudice; for what is slavery but the legalized survival of the unfit and the nullification of the work of natural internal leadership? Negro leadership, therefore, sought from the first to rid the race of this awful incubus that it might make way for natural selection and the survival of the fittest. . . .

In 1831 there met that first Negro convention in Philadelphia, at which the world gaped curiously but which bravely attacked the problems of race and slavery, crying out against persecution and declaring that "Laws as cruel in themselves as they were unconstitutional and unjust have in many places been enacted against our poor, unfriended and unoffending brethren (without a shadow of provocation on our part), at whose bare recital the very savage draws himself up for fear of contagion—looks noble and prides himself because he bears not the name of Christian." Side by side this free Negro movement, and the movement for abolition, strove until they merged into one strong stream. Too little notice has been taken of the work which the Talented Tenth among Negroes took in the great abolition crusade. From the very

161

day that a Philadelphia colored man became the first subscriber to [William] Garrison's "Liberator," to the day when Negro soldiers made the Emancipation Proclamation possible, black leaders worked shoulder to shoulder with white men in a movement, the success of which would have been impossible without them. . . .

Forsaken Opportunities

Ida B. Wells-Barnett, a prominent black activist who wrote extensively against lynching, criticizes Booker T. Washington's focus on industrial education in a 1904 article in The World Today. *She writes that other black colleges have suffered as funding from white philanthropists has been lost to Washington's Tuskegee Institute, to the detriment of African Americans as a whole.*

No human agency can tell how many black diamonds lie buried in the black belt of the South, and the opportunities for discovering them become rarer every day as the schools for thorough training become more cramped and no more are being established. The presidents of Atlanta University and other such schools remain in the North the year round, using their personal influence to secure funds to keep these institutions running. Many are like the late Collis P. Huntington, who had given large amounts to Livingston College, Salisbury, North Carolina. Several years before his death he told the president of that institution that as he believed Booker Washington was educating Negroes in the only sensible way, henceforth his money for that purpose would go to Tuskegee. All the schools in the South have suffered as a consequence of this general attitude, and many of the oldest and best which have regarded themselves as fixtures now find it a struggle to maintain existence. . . .

Does this mean that the Negro objects to industrial education? By no means. It simply means that he knows by sad experience that industrial education will not stand him in place of political, civil and intellectual liberty, and he objects to being deprived of fundamental rights of American citizenship to the end that one school for industrial training shall flourish. To him it seems like selling a race's birthright for a mess of pottage.

Where were these black abolitionists trained? Some, like Frederick Douglass, were self-trained, but yet trained liberally; others, like Alexander Crummell and McCune Smith, graduated from famous foreign universities. Most of them rose up through the colored schools of New York and Philadelphia and Boston, taught by college-bred men like [John] Russworm of Dartmouth, and college-bred white men like Neau and [Anthony] Benezet.

After emancipation came a new group of educated and gifted leaders: [John M.] Langston, [Blanche K.] Bruce and [Robert B.]

Elliot, [Richard T.] Greener, [George W.] Williams and [Daniel A.] Payne. Through political organization, historical and polemic writing and moral regeneration, these men strove to uplift their people. It is the fashion of to-day to sneer at them and to say that with freedom Negro leadership should have begun at the plow and not in the Senate—a foolish and mischievous lie; two hundred and fifty years that black serf toiled at the plow and yet that toiling was in vain till the Senate passed the war amendments; and two hundred and fifty years more the half-free serf of to-day may toil at his plow, but unless he have political rights and righteously guarded civic status, he will still remain the poverty-stricken and ignorant plaything of rascals, that he now is. This all sane men know even if they dare not say it.

And so we come to the present—a day of cowardice and vacillation, of strident wide-voiced wrong and faint hearted compromise; of double-faced dallying with Truth and Right. Who are to-day guiding the work of the Negro people? The "exceptions" of course. And yet so sure as this Talented Tenth is pointed out, the blind worshippers of the Average cry out in alarm: "These are exceptions, look here at death, disease and crime—these are the happy rule." Of course they are the rule, because a silly nation made them the rule: Because for three long centuries this people lynched Negroes who dared to be brave, raped black women who dared to be virtuous, crushed dark-hued youth who dared to be ambitious, and encouraged and made to flourish servility and lewdness and apathy. But not even this was able to crush all manhood and chastity and aspiration from black folk. A saving remnant continually survives and persists, continually aspires, continually shows itself in thrift and ability and character. Exceptional it is to be sure, but this is its chiefest promise; it shows the capability of Negro blood, the promise of black men. Do Americans ever stop to reflect that there are in this land a million men of Negro blood, well-educated, owners of homes, against the honor of whose womanhood no breath was ever raised, whose men occupy positions of trust and usefulness, and who, judged by any standard, have reached the full measure of the best type of modern European culture? Is it fair, is it decent, is it Christian to ignore these facts of the Negro problem, to belittle such aspiration, to nullify such leadership and seek to crush these people back into the mass out of which by toil and travail, they and their fathers have raised themselves?

Raising the Masses

Can the masses of the Negro people be in any possible way more quickly raised than by the effort and example of this aristocracy of talent and character? Was there ever a nation on God's fair earth civilized from the bottom upward? Never; it is, ever was and ever will be from the top downward that culture filters. The Talented Tenth rises and pulls all that are worth the saving up to their vantage ground. This is the history of human progress; and the two historic mistakes which have hindered that progress were the thinking first that no more could ever rise save the few already risen; or second, that it would better the unrisen to pull the risen down.

How then shall the leaders of a struggling people be trained and the hands of the risen few strengthened ? There can be but one answer: The best and most capable of their youth must be schooled in the colleges and universities of the land. We will not quarrel as to just what the university of the Negro should teach or how it should teach it—I willingly admit that each soul and each race-soul needs its own peculiar curriculum. But this is true: A university is a human invention for the transmission of knowledge and culture from generation to generation, through the training of quick minds and pure hearts, and for this work no other human invention will suffice, not even trade and industrial schools.

All men cannot go to college but some men must; every isolated group or nation must have its yeast, must have for the talented few centers of training where men are not so mystified and befuddled by the hard and necessary toil of earning a living, as to have no aims higher than their bellies, and no God greater than Gold. This is true training, and thus in the beginning were the favored sons of the freedmen trained. Out of the colleges of the North came, after the blood of war, [Edmund] Ware, [Erastus M.] Cravath, Chase, Andrews, Bumstead and Spence to build the foundations of knowledge and civilization in the black South. Where ought they to have begun to build? At the bottom of course, quibbles the mole with his eyes in the earth. Aye! truly at the bottom, at the very bottom; at the bottom of knowledge, down in the very depths of knowledge there where the roots of justice strike into the lowest soil of Truth. And so they did begin; they founded colleges, and up from the colleges shot normal schools, and out from the normal schools went teachers, and around the normal teachers clustered other teachers to teach the public schools; the college trained in Greek and Latin and mathematics, 2,000 men; and these men trained full 50,000 others in morals and manners, and they in turn taught thrift and the alphabet to nine millions of men, who to-day hold $300,000,000 of property. It was a miracle—the most wonderful peace-battle of the 19th century, and yet to-day men smile at it, and in fine superiority tell us that it was all a strange mistake; that a proper way to found a system of education is first to gather the children and buy them spelling books and hoes; afterward men may look about for teachers, if haply they may find them; or again they would teach men Work, but as for Life—why, what has Work to do with Life, they ask vacantly.

Was the work of these college founders successful; did it stand the test of time? Did the college graduates, with all their fine theories of life, really live? Are they useful men helping to civilize and elevate their less fortunate fellows? Let us see....

Six institutions—Atlanta, Fisk, Howard, Shaw, Wilberforce and Leland, are the important Negro colleges so far as actual work and number of students are concerned. In all these institutions, seven hundred and fifty Negro college students are enrolled. In grade the best of these colleges are about a year behind the smaller New England colleges and a typical curriculum is that of Atlanta University. Here students from the grammar grades, after a three years' high school course, take a college course of 136 weeks. One-fourth of this time is given to Latin and Greek; one-fifth, to English and modern languages; one-sixth, to history and social science; one-seventh, to natural science; one-eighth to mathematics, and one-eighth to philosophy and pedagogy.

In addition to these students in the South, Negroes have attended Northern colleges for many years. As early as 1826 one was graduated Bowdoin College, and from that time till to-day nearly every year has seen elsewhere, other such graduates. They have, of course, met much color prejudice. Fifty years ago very few colleges would admit them at all. Even to-day no Negro has ever been admitted to Princeton, and at some other leading institutions they are rather endured than encouraged. Oberlin was the great pioneer in the work of blotting out the color line in colleges, and has more Negro graduates by far than any other Northern college.

The total number of Negro college graduates up to 1899, (several of the graduates of that year not being reported), was as follows:

	Negro Colleges.	White Colleges.
Before '76	137	75
'75–80	143	22
'80–85	250	31
'85–90	413	43
'90–95	465	66
'95–99	475	88
Class Unknown	57	64
Total	1,914	390

Of these graduates 2,079 were men and 252 were women; 50 per cent. of Northern-born college men come South to work among the masses of their people, at a sacrifice which few people realize; nearly 90 per cent. of the Southern-born graduates instead of seeking that personal freedom and broader intellectual atmosphere which their training has led them, in some degree, to conceive, stay and labor and wait in the midst of their black neighbors and relatives.

The most interesting question, and in many respects the crucial question, to be asked concerning college-bred Negroes, is: Do they earn a living? It has been intimated more than once that the higher training of Negroes has resulted in sending into the world of work, men who could find nothing to do suitable to their talents. Now and then there comes a rumor of a colored college man working at menial service, etc. Fortunately, returns as to occupations of college-bred Negroes, gathered by the Atlanta conference, are quite full—nearly sixty per cent. of the total number of graduates.

This enables us to reach fairly certain conclusions as to the occupations of all college-bred Negroes. Of 1,312 persons reported, there were:

	Per Cent.
Teachers,	53.4
Clergymen,	16.8
Physicians, etc.,	6.3
Students,	5.6
Lawyers,	4.7
In Govt. Service,	4.0
In Business,	3.6
Farmers and Artisans,	2.7
Editors, Secretaries and Clerks,	2.4
Miscellaneous.	.5

Over half are teachers, a sixth are preachers, another sixth are students and professional men; over 6 per cent. are farmers, artisans and merchants, and 4 per cent. are in government service. . . .

The Need for Leaders

These figures illustrate vividly the function of the college-bred Negro. He is, as he ought to be, the group leader, the man who sets the ideals of the community where he lives, directs its thoughts and heads its social movements. It need hardly be argued that the Negro people need social leadership more than most groups: that they have no traditions to fall back upon, no long established customs, no strong family ties, no well defined social classes. All these things must be slowly and painfully evolved. The preacher was, even before the war, the group leader of the Negroes, and the church their greatest social institution. Naturally this preacher was ignorant and often immoral, and the problem of replacing the older type by better educated men has been a difficult one. Both by direct work and by direct influence on other preachers, and on congregations, the college-bred preacher has an opportunity for reformatory work and moral inspiration, the value of which cannot be overestimated.

It has, however, been in the furnishing of teachers that the Negro college has found its peculiar function. Few persons realize how vast a work, how mighty a revolution has been thus accomplished. To furnish five millions and more of ignorant people with teachers of their own race and blood, in one generation, was not only a very difficult undertaking, but very important one, in that, it placed before the eyes of almost every Negro child an attainable ideal. It brought the masses of the blacks in contact with modern civilization, made black men the leaders of their communities and trainers of the new generation. In this work college-bred Negroes were first teachers, and then teachers of teachers. And here it is that the broad culture of college work has been of peculiar value. Knowledge of life and its wider meaning, has been the point of the Negro's deepest ignorance, and the sending out of teachers whose training has not been simply for bread winning, but also for human culture, has been of inestimable value in the training of these men.

In earlier years the two occupations of preacher and teacher were practically the only ones open to the black college graduate. Of later years a larger diversity of life among his people, has opened new avenues of employment. Nor have these college men been paupers and spendthrifts; 557 college-bred Negroes owned in 1899, $1,342,862.50 worth of real estate, (assessed value) or $2,411 per family. The real value of the total accumulations of the whole group is perhaps about $10,000,000, or $5,000 a piece. Pitiful, is it not, beside the fortunes of oil kings and steel trusts, but after all is the fortune of the millionaire the only stamp of true and successful living? Alas! it is, with many, and there's the rub. . . .

The Main Question

The main question, so far as the Southern Negro is concerned, is: What under the present circumstance, must a system of education do in order to raise the Negro as quickly as possible in the scale of civilization? The answer to this question seems to me clear: It must strengthen the Negro's character, increase his knowledge and teach him to earn a living. Now it goes without saying, that it is hard to do all these things simultaneously or suddenly, and that at the same time it will not do to give all the attention to one and neglect the others; we could give black boys trades, but that alone will not civilize a race of ex-slaves; we might simply increase their knowledge of the world, but this would not necessarily make them wish to use this knowledge honestly; we might seek to strengthen character and purpose, but to what end if this people have nothing to eat or to wear? A system of education is not one thing, nor does it have a single definite object, nor is it a mere matter of schools. Education is that whole system of human training within and without the school house walls, which molds and develops men. If then we start out to train an ignorant and unskilled people with a heritage of bad habits, our system of training must set before itself two great aims—the one dealing with knowledge and character, the other part seeking to give the child the technical knowledge necessary for him to earn a living under the present circumstances. These objects are accomplished in part by the opening of the common schools on the one, and of the industrial schools on the other. But only in part, for there must also be trained those who are to teach these schools—men and women of knowledge and culture and technical skill who understand modern civilization, and have the training and aptitude to impart it to the children under them. There must be teachers, and teachers of teachers, and to attempt to establish any sort of a system of common and industrial school training, without *first* (and I say *first* advisedly) without *first* providing for the higher training of the very best teachers, is simply throwing your money to the winds. School houses do not teach themselves—piles of brick and mortar and machinery do not send out *men*. It is the trained, living human soul, cultivated and strengthened by long study and thought, that breathes the real breath of life into boys and girls and makes them human, whether they be black or white, Greek, Russian or American. Nothing, in these latter days, has so dampened the faith of thinking Negroes in recent educational movements, as the fact that such movements have been accompanied by ridicule and denouncement and decrying of those very institutions of higher training which made the Negro public school possible, and make Negro industrial schools thinkable. It was Fisk, Atlanta, Howard and Straight, those colleges born of the faith and sacrifice of the abolitionists, that placed in the black schools of the South the 30,000 teachers and more, which some, who depreciate the work of these higher schools, are using to teach their own new experiments. If Hampton, Tuskegee and the hundred other industrial schools prove in the future to be as successful as they deserve to be, then their success in training black artisans for the South, will be due primarily to the white colleges of the North and the black colleges of the South, which trained the teachers who to-day conduct these institutions. . . .

I would not deny, or for a moment seem to deny, the paramount necessity of teaching the Negro to work, and to work steadily and skillfully; or seem to depreciate in the slightest degree the important part industrial schools must play in the accomplishment of these ends, but I *do* say, and insist upon it, that it is industrialism drunk with its vision of success, to imagine that its own work can be accomplished without providing for the training of broadly cultured men and women to teach its own teachers, and to teach the teachers of the public schools.

But I have already said that human education is not simply a matter of schools; it is much more a matter of family and group life—the training of one's home, of one's daily companions, of one's social class. Now the black boy of the South moves in a black world—a world with its own leaders, its own thoughts, its own ideals. In this world he gets by far the larger part of his life training, and through the eyes of this dark world he peers into the veiled world beyond. Who guides and determines the education which he receives in his world? His teachers here are the group-leaders of the Negro people—the physicians and clergymen, the trained fathers and mothers, the influential and forceful men about him of all kinds; here it is, if at all, that the culture of the surrounding world trickles through and is handed on by the graduates of the higher schools. Can such culture training of group leaders be neglected? Can we afford to ignore it? Do you think that if the leaders of thought among Negroes are not trained and educated thinkers, that they will have no leaders? On the contrary a hundred half-trained demagogues will still hold the places they so largely occupy now, and hundreds of vociferous busy-bodies will multiply. You have no choice; either you must help furnish this race from within its own ranks with thoughtful men of trained leadership, or you must suffer the evil consequences of a headless misguided rabble.

The Object of True Education

I am an earnest advocate of manual training and trade teaching for black boys, and for white boys, too. I believe that next to the founding of Negro colleges the most valuable addition to Negro education since the war, has been industrial training for black boys. Nevertheless, I insist that the object of all true education is not to make men carpenters, it is to make carpenters men; there are two means of making the carpenter a man, each equally important: the first is to give the group and community in which he works, liberally trained teachers and leaders to teach him and his family what life means; the second is to give him sufficient intelligence and technical skill to make him an efficient workman; the first object demands the Negro college and college-bred men—not a quantity of such colleges, but a few of excellent quality; not too many college-bred men, but enough to leaven the lump, to inspire the masses, to raise the Talented Tenth to leadership; the second object demands a good system of common schools, well-taught, conveniently located and properly equipped. . . .

We need Negro teachers for the Negro common schools, and we need first-class normal schools and colleges to train them. This is the work of higher Negro education and it must be done. . . .

Indeed the demand for college-bred men by a school like Tuskegee, ought to make Mr. Booker T. Washington the firmest friend of higher training. Here he has as helpers the son of a Negro senator, trained in Greek and the humanities, and graduated at Harvard; the son of a Negro congressman and lawyer, trained in Latin and mathematics, and graduated at Oberlin; he has as his wife, a woman who read Virgil and Homer in the same class room with me; he has as college chaplain, a classical graduate of Atlanta University; as teacher of science, a graduate of Fisk; as teacher of history, a graduate of Smith,—indeed some thirty of his chief teachers are college graduates, and instead of studying French grammars in the midst of weeds, or buying pianos for dirty cabins, they are at Mr. Washington's right hand helping him in a noble work. And yet one of the effects of Mr. Washington's propaganda has been to throw doubt upon the expediency of such training for Negroes, as these persons have had.

Men of America, the problem is plain before you. Here is a race transplanted through the criminal foolishness of your fathers. Whether you like it or not the millions are here, and here they will remain. If you do not lift them up, they will pull you down. Education and work are the levers to uplift a people. Work alone will not do it unless inspired by the right ideals and guided by intelligence. Education must not simply teach work—it must teach Life. The Talented Tenth of the Negro race must be made leaders of thought and missionaries of culture among their people. No others can do this work and Negro colleges must train men for it. The Negro race, like all other races, is going to be saved by its exceptional men.

"The trouble with Mr. Booker T. Washington's work is that he is . . . attempting to build a nation inside a nation of two hostile races."

The Negro Has No Place in America

Thomas Dixon Jr. (1864–1946)

Booker T. Washington was praised by many whites for being a "safe" and conciliatory leader who was comparatively silent on the issue of political and civil rights (a fact that disturbed some of his black critics). Not all whites were favorably disposed to Washington and his program, however. The following viewpoint is excerpted from a 1905 *Saturday Evening Post* article by Thomas Dixon Jr., a Baptist minister who became a popular novelist and playwright. The North Carolina resident's fictional works, such as *The Clansmen* (which became the basis for D.W. Griffith's motion picture *Birth of a Nation*) and *The Leopard's Spots*, often portrayed blacks as bestial and depraved. In the *Post* article, Dixon professes admiration for Washington but argues that his program of economic self-improvement for blacks will never succeed in the long term because of uneradicable racial differences and white resistance to black advancement.

For Mr. Booker T. Washington as a man and leader of his race I have always had the warmest admiration. His life is a romance which appeals to the heart of universal humanity. The story of a little ragged, barefooted pickaninny who lifted his eyes from a

From Thomas Dixon Jr., "Booker T. Washington and the Negro," *Saturday Evening Post*, August 19, 1905.

cabin in the hills of Virginia, saw a vision and followed it, until at last he presides over the richest and most powerful institution of harmony in the South, and sits down with crowned heads and Presidents, has no parallel in the Tales of the Arabian Nights.

The spirit of the man, too, has always impressed me with its breadth, generosity and wisdom. The aim of his work is noble and inspiring. As I understand it from his own words, it is "to make Negroes producers, lovers of labor, honest, independent, good." His plan for doing this is to lead the Negro to the goal through the development of solid character, intelligent industry and material acquisition.

Only a fool or a knave can find fault with such an ideal. It rests squarely on the eternal verities. And yet it will not solve the Negro problem nor bring us within sight of its solution. Upon the other hand, it will only intensify that problem's danger-features, complicate and make more difficult its ultimate settlement.

It is this tragic fact to which I am trying to call the attention of the nation.

Pity for the Negro Race

I have for the Negro race only pity and sympathy. . . .

As a friend of the Negro race I claim that he should have the opportunity for the highest, noblest and freest development of his full, rounded manhood. He has never had this opportunity in America, either north or south, and he never can have it. . . .

My books are simply merciless records of conditions as they exist, conditions that can have but one ending if they are not honestly and fearlessly faced. The Civil War abolished chattel slavery. It did not settle the Negro problem. It settled the Union question and created the Negro problem. . . .

A Grave Problem

If allowed to remain here the Negro race in the United States will number 60,000,000 at the end of this century by their present rate of increase. Think of what this means for a moment and you face the gravest problem which ever puzzled the brain of statesman or philosopher. No such problem ever before confronted the white man in his recorded history. It cannot be whistled down by opportunists, politicians, weak-minded optimists or female men. It must be squarely met and fought to a finish.

Several classes of people at present obstruct any serious consideration of this question—the pot-house politician, the ostrich man, the pooh-pooh man, and the benevolent old maid. The politician is still busy over the black man's vote in doubtful States. The pooh-pooh man needs no definition—he was born a fool. The benevolent old maid contributes every time the hat is passed and is pretty sure to do as much harm as good in the long run to any cause. The ostrich man is the funniest of all this group of obstructionists, for he is a man of brains and capacity.

I have a friend of this kind in New York. He got after me the other day somewhat in this fashion:

"What do you want to keep agitating this infernal question for? There's no danger in it unless you stir it. Let it alone. I grant you that the Negro race is a poor, worthless parasite, whose criminal and animal instincts threaten society. But the Negro is here to stay. We must train him. It is the only thing we can do. So what's the use to waste your breath?"

Raising False Hopes

Senator Ben Tillman of South Carolina, speaking before the Senate on February 24, 1903, expresses sentiments similar to those of Thomas Dixon Jr.

Some people have been ready to believe and to contend that the Negro is a white man with a black skin. All history disproves that. Go to Africa. What do you find there? From one hundred and fifty million to two hundred million savages. . . .

I warn you that in proportion as you arouse false hopes in these people's minds as to their future, keeping the door of hope open by giving them offices, you are only sowing the wind which will whirl up into a whirlwind later on. You cannot keep that door open without shutting it on the whites. The Northern millions which have gone down there have gone into Negro colleges and schools to equip these people to compete with their white neighbors.

All of the millions that are being sent there by Northern philanthropy has been but to create an antagonism between the poorer classes of our citizens and these people upon whose level they are in the labor market. There has been no contribution to elevate the white people in the South, to aid and assist the Anglo-Saxon Americans. . . . They are allowed to struggle in poverty and in ignorance, and to do everything they can to get along, and they see Northern people pouring in thousands and thousands to help build up an African domination.

"But what about the future when you have educated the Negro?" I asked timidly.

"Let the future take care of itself!" the ostrich man snorted. "We live in the present. What's the use to worry about Hell? If I can scramble through this world successfully I'll take my chances with the Hell problem!"

My friend forgets that this was precisely the line of argument of our fathers over the question of Negro slavery. When the constructive statesmen of Virginia (called pessimists and infidels in their day) foresaw the coming baptism of fire and blood ('61 to '65) over the Negro slave, they attempted to destroy the slave trade and abolish slavery. My friend can find his very words in the answers of their opponents. "Let the future take care of itself! The slaves are here and here to stay. Greater evils await their freedom. We need their labor. Let the question alone. There is no danger in it unless you stir it."

The truth which is gradually forcing itself upon thoughtful students of our national life is that no scheme of education or religion can solve the race problem, and that Mr. Booker T. Washington's plan, however high and noble, can only intensify its difficulties.

This conviction is based on a few big fundamental facts, which no pooh-poohing, ostrich-dodging, weak-minded philanthropy or political rant can obscure.

Racial Differences

The first one is that no amount of education of any kind, industrial, classical or religious, can make a Negro a white man or bridge the chasm of the centuries which separate him from the white man in the evolution of human civilization.

Expressed even in the most brutal terms of Anglo-Saxon superiority there is here an irreducible fact. It is possibly true, as the Negro, Professor Kelly Miller, claims, that the Anglo-Saxon is "the most arrogant and rapacious, the most exclusive and intolerant race in history." Even so, what answer can be given to his cold-blooded proposition: "Can you change the color of the Negro's skin, the kink of his hair, the bulge of his lip or the beat of his heart with a spelling-book or a machine?"

Whence this physical difference? Its secret lies in the gulf of thousands of years of inherited progress which separates the child of the Aryan from the child of the African.

Judged by this supreme test, what contribution to human progress have the millions of Africans who inhabit this planet made during the past four thousand years? Absolutely nothing. And yet, Mr. Booker T. Washington in a recent burst of eloquence over his educational work boldly declares:

"The Negro race has developed more rapidly in the thirty years of its freedom than the Latin race has in one thousand years of freedom."

Think for a moment of the pitiful puerility of this statement falling from the lips of the greatest and wisest leader the Negro race has yet produced!

Education is the development of that which *is*. The Negro has held the Continent of Africa since the dawn of history, crunching acres of diamonds beneath his feet. Yet he never picked one up from the dust until a white man showed to him its light. His land swarmed with powerful and docile animals, yet he never built a harness, cart or sled. A hunter by necessity, he never made an ax, spear or arrowhead worth preserving beyond the moment of its use. In a land of stone and timber, he never carved a block, sawed a foot of lumber or built a house save of broken sticks and mud, and for four thousand years he gazed upon the sea yet never dreamed a sail. . . .

I repeat, education is the development of that which *is*. Behold the man whom the rags of slavery once concealed—nine millions strong! This creature, with a racial record of four thousand years of incapacity, half-child, half-animal, the sport of impulse, whim and conceit, pleased with a rattle, tickled with a straw, a being who, left to his will, roams at night and sleeps in the day, whose native tongue has framed no word of love, whose passions once aroused are as the tiger's—equality is the law of our life!—when he is educated and ceases to fill his useful sphere as servant and peasant, what are you going to do with him?

The second big fact which confronts the thoughtful, patriotic American is that the greatest calamity which could possibly befall this Republic would be the corruption of our national character by the assimilation of the Negro race. I have never seen a white man of any brains who disputes this fact. I have never seen a Negro of any capacity who did not deny it.

One thought I would burn into the soul of every young American (and who thinks of a Negro when he says "American"?)—this: Our Republic is great not by reason of the amount of dirt we possess, or the size of our census roll, but because of the genius of the race of pioneer white freemen who settled this continent, dared the might of kings, and blazed the way through our wilderness for the trembling feet of liberty. . . .

What is the attitude of Mr. Booker T. Washington on this vital issue? You will search his books and listen to his lectures in vain for any direct answer. Why? Because, if he dared to say what he really in his soul of soul believes, it would end his great career, both North and South. In no other way has he shown his talent as an organizer and leader of his people with such consummate skill as in the dexterity with which he has for twenty years dodged this issue, holding steadily the good-will of the Southern white man and the Northern philanthropist. He is the greatest diplomat his race has ever produced.

The trouble with Mr. Booker T. Washington's work is that he is really silently preparing us for the future heaven of Amalgamation—or he is doing something equally dangerous, namely he is attempting to build a nation inside a nation of two hostile races. In this event he is storing dynamite beneath the pathway of our children—the end at last can only be in bloodshed.

Mr. Washington is not training Negroes to take their place in any industrial system of the South in which the white man can direct or control him. He is not training his students to be servants and come at the beck and call of any man. He is training them all to be masters of men, to be independent, to own and operate their own industries, plant their own fields, buy and sell their own goods, and in every shape and form destroy the last vestige of dependence on the white man for anything. . . .

The Negro remains on this continent for one reason only. The Southern white man has needed his labor, and therefore has fought every suggestion of his removal. But when he refuses longer to work for the white man, then what? . . .

Education Drives the Races Apart

The point I raise is that education necessarily drives the races further and further apart, and Mr. Washington's brand of education makes the gulf between them if anything a little deeper. If there is one thing a Southern white man cannot endure it is an educated Negro. What's to be the end of it if the two races are to live forever side by side in the South?

Mr. Washington says: "Give the black man so much skill and brains that he can cut oats like the white man—then he can compete with him."

And then the real tragedy will begin. Does any sane man believe that when the Negro ceases to work under the direction of the Southern white man this . . . [white] race will allow the Negro to master his industrial system, take the bread from his mouth, crowd him to the wall and place a mortgage on his house? Competition is war—the most fierce and brutal of all its forms. Could fatuity reach a sublimer height than the idea that the white man will stand idly by and see this performance? What will he do when put to the test? He will do exactly what his white neighbor in the North does when the Negro threatens his bread—kill him! . . .

We have spent about $800,000,000 on Negro education since the war. One-half of this sum would have been sufficient to make Liberia a rich and powerful Negro state. Liberia is capable of supporting every Negro in America. Why not face this question squarely? We are temporizing and playing with it. All our educational schemes are compromises and temporary makeshifts. Mr. Booker T. Washington's work is one of noble aims. A branch of it should be immediately established at Monrovia, the capital of Liberia. A gift of ten millions would do this, and establish a colony of half a million Negroes, within two years. They could lay the foundation of a free black republic which within twenty-five years would serve our race problem on the only rational basis within human power. Colonization is not a failure. It has never been tried.

We owe this to the Negro. At present we are deceiving him and allowing him to deceive himself. He hopes and dreams of amalgamation, forgetting that self-preservation is the first law of Nature. Our present attitude of hypocrisy is inhuman toward a weaker race brought to our shores by the sins of our fathers. We owe him a square deal, and we will never give it to him on this continent.

"Race hatred is the most malignant poison that can afflict the mind."

Racism Has No Place in America

Kelly Miller (1863–1939)

Kelly Miller, born into slavery in South Carolina during the Civil War, was for many years a professor of mathematics and dean at Howard University, an African-American college in Washington, D.C. Miller was also a prolific writer and lecturer on racial, educational, and civil rights issues. In his writings Miller usually positioned himself somewhere between Booker T. Washington and Washington's black militant critics.

The following viewpoint was written by Miller in direct response to a 1905 *Saturday Evening Post* article by Thomas Dixon Jr. in which the white author criticized Booker T. Washington and disparaged the black race (see opposing viewpoint). Miller refutes Dixon's declarations that blacks are inferior and attacks his writings for inciting violence against African Americans. Among the arguments Miller makes in this viewpoint are several concerning Dixon's alarm over racial "amalgamation." Miller writes that fears of racial mixing are unjustified and that such intermingling would in fact decline if African Americans were given social and political equality.

M R. THOMAS DIXON, JR.

Dear Sir: I am writing you this letter to express the attitude and feeling of ten million of your fellow-citizens toward the evil propagandism of race animosity to which you have lent your great lit-

From Kelly Miller, "As to the Leopard's Spots: An Open Letter to Thomas Dixon Jr.," September 1905; reprinted in Kelly Miller, *Race Adjustment*, (New York: Neale, 1908).

erary powers. Through the widespread influence of your writings you have become the chief priest of those who worship at the shrine of race hatred and wrath. This one spirit runs through all your books and published utterances, like the recurrent theme of an opera. As the general trend of your doctrine is clearly epitomized and put forth in your contribution to the *Saturday Evening Post* of August 19 [1905], I beg to consider chiefly the issues therein raised. You are a white man born in the midst of the Civil War; I am a Negro born during the same stirring epoch. You were born with a silver spoon in your mouth; I was born with an iron hoe in my hand. Your race has afflicted accumulated injury and wrong upon mine; mine has borne yours only service and good will. You express your views with the most scathing frankness; I am sure you will welcome an equally candid expression from me. . . .

A Discredited Doctrine

Your fundamental thesis is that "no amount of education of any kind, industrious, classical or religious, can make a Negro a white man or bridge the chasm of the centuries which separates him from the white man in the evolution of human history." This doctrine is as old as human oppression. [John C.] Calhoun made it the arch-stone in the defense of Negro slavery—and lost.

This is but a recrudescence of the doctrine which was exploited and exploded during the anti-slavery struggle. Do you recall the school of pro-slavery scientists who demonstrated beyond doubt that the Negro's skull was too thick to comprehend the substance of Aryan knowledge? Have you not read in the now discredited scientific books of that period with what triumphant acclaim it was shown that the shape and size of the Negro's skull, facial angle, and cephalic configuration rendered him forever impervious to the white man's civilization? But all enlightened minds are now as ashamed of that doctrine as they are of the one-time dogma that the Negro had no soul. We become aware of mind through its manifestations. Within forty years of only partial opportunity, while playing, as it were, in the back yard of civilization, the American Negro has cut down his illiteracy by over fifty per cent.; has produced a professional class, some fifty thousand strong, including ministers, teachers, doctors, editors, authors, architects, engineers, and is found in all higher lines of listed pursuits in which white men are engaged; some three thousand Negroes have taken collegiate degrees, over three hundred being from the best institutions in the North and West established for the most favored white youth; there is scarcely a first-class institution in America, excepting some three or four in the South, that is without colored students, who pursue their studies generally with success, and sometimes with distinction; Negro inventors have taken out four hundred patents as a contribution to the mechanical genius of America; there are scores of Negroes who, for conceded ability and achievements, take respectable rank in the company of distinguished Americans.

It devolves upon you, Mr. Dixon, to point out some standard, either of intelligence, character, or conduct, to which the Negro cannot conform. Will you please tell a waiting world just what is the psychological difference between the races? No reputable authority, either of the old or of the new school of psychology, has yet pointed out any sharp psychic discriminant. There is not a single intellectual, moral, or spiritual excellence attained by the white race to which the Negro does not yield an appreciative response. If you could show that the Negro is incapable of mastering the intricacies of Aryan speech; that he could not comprehend the intellectual basis of European culture, or apply the apparatus of practical knowledge; that he could not be made amenable to the white man's ethical code or appreciate his spiritual motive— then your case would be proved. But in default of such demonstration we must relegate your eloquent pronouncement to the realm of generalization and prophecy, an easy and agreeable exercise of the mind in which the romancer is ever prone to indulge.

Questioning Racial Differences

The inherent, essential and unchangeable inferiority of the Negro to the white man lies at the basis of your social philosophy. . . .

That Negroes in the average are not equal in developed capacity to the white race, is a proposition which it would be as simple to affirm as it is silly to deny. The Negro represents a belated race which has not yet taken a commanding part in the progressive movement of the world. In the great cosmic scheme of things, some races reach the lime-light of civilization ahead of others. But that temporary forwardness does not argue inherent superiority is as evident as any fact of history. An unfriendly environment may hinder and impede the one, while fortunate circumstances may quicken and spur the other. Relative superiority is only a transient phase of human development. . . .

There is no hard and fast line dividing the two races on the scale of capacity. There is the widest possible range of variation within the limits of each. A philosopher and a fool may not only be members of the same race but of the same family. No scheme of classification is possible which will include all white men and shut out all Negroes. According to any test of excellence that your . . . ingenuity can devise, some Negroes will be superior to most white men; no stretch of ingenuity or strain of conscience has yet devised a plan of franchise which includes all of the members of one race and excludes all those of the other. . . .

Prof. N.F. Shaler, a native of the South, and Professor in Harvard University, writes in the *Arena:* "There are hundreds and thousands of black men who in capacity are to be ranked with the superior persons of the dominant race, and it is hard to say that in any evident feature of mind they characteristically differ from their white fellow-citizens."

Benjamin Kidd, in his work on Social Evolution, declares that the Negro child shows no inferiority, and that the deficiency which he seems to manifest in after life is due to his dwarfing and benumbing environment. Prof. John Spencer Bassett, of Trinity College, North Carolina, has had the courage to state the belief that the Negro would gain equality some day. He also tells us that Dr. Booker Washington . . . is the greatest man, with a single exception, that the South has produced in a hundred years. This is indeed a suggestion of Negro superiority with a vengeance. In the judgment of this distinguished Southerner, one Negro, at least, is superior to millions of his white fellow-citizens, including the author of "The Leopard's Spots" [Dixon]. . . .

Your position as to the work and worth of Booker T. Washington is pitiably anomalous. . . .

Mr. Washington's motto, in his own words, is that "The Negro has been worked; but now he must learn to work." The man who works for himself is of more service to any community than the man whose labor is exploited by others. You bring forward the traditional bias of the slave regime to modern conditions, viz., that the Negro did not exist in his own right and for his own sake, but for the benefit of the white man. This principle is as false in nature as it is in morals. The naturalists tell us that throughout all the range of animal creation there is found no creature which exists for the sake of any other, but each is striving after its own best welfare. Do you fear that the Negro's welfare is incompatible with that of the white man? I commend to you a careful perusal of the words of Mr. E. Gardner Murphy, who, like yourself, is a devoted Southerner, and is equally zealous to promote the highest interest of that section: "Have prosperity, peace, and happiness ever been successfully or permanently based upon indolence, inefficiency, and hopelessness? Since time began, has any human thing that God has made taken damage to itself or brought damage to the world through knowledge, truth, hope, and honest toil?" Read these words of your fellow Southerner, Mr. Dixon, and meditate upon them; they will do you good as the truth doeth the upright in heart.

Racial Amalgamation

You quote me as being in favor of the amalgamation of the races. A more careful reading of the article referred to would have convinced you that I was arguing against amalgamation as a probable solution of the race problem. I merely stated the intellectual conviction that two races cannot live indefinitely side by side, under the same general regime, without ultimately fusing. This was merely the expression of a belief, and not the utterance of a preference nor the formulation of a policy. I know of no colored man who advocates amalgamation as a feasible policy of solution. You are mistaken. The Negro does not "hope and dream of amalgamation." This would be self-stultification with a vengeance. If such a policy were allowed to dominate the imagination of the colored race its women would give themselves over to the unrestrained passion of white men, in quest of tawny offspring, which would give rise to a state of indescribable moral debauchery. At the same time, you would hardly expect the Negro, in derogation of his common human qualities, to proclaim that he is so diverse from God's other human creatures as to make the blending of the races contrary to the law of nature. The Negro refuses to become excited or share in your frenzy on this subject. The amalgamation of the races is an ultimate possibility, though not an immediate probability. But what have you and I to do with ultimate questions, anyway? Our concern is with duty, not destiny. . . .

Crossing the Color Line

But do you know, Mr. Dixon, that you are probably the foremost promoter of amalgamation between the two oceans? Wherever you narrow the scope of the Negro by preaching the doctrine of hate you drive thousands of persons of lighter hue over to the white race, carrying more or less Negro blood in their train. The blending of the races is less likely to take place if the self-respect and manly opportunity of the Negro are respected and encouraged than if he is to be forever crushed beneath the level of his faculties for dread of the fancied result. Hundreds of the composite progeny are daily crossing the color line and carrying as much of the despised blood as an albicant skin can conceal without betrayal. I believe that it was Congressman [George] Tillman, brother of the more famous Senator of that name, who stated on the floor of the [1895] Constitutional Convention of South Carolina that he knew of four hundred white families in that State who had a taint of Negro blood in their veins. I personally know, or know of, fifty cases of transition in the city of Washington. It is a momentous thing for one to change one's caste. The man or woman who affects to deny, ignore, or scorn the class with whom he previously associated is usually deemed deficient in the nobler qualities of human nature. It is not conceivable that persons of this class would undergo the self-degradation and humiliation of soul necessary to cross the great "social divide" unless it be to escape for themselves and their descendants an odious and despised status. Your oft expressed and passionately avowed belief that the progressive development of the Negro would hasten amalgamation is not borne out by the facts of observation. The refined and cultivated class among colored people are as much disinclined to such unions as the whites themselves. . . .

Degradation would soonest lead to race blending through illicitness. Had the institution of slavery existed for another century without fresh African importation there would scarcely have remained an unbleached Negro on the continent. The best possible evidence that the development of self-respect does not lead to amalgamation is furnished by Oberlin College in Ohio and by Berea College in Kentucky. These institutions have had thousands of students of the two races, male and female, associating on terms of personal equality, mutual respect, and good will, and yet in all these years not a single case of miscegenation has resulted. Contrast this record with the concubinage of the Southern plantation and the illicit relations of the city slum, and it is easy to see where the chief stress should be placed by those who so frantically dread race admixture. . . .

Misstatements of Fact

You say that "we have spent about $800,000,000 on Negro education since the war." This statement is so very wide of the mark that I was disposed to regard it as a misprint, if you had not reinforced it with an application implying a like amount. In the report of the Bureau of Education for 1901 the estimated expenditure for Negro education in all the former slave States since the Civil War is put down at $121,184,568. The amount contributed by Northern philanthropy during that interval is variously estimated from fifty to seventy-five millions. Your estimate is four times too large. It would be interesting and informing to the world if you would reveal the source of your information. These misstatements of fact are not of so much importance in themselves as that they serve to warn the reader against the accuracy and value of your general judgments. It would seem that you derive your figures of arithmetic from the same source from which you fashion your figures of speech. You will not blame the reader for not paying much heed to your sweeping generalizations when you are at such little pains as to the accuracy of easily ascertainable data.

Your proposed solution of the race problem by colonizing the Negroes in Liberia reaches the climax of absurdity. It is difficult to see how such a proposition could emanate from a man of your reputation. Did you consult Cram's Atlas about Liberia? Please do so. You will find that it has an area of 48,000 square miles and a population of 1,500,000, natives and immigrants. The area and population are about the same as those of North Carolina, which, I believe, is your native State. When you tell us that this restricted area, without commerce, without manufacture, without any system of organized industry, can support every Negro in America, in addition to its present population, I beg mildly to suggest that you recall your plan for revision before submitting it to the judgment of a critical world. Your absolute indifference to the facts, and your heedlessness of the circumstances and conditions involved in the scheme of colonization, well befit the absurdity of the general proposition.

Dangerous Words

The solution of the race problem in America is indeed a grave and serious matter. It is one that calls for statesmanlike breadth of view, philanthropic tolerance of spirit, and exact social knowledge. The whole spirit of your propaganda is to add to its intensity and aggravation. You stir the slumbering fires of race wrath into an uncontrollable flame. . . . You openly urge your fellow-citizens to override all law, human and divine. Are you aware of the force and effect of these words? "Could fatuity reach a sublimer height than the idea that the white man will stand idly by and see the performance? What will he do when put to the test? He will do exactly what his white neighbor in the North does when the Negro threatens his bread—kill him!" These words breathe out hatred and slaughter and suggest the murder of innocent men whose only crime is quest for the God-given right to work. You poison the mind and pollute the imagination through the subtle influence of literature. Are you aware of the force and effect of evil suggestion when the passions of men are in a state of unstable equilibrium? A heterogeneous population, where the elements are, on any account, easily distinguishable, is an easy prey for the promoter of wrath. The fuse is already prepared for the spark. The soul of the mob is stirred by suggestion of hatred and slaughter, as a famished beast at the smell of blood. Hatred is the ever-handy dynamic of the demagogue. The rabble responds much more readily to an appeal to passion than to reason. To stir wantonly the fires of race antipathy is as execrable a deed as flaunting a red rag in the face of a bull at a summer's picnic, or raising a false cry of "fire" in a crowded house. Human society could not exist one hour except on the basis of law which holds the baser passions of men in restraint.

In our complex situation it is only the rigid observance of law reinforced by higher moral restraint that can keep these passions in bound. You speak about giving the Negro a "square deal."

Even among gamblers, a "square deal" means to play according to the rules of the game. The rules which all civilized States have set for themselves are found in the Ten Commandments, the Golden Rule, the Sermon on the Mount, and the organic law of the land. You acknowledge no such restraints when the Negro is involved, but waive them all aside with frenzied defiance. You preside at every crossroad lynching of a helpless victim; wherever the midnight murderer rides with rope and torch in quest of the blood of his black brother, you ride by his side; wherever the cries of the crucified victim go up to God from the crackling flame, behold, you are there; when women and children, drunk with ghoulish glee, dance around the funeral pyre and mock the death groans of their fellow-man and fight for ghastly souvenirs, you have your part in the inspiration of it all. When guilefully guided workmen in mine and shop and factory, goaded by a real or imaginary sense of wrong, begin the plunder and pillage of property and murder of rival men, your suggestion is justifier of the dastardly doings. Lawlessness is gnawing at the very vitals of our institutions. It is the supreme duty of every enlightened mind to allay rather than spur on this spirit. . . .

But do not think, Mr. Dixon, that when you evoke the evil spirit you can exorcise him at will. The Negro in the end will be the least of his victims. Those who become inoculated with the virus of race hatred are more unfortunate than the victims of it. Voltaire tells us that it is more difficult and more meritorious to wean men of their prejudices than it is to civilize the barbarian. Race hatred is the most malignant poison that can afflict the mind. It freezes up the font of inspiration and chills the higher faculties of the soul. You are a greater enemy to your own race than you are to mine. . . .

I have written you thus fully in order that you may clearly understand how the case lies in the Negro's mind. If any show of feeling or bitterness of spirit crops out in my treatment of the subject, or between the lines, my letter is, at least, wholly without vindictive intent; but is the inevitable outcome of dealing with issues that verge upon the deepest human passion.

CHAPTER 5

The Great Migration and the Harlem Renaissance

Chapter Preface

During the first half of the twentieth century the lives of African Americans were influenced and shaped by two world wars, the Great Depression, President Franklin D. Roosevelt's New Deal, and other momentous events and issues that affected all Americans. Perhaps the most significant single trend of African-American life in the early twentieth century, however, was migration. As late as 1900 almost 90 percent of African Americans resided in rural areas in the South. But between 1910 and 1920 approximately half a million southern blacks moved to northern cities such as Chicago and New York. By 1940, 1.75 million southern blacks had migrated northward, where they created new communities and ways of living and also faced new problems.

The causes of the migration included the continuing repression many blacks faced in the South, the limited opportunities of agricultural work, and floods and boll-weevil infestations that created economic woes in the region. African Americans were also attracted to the North by the unprecedented economic opportunities created by World War I and by the curtailment of foreign immigration. Most black men who made the move north found employment as unskilled industrial laborers, while black women obtained jobs as domestic workers; few blacks were employed as skilled workers.

Most migrants lived in crowded and segregated black communities. These areas, known as slums or ghettos, were often plagued with poverty and crime. But some also became the centers of a vibrant new African-American culture. Observers began to speak of the "New Negro" to describe this new black population, the newness referring not just to their urbanization but also to fresh bursts of political assertiveness, literary creativity, and ethnic pride.

World War I affected the lives of black Americans beyond its creation of industrial jobs. Around 367,000 African Americans served overseas as part of the American war effort. African-American support for the war was high, buoyed in part by President Woodrow Wilson's statements that the war was being fought to make the world "safe for democracy." Among the patriotic supporters was civil rights activist W.E.B. Du Bois. "Let us, while this war lasts," he wrote in a July 1918 editorial in the *Crisis*, "forget our special grievances and close our ranks shoulder to shoulder with our white citizens and the allied nations that are fighting for democracy."

However, the black soldiers returned from Europe to find an America beset by growing racial antagonism, especially in places with large new black populations. In the "red summer" of 1919 riots between whites and blacks took place in twenty-five cities in all parts of the nation. Most blacks still faced severe restrictions on their economic and political activities. Du Bois expressed both the disappointment and resolve of many returning black soldiers when he wrote in May 1919:

> We stand again to look America squarely in the face and call a spade a spade. We sing: This country of ours . . . is yet a shameful land. . . .
>
> We *return. We return from fighting. We return fighting.*
>
> Make way for Democracy!

The two decades following World War I witnessed significant challenges and developments for African Americans. During the 1920s the "Harlem Renaissance"—the literary, intellectual, and artistic outpouring centered around Harlem, a community of New York City—was at its height. The decade also witnessed the rise of a black nationalist movement led by Marcus Garvey, a failed campaign by the National Association for the Advancement of Colored People (NAACP) to make lynching a federal crime, and the rise and fall of a reborn Ku Klux Klan. During the 1930s, the Harlem Renaissance faded and economic concerns came to the fore as the Great Depression, which affected all Americans, significantly reduced the employment and wages of blacks. The economic woes helped precipitate a major political shift; most black voters abandoned their traditional allegiance to the Republican Party and supported Democratic president Franklin D. Roosevelt and his New Deal.

During this time, many of the debates within and about the African-American community revolved around a few fundamental and familiar questions. How were blacks to attain their standing as first-class American citizens? Should urbanized blacks follow the footsteps of white foreign immigrants and attempt to become part of the American "melting pot"? Or should African Americans concentrate on attaining political and economic power while maintaining a clear and separate identity as blacks? The viewpoints in this chapter present a sampling of some of the issues African Americans faced as they transformed themselves from a southern rural to a national and urbanized population.

Viewpoint 1

"We believe that the white race should uphold its racial pride and perpetuate itself, and that the black race should do likewise."

Blacks Must Promote Racial Pride and Purity

Marcus Garvey (1887–1940)

The Jamaican-born Marcus Garvey was the most prominent and controversial black leader of the 1920s. His Universal Negro Improvement Association (UNIA), founded in Jamaica in 1914 and relocated to Harlem, New York, in 1916, was, at its peak in 1921, the largest black movement in U.S. history, attracting perhaps as many as several million followers from the United States, the Caribbean, and Africa. Elements of Garvey's movement included the *Negro World* newspaper and several black businesses, including the Black Star Line, a shipping company. Many African Americans who had migrated to Harlem and other northern cities were attracted to Garvey's dramatic speechmaking and black nationalist ideas. A central part of his program was the belief that the future for blacks lay not in the United States, where they would remain forever under the rule of the white majority, but instead in an Africa liberated from colonial rule. Toward this end he held several all-black conventions that produced a Declaration of Rights for the world's blacks and elected Garvey "Provisional President-General of Africa."

The following viewpoint is taken from a 1923 speech that was later published in a two-volume set of Garvey's writings and lectures. In it, Garvey describes what he considers to be the basic goals of the UNIA and contrasts these goals with those of other important black leaders, especially those of W.E.B. Du Bois of the National Association for the Advancement of Colored People (NAACP).

From Marcus Garvey, "Aims and Objects of Movement for Solution of Negro Problem" (1923); reprinted in *Philosophy and Opinions of Marcus Garvey*, edited by Amy Jacques-Garvey (New York: Universal, 1925).

Garvey's downfall came after his Black Star Line went bankrupt and he was convicted of mail fraud in 1923—charges that his supporters have argued were politically motivated. Imprisoned in 1925, Garvey was deported to Jamaica in 1927, where he tried with limited success to create a similar mass movement. Garvey's ideas, especially on racial pride and black nationalism, influenced similar black nationalist movements in subsequent decades.

Generally the public is kept misinformed of the truth surrounding new movements of reform. Very seldom, if ever, reformers get the truth told about them and their movements. Because of this natural attitude, the Universal Negro Improvement Association has been greatly handicapped in its work, causing thereby one of the most liberal and helpful human movements of the twentieth century to be held up to ridicule by those who take pride in poking fun at anything not already successfully established.

The white man of America has become the natural leader of the world. He, because of his exalted position, is called upon to help in all human efforts. From nations to individuals the appeal is made to him for aid in all things affecting humanity, so, naturally, there can be no great mass movement or change without first acquainting the leader on whose sympathy and advice the world moves.

It is because of this, and more so because of a desire to be Christian friends with the white race, why I explain the aims and objects of the Universal Negro Improvement Association.

The Universal Negro Improvement Association is an organization among Negroes that is seeking to improve the condition of the race, with the view of establishing a nation in Africa where Negroes will be given the opportunity to develop by themselves, without creating the hatred and animosity that now exist in countries of the white race through Negroes rivaling them for the highest and best positions in government, politics, society and industry. The organization believes in the rights of all men, yellow, white and black. To us, the white race has a right to the peaceful possession and occupation of countries of its own and in like manner the yellow and black races have their rights. It is only by an honest and liberal consideration of such rights can the world be blessed with the peace that is sought by Christian teachers and leaders.

What the Organization Stands For

The following preamble to the constitution of the organization speaks for itself:

The Universal Negro Improvement Association and African Communities' League is a social, friendly, humanitarian, charitable, educational, institutional, constructive, and expansive society, and is founded by persons, desiring to the utmost to work for the general uplift of the Negro peoples of the world. And the members pledge themselves to do all in their power to conserve the rights of their noble race and to respect the rights of all mankind, believing always in the Brotherhood of Man and the Fatherhood of God. The motto of the organization is: One God! One Aim! One Destiny! Therefore, let justice be done to all mankind, realizing that if the strong oppresses the weak confusion and discontent will ever mark the path of man, but with love, faith and charity toward all the reign of peace and plenty will be heralded into the world and the generation of men shall be called Blessed.

The declared objects of the association are:

To establish a Universal Confraternity among the race; to promote the spirit of pride and love; to reclaim the fallen; to administer to and assist the needy; to assist in civilizing the backward tribes of Africa; to assist in the development of Independent Negro Nations and Communities; to establish a central nation for the race; to establish Commissaries or Agencies in the principal countries and cities of the world for the representation of all Negroes; to promote a conscientious Spiritual worship among the native tribes of Africa; to establish Universities, Colleges, Academies and Schools for the racial education and culture of the people; to work for better conditions among Negroes everywhere.

The organization of the Universal Negro Improvement Association has supplied among Negroes a long-felt want. Hitherto the other Negro movements in America, with the exception of the Tuskegee effort of Booker T. Washington, sought to teach the Negro to aspire to social equality with the whites, meaning thereby the right to intermarry and fraternize in every social way. This has been the source of much trouble and still some Negro organizations continue to preach this dangerous "race destroying doctrine" added to a program of political agitation and aggression. The Universal Negro Improvement Association on the other hand believes in and teaches the pride and purity of race. We believe that the white race should uphold its racial pride and perpetuate itself, and that the black race should do likewise. We believe that there is room enough in the world for the various race groups to grow and develop by themselves without seeking to destroy the Creator's plan by the constant introduction of mongrel types.

The unfortunate condition of slavery as imposed upon the Negro, and which caused the mongrelization of the race, should not be legalized and continued now to the harm and detriment of both races.

The time has really come to give the Negro a chance to develop himself to a moral-standard-man, and it is for such an opportunity that the Universal Negro Improvement Association seeks in the creation of an African nation for Negroes, where the greatest latitude would be given to work out this racial ideal.

Marcus Garvey, shown here in uniform at a parade through Harlem, preached black pride and "Africa for the Africans" during the 1920s.

There are hundreds of thousands of colored people in America who desire race amalgamation and miscegenation as a solution of the race problem. These people are, therefore, opposed to the race pride ideas of black and white; but the thoughtful of both races will naturally ignore the ravings of such persons and honestly work for the solution of a problem that has been forced upon us.

Liberal white America and race loving Negroes are bound to think at this time and thus evolve a program or plan by which there can be a fair and amicable settlement of the question.

We cannot put off the consideration of the matter, for time is pressing on our hands. The educated Negro is making rightful constitutional demands. The great white majority will never grant them, and thus we march on to danger if we do not now stop and adjust the matter.

The time is opportune to regulate the relationship between both races. Let the Negro have a country of his own. Help him to return to his original home, Africa, and there give him the opportunity to climb from the lowest to the highest positions in a state of his own. If not, then the nation will have to hearken to the demand of the aggressive, "social equality" organization, known as the National Association for the Advancement of Colored People, of which W.E.B. Du Bois is leader, which declares vehemently for social and political equality, viz.: Negroes and whites in the same hotels, homes, residential districts, public and private places, a Negro as president, members of the Cabinet, Governors of States, Mayors of cities, and leaders of society in the United States. In this agitation, Du Bois is ably supported by the "Chicago Defender," a colored newspaper published in Chicago. This paper advocates Negroes in the Cabinet and Senate. All these, as everybody knows, are the Negroes' constitutional rights, but reason dictates that the masses of the white race will never stand by the ascendancy of an opposite minority group to the favored positions in a government, society and industry that exist by the will of the majority, hence the demand of the Du Bois group of colored leaders will only lead, ultimately, to further disturbances in riots, lynching and mob rule. The only logical solution therefore, is to supply the Negro with opportunities and environments of his own, and there[by] point him to the fullness of his ambition.

The Negro who seeks the White House in America could find ample play for his ambition in Africa. The Negro who seeks the office of Secretary of State in America would have a fair chance of demonstrating his diplomacy in Africa. The Negro who seeks a seat in the Senate or of being governor of a State in America, would be provided with a glorious chance for statesmanship in Africa.

A Claim on White Sympathy

The Negro has a claim on American white sympathy that cannot be denied. The Negro has labored for 300 years in contributing to America's greatness. White America will not be unmindful, therefore, of this consideration, but will treat him kindly. Yet it is realized that all human beings have a limit to their humanity. The humanity of white America, we realize, will seek self-protection and self-preservation, and that is why the thoughtful and reasonable Negro sees no hope in America for satisfying the aggressive program of the National Association for the Advancement of Colored People, but advances the reasonable plan of the Universal Negro Improvement Association, that of creating in Africa a nation and government for the Negro race.

This plan when properly undertaken and prosecuted will solve the race problem in America in fifty years. Africa affords a wonderful opportunity at the present time for colonization by the Negroes of the Western world. There is Liberia, already established as an independent Negro government. Let white America assist

Afro-Americans to go there and help develop the country. Then, there are the late German colonies; let white sentiment force England and France to turn them over to the American and West Indian Negroes who fought for the Allies in the World's War. Then, France, England and Belgium owe America billions of dollars which they claim they cannot afford to repay immediately. Let them compromise by turning over Sierre Leone and the Ivory Coast on the West Coast of Africa and add them to Liberia and help make Liberia a state worthy of her history.

The Negroes of Africa and America are one in blood. They have sprung from the same common stock. They can work and live together and thus make their own racial contribution to the world.

Will deep thinking and liberal white America help? It is a considerate duty.

It is true that a large number of self-seeking colored agitators and so-called political leaders, who hanker after social equality and fight for the impossible in politics and governments, will rave, but remember that the slave-holder raved, but the North said, "Let the slaves go free"; the British Parliament raved when the Colonists said, "We want a free and American nation"; the Monarchists of France raved when the people declared for a more liberal form of government.

The masses of Negroes think differently from the self-appointed leaders of the race. The majority of Negro leaders are selfish, self-appointed and not elected by the people. The people desire freedom in a land of their own, while the colored politician desires office and social equality for himself in America, and that is why we are asking white America to help the masses to realize their objective. . . .

Surely the time has come for the Negro to look homeward. He has won civilization and Christianity at the price of slavery. The Negro who is thoughtful and serviceable, feels that God intended him to give to his brothers still in darkness, the light of his civilization. The very light element of Negroes do not want to go back to Africa. They believe that in time, through miscegenation, the American race will be of their type. This is a fallacy and in that respect the agitation of the mulatto leader, Dr. W.E.B. Du Bois and the National Association for the Advancement of Colored People is dangerous to both races.

Racial Purity

The off-colored people, being children of the Negro race, should combine to re-establish the purity of their own race, rather than seek to perpetuate the abuse of both races. That is to say, all elements of the Negro race should be encouraged to get together and form themselves into a healthy whole, rather than seeking to lose their identities through miscegenation and social intercourse with the white race. These statements are made because we desire an honest solution of the problem and no flattery or deception will bring that about.

Let the white and Negro people settle down in all seriousness and in true sympathy and solve the problem. When that is done, a new day of peace and good will will be ushered in.

The natural opponents among Negroes to a program of this kind are that lazy element who believe always in following the line of least resistance, being of themselves void of initiative and the pioneering spirit to do for themselves. The professional Negro leader and the class who are agitating for social equality feel that it is too much work for them to settle down and build up a civilization of their own. They feel it is easier to seize on to the civilization of the white man and under the guise of constitutional rights fight for those things that the white man has created. Natural reason suggests that the white man will not yield them, hence such leaders are but fools for their pains. Teach the Negro to do for himself, help him the best way possible in that direction; but to encourage him into the belief that he is going to possess himself of the things that others have fought and died for, is to build up in his mind false hopes never to be realized. As for instance, Dr. W.E.B. Du Bois, who has been educated by white charity, is a brilliant scholar, but he is not a hard worker. He prefers to use his higher intellectual abilities to fight for a place among white men in society, industry and in politics, rather than use that ability to work and create for his own race that which the race could be able to take credit for. He would not think of repeating for his race the work of the Pilgrim Fathers or the Colonists who laid the foundation of America, but he prefers to fight and agitate for the privilege of dancing with a white lady at a ball at the Biltmore or at the Astoria hotels in New York. That kind of leadership will destroy the Negro in America and against which the Universal Negro Improvement Association is fighting.

The Universal Negro Improvement Association is composed of all shades of Negroes—blacks, mulattoes and yellows, who are all working honestly for the purification of their race, and for a sympathetic adjustment of the race problem.

VIEWPOINT 2

"A movement of White against Black, like the Klan, or a movement of Black in contradistinction to White, like Garveyism, must do more harm than good."

A Critique of Marcus Garvey and Garveyism

William Pickens (1881–1954)

Many African-American leaders of the 1920s were perplexed, and in some cases dismayed, by the great popularity of Marcus Garvey and his Universal Negro Improvement Association (UNIA). They regarded his emphasis on racial pride as a simplistic and dangerous reversal of white racism and viewed many of his activities, parades, and conventions as showy spectacles with little practical use for black Americans.

The following viewpoint, an attack on Garvey and his movement, was written by William Pickens, a college professor and author. From 1920 to 1942, Pickens was a field secretary for the National Association for the Advancement of Colored People (NAACP), an organization that was severely criticized by Garvey for not serving the true interests of African Americans. Pickens was one of several black leaders who embarked on a "Garvey Must Go" campaign of speeches, articles, and meetings. His article, published in *Forum* in 1923, is a critical overview of Garvey's doctrines and activities, including his arrest and conviction for mail fraud.

From William Pickens, "The Emperor of Africa," *Forum*, August 1923.

On June 18th, 1923, Marcus Garvey, "Provisional President of Africa," after five weeks of serious trial interspersed with little comedies, was found guilty by a federal court in New York City of using the mails to defraud investors in the "Black Star Line" of dilapidated and mythical ships. This man Garvey was a fast worker: when he arrived from Jamaica just six years ago his friends in New York had to supply him with clothes and food, but when Judge [Julian] Mack pronounced sentence against him he was paying one hundred and fifty dollars a month for a New York apartment furnished in the bizarre south-sea fashion, was drawing ten thousand dollars a year as "President General of the Universal Negro Improvement Association," an additional eleven thousand dollars as "Provisional President of Africa," and boasted a longer string of magniloquent titles than the King of England.

When Marcus Garvey was sentenced to the penitentiary, we wonder if the judge realized how many different personages were to be locked up in that one cell: "The Provisional President of Africa," "The President General of the Universal Negro Improvement Association," "The President of the Black Star Line" of ships, "The Commander in Chief of the African Legion," head of the "Distinguished Service Order of Ethiopia," "The President of the Negro Factories Corporation" and of the "African Communities League," the head of the "Booker Washington University," and the managing editor of *The Negro World* (a weekly), *The Black Man* (a monthly of odd months), and *The Negro Times* (an occasional "daily").

Endless Pleas for Money

In a brief six years he had not only made a place, and perhaps laid away a fortune, for himself, but he had also wasted at the very lowest figure one million dollars for Negro washerwomen and workingmen. When the business of his "Black Star Line," for example, wound up, it owed about three-quarters of a million and had on hand just thirty-one dollars and seventy-five cents!

He probably received, managed, and disbursed, or rather disposed of, a greater variety of unaccounted-for "funds" than any other man of his decade. At frequent intervals *The Negro World* announced the opening of some new "fund" drive, without accounting adequately for the closing of the preceding one. There were "The African Redemption Fund," but Africa is still unredeemed; "The Liberian Loan Fund," and Liberia is still in need of the loan; the perennial "Convention Fund"; funds for factories, stores, and laundries, all of brief duration; "Black Star" funds; "Marcus Garvey Defense" funds, whenever somebody sued him for back salary or other debts; *Negro World* funds, daily paper funds, monthly magazine funds; funds to send emissaries to Liberia, who were allowed to become stranded there, to be a burden on Liberian charity, and to get back however they could; funds for "delegates to the League of Nations," to sit in the galleries and look on, when possible; and each time he married a new wife, his devoted people were inspired to raise an "appreciation" fund which however did not keep him from raiding the "Black Star" funds to the tune of nine hundred dollars for one of his honeymoons to Canada. He claimed Napoleon Bonaparte as his "ideal hero," and he even had his Josephine.

He is himself a Jamaican Negro and his organization began among West Indians in Harlem. Among his American Negro followers the "dues-paying" portion are below the average of intelligence for blacks of the continent, while most of the intelligent United States Negroes who joined the movement were in it for the sake of salaries, titles, and honors.

In the western hemisphere Negroes may be divided into three divisions, according to their relationships to the whites among whom they live: the Latin-American group, where amalgamation is the rule; the British-American group, where subjection with benevolent paternalism is customary; and United States Negroes, where constitutional equality with "racial integrity," supported by varying degrees of segregation, is at present essayed. These differences account for the differing attitudes of these respective groups toward world problems and such schemes as Garvey's Black Republic of Africa.

A British Phenomenon

A comparison of British-American Negroes with those of the United States shows that the phenomena of Garveyism are rather British. British West Indian Negroes are free from spectacular horrors, such as lynchings and mob massacres, yet a settled and fixed policy of caste makes their future outlook more hopeless than that of the Negroes in the Southern United States. The United States Negro, on the other hand, is constitutionally a part of the general citizenship, and although sentiment, maladministration, and unconstitutional procedure may deprive him temporarily of the full exercise of his rights, the *basis* of his claim is broader and better.

The Negro of the States is physically a part of his nation, while the West Indian Negro is a colonial, separated by an ocean from the power which rules over him. And like British colonials of many races he has an idea, tinged with hope, that some time he may become entirely independent. The West Indian blacks whom Garvey found in New York were therefore the first to be moved by the idea of entire racial separateness, even to the absurd extent of having a continent assigned to a color,—a condition which commercial interdependence and scientific intercommunication make impossible.

There are other differences in these group complexes that help to explain Garveyism: the American Negro is used to the theory, and more or less to the actuality, of democracy and equality. If American Negroes had planned the "Republic of Africa," we should have heard nothing of "Knights and Ladies of Ethiopia," "Knights Commander of the Nile," and "Dukes of Uganda." Those are reactions of the British substratum. When Garvey was traveling through the States, advertising "Black Star" stock and "Back to Africa" schemes, he required the men and women of his retinue to address him as "Your Highness," and what was the amused astonishment of a colored American housewife in Ohio, who had rented rooms to Garvey and his followers, when one of Garvey's female attendants descended the stairway and announced: "His Highness would like ham and eggs, or pork chops and gravy, for his supper.". . .

Color Prejudice

Another insular complex led Garvey astray when he appealed to the color-prejudice of "black" colored Americans. Being a black man himself, Garvey tried to draw the black Negroes of America away from those of lighter skin. But the color line of the whites against the whole Negro group in this country gives that many-colored group a consciousness of common interests. The British in the islands have three castes: white, colored, and black (or dark brown),—because that makes the matter easier for the whites. A united colored group in the West Indies would be an overwhelming majority, while in the States all the colored blood of every shade and degree added together constitutes only a one-tenth minority.

The American white, therefore, did not feel it necessary to make the triple distinction. Individual Negroes may have color senti-ment, like any other "taste," and it is a vanishing tradition in a few localities where it originated in the pre-Civil War status of free mulattoes, as in Charleston, S.C., and New Orleans, La. But the color question has never made a group division of the colored people of the United States. With the consciousness of a black West Indian, Garvey had a chip on his shoulder for the lighter skins of the continent, and even after he was put in jail, he voiced the opinion that the whites and light skins were his worst ene-mies, although these colors had not been distinguished in the trial against him, and in spite of a fact which he knew well: that the four men who during the previous twelve months had done most to expose his frauds and destroy his influence in America, were dark Negroes of the average American type, one of them very dark, none of them a mulatto, and all of them Southern in origin: Chandler Owen and A.P. Randolph, editors, Robert W. Bagnall, and the present writer, citizens of Harlem.

He seemed not to realize that he would have to rule over every race and color under the sun, if he was to be Emperor of Africa,—

A Lunatic or a Traitor

In a May 1924 editorial in the Crisis, *W.E.B. Du Bois made one of his harshest attacks on Marcus Garvey and his program.*

Marcus Garvey is, without doubt, the most dangerous enemy of the Negro race in America and in the world. He is either a lunatic or a traitor. He is sending all over this country tons of letters and pamphlets appealing to Congressmen, business men, philanthropists and educators to join him on a platform whose half concealed planks may be interpreted as follows:

That no person of Negro descent can ever hope to become an American citizen.

That forcible separation of the races and the banishment of Negroes to Africa is the only solution of the Negro problem.

That race war is sure to follow any attempt to realize the program of the N.A.A.C.P.

We would have refused to believe that any man of Negro descent could have fathered such a propaganda if the evidence did not lie before us in black and white signed by this man. . . .

Everybody, including the writer, who has dared to make the slightest criticism of Garvey has been intimidated by threats and threatened with libel suits. Over fifty court cases have been brought by Garvey in ten years. After my first unfavorable article on Garvey, I was not only threatened with death by men declaring themselves his followers, but received letters of such unbelievable filth that they were absolutely unprintable. When I landed in this country from my trip to Africa I learned with disgust that my friends stirred by Garvey's threats had actually felt compelled to have secret police protection for me on the dock!

Friends have even begged me not to publish this editorial lest I be assassinated. To such depths have we dropped in free black America! I have been exposing white traitors for a quarter century. If the day has come when I cannot tell the truth about black traitors it is high time that I died.

The American Negroes have endured this wretch all too long with fine restraint and every effort at cooperation and understanding. But the end has come. Every man who apologizes for or defends Marcus Garvey from this day forth writes himself down as unworthy of the countenance of decent Americans. As for Garvey himself, this open ally of the Ku Klux Klan should be locked up or sent home.

from yellow Hottentots in the south to white Frenchmen and brunette Spaniards in the north; from the western Liberians, descended from American Negroes to the eastern Abyssinians, claiming descent from ancient Jews; stalwart Zulus and pigmy Bushmen, black Bantus, brown Moors, copper Egyptians; white South Africans, white settlers everywhere, and even Asiatics on the south and east. Nor did he realize how varied his subjects would be in national traditions; he ignored all problems of religious conflict, such as the inroads of Mohammedanism in unexpected corners of Africa; he was not aware that the Liberians are as different from the people of Abyssinia, as Mexicans are different from Russians; that there is no more in common between South Africa and North Africa than between Texas and Turkey. He did not know that the worst enemy a foreign usurper would find in Africa would be the Africans themselves. He had not a grammar grade understanding of Africa. . . .

We will not be so hard upon the British as to charge also to their training or example the colossal conceit of Marcus Garvey. His megalomania and love of exaggeration are individual freaks, rather than either national or racial traits. During the period of his empire building, perhaps to boost the imaginary grandeur of his sway, he always spoke of "the 400,000,000 Negroes of the world," when there are only about 150,000,000. Two years ago he claimed to have four million members; to-day he claims six million; while most analyses of his other figures and data indicate that he has never had more than twenty or thirty thousand dues-paying members. He loudly announced that his 1922 convention would have "one hundred and fifty thousand delegates," but when his convention had been in session for a month, the most hotly contested issues, like those for offices and salaries, registered a vote of less than two hundred yeas and nays.

Yet his naïve-minded followers accept the myth of "the greatest Negro organization in the world," and look forward confidently to an early conquest of Africa against all the powers of Europe. Indeed Garvey announced, amid thunderous applause, at the opening of his 1922 convention: "If England wants peace, if France wants peace, if Italy wants peace, I advise them to pack up bag and baggage and get out of Africa!" And to substantiate the threat he marched through the streets of Harlem with an "army" assembled from "all over the world" and numbering less than six thousand men, women, little children, "Black Cross Nurses," local sympathizers, and unorganized camp followers. The "President" headed the procession, uniformed and plumed like a German field marshal, and pursued by various kinds of nobles in bright-colored robes and tassels.

Garvey understands mass psychology, with perhaps little formal knowledge of the subject, and the post-war spirit of the world was his ally, as exemplified in "Zionism," the Irish struggle, "self-determination" of peoples, and the great Negro migrations from South to North in this country. Some of these migrants had greatly improved their condition by one move, and, as simple minds run, a longer and more daring move, to Africa, or somewhere, would make their happiness complete. He declared for a "Black House" in Washington, to match the White House. He organized a ten million dollar ship corporation, without any money, and called it the "Black Star Line," to match the "White Star Line."

Each year he held a thirty-one days' convention to dispose of the affairs of the non-existent state of Africa. Before the opening of each big meeting in "Liberty Hall" on West 138th Street, he marched up and down the aisles and finally to the platform, surrounded by a bodyguard and followed by a chorus, carrying the red, black and green tricolor of the African Republic and singing: "God bless our President!" Garvey made these people at least *feel* important. There were the "Black Cross Nurses," for the most part uneducated working women who did not know the first principles of first aid, and there were the soldiers, with uniforms and arms, feeling as heroic tramping through the aisles of "Liberty Hall" as if treading the highways of an empire.

The human mind may dwell so long on an illusion that it will conceive that illusion as a reality. From the Tombs Prison in New York, Garvey proclaims to his subjects that he is "the victim of an international frame-up." He compares himself with O'Connell, MacSwiney, Gandhi, and Jesus. He regarded the judge and the United States district attorney as international and interracial tools. Petulant and suspicious, he dismissed his attorney and took charge of his own case, greatly delaying the progress of the court by his ignorance of the law, and creating a sort of "comedy of errors" by presenting the attorney Marcus Garvey, for the defendant Marcus Garvey, examining the witness Marcus Garvey. In summing up his case to the jury he talked for three hours, in true "Liberty Hall" propaganda style, expecting to overcome the evidence by the sheer multitudinousness and vehemency of his words. If sincere, he did not realize that he was *not* being tried for being the "President of Africa," for attempting to build a ship line, for rating himself as the only saviour of "the 400,000,000 Negroes of the world," nor for meeting the arrogant claim of Caucasian superiority with the equally absurd claim of black superiority,—but that he was being tried for the ordinary private crime of using the United States mail to defraud investors in a mythical ship. For stealing from his own subjects and supporters he was condemned on *their* testimony.

Some of his followers, believing that he was being persecuted for his doctrines, intimidated witnesses, wrote threats to the prosecutor and the court, and when on the last day he was being led away to prison, some of these dropped to their knees on the crowded pavement and asked God to intervene, informing Him that Garvey was being punished for the same reason that Jesus was crucified, ignoring the fact that the Man of Nazareth was never connected with financial fraud and debacle.

A Pact with the Ku Klux Klan

Intelligent American Negroes had only laughed at Garveyism, but became almost solid against him when in 1922 he launched the African Republic into the treaty-making business by apparently concluding the first pact with the Ku Klux Klan,—the Klan getting all the advantage in the diplomatic exchanges. When the invisible "government of Africa" came to an understanding with the "invisible empire of America," naturally the terms of agreement had to be a secret but they are easily inferred from Garvey's voluminous speeches immediately following his visit to Atlanta, where he had conferred with the "Imperial Wizard." The Ku Klux Klan were to be given America, so far as Garvey was concerned, and in return for his preaching that "this is a white man's country" he and his followers were to be allowed to take Africa,—so far as the "Imperial Wizard" was concerned.

Then it was that the greater number of intelligent American Negroes decided that Garveyism had passed from the stage of amusing parade into a phase of actual menace to interracial tranquility. Nobody had ever feared that he would lead all Negroes back to Africa,—England and France would see to that,—nor that he could lead as many as one out of every ten thousand American Negroes anywhere. But there was the real danger of robbing the ignorant blacks of the South, thus rousing interracial suspicion and antagonism. It was decided that "Garvey must go!" And the four colored Americans whom we have named, issued a circular bearing that title and arranged a series of meetings to expose Garveyism in Harlem. Some of his uniformed legionaries and fanatics came to break up the meeting with knives and clubs. Police protection was secured and the exposé went on, every meeting drawing a bigger and bigger crowd of determined colored Americans, and the menace and folly of the "back to Africa" program was made plainer than it had ever before been made.

Garveyism and American Repression

And there is a moral to the tale: it must be considered that Garveyism could never happen simply because there was a Marcus Garvey. There was an opportunity for him and a response to him.

This opportunity consists in the general repression of the Negro and Negroid peoples of parts of North America and parts of Africa. Like all humans the Negro is striving for self-expression and self-realization. And if these normal instincts are abnormally repressed, it will make him a prey to sharks and a menace to society. The very nature of this "black world" organization attracted into it sharks who would rend it to pieces, but the instinct for self-realization will still persist and must be invited and guided into useful channels or it will break out again in some new direction of waste and folly.

Life must somehow be made more normal for the colored minorities who live among white populations or who are in the power of governments dominated by whites. Movements for the advancement of the interests of such colored people must involve the co-operation of white and black. A movement of White against Black, like the Klan, or a movement of Black in contradistinction to White, like Garveyism, must do more harm than good.

Human science and intercommunication have made it improbable that the earth will ever again be divided geographically among monochromatic populations. The idea that one race should be set, geographically or otherwise, over against another is a reversion in civilization. Twelve million colored people of the United States can only consider plans for progress *in America*, but no fantastic schemes for egress from America. Any movement pivoted on any outside world is doomed to failure among this people.

"This is the mountain standing in the way of any true Negro art in America—this urge . . . toward whiteness, the desire to pour racial individuality into the mold of American standardization, and to be as little Negro and as much American as possible."

African-American Artists Should Emphasize Their Black Heritage

Langston Hughes (1902–1967)

In addition to urban migration and the mass movement led by Marcus Garvey, another important chapter in African-American history in the 1920s was the artistic and literary flowering known as the Harlem Renaissance. Harlem, a section of New York City that was the destination of many black migrants from the southern states and the Caribbean, became a haven for such writers as Countee Cullen, Claude McKay, Jean Toomer, and Zora Neale Hurston. Similar artistic movements occurred in other northern cities that had attracted black migrants.

Langston Hughes, a central figure of the Harlem Renaissance, is viewed today as one of the leading American writers of the twentieth century. Known primarily for his poetry, in which he made use of racial themes and jazz and blues rhythms, Hughes also wrote plays, song lyrics, and fiction. The following viewpoint is taken from an article published in the *Nation* in 1926. Hughes argues that African-American artists should embrace and celebrate their black heritage, in part to combat what he sees as the unconscious desire of the black middle class to imitate whites.

From Langston Hughes, "The Negro Artist and the Racial Mountain," *Nation*, June 23, 1926. Reprinted with permission from the *Nation* magazine; © The Nation Company, L.P.

One of the most promising of the young Negro poets said to me once, "I want to be a poet—not a Negro poet," meaning, I believe, "I want to write like a white poet"; meaning subconsciously, "I would like to be a white poet"; meaning behind that, "I would like to be white." And I was sorry the young man said that, for no great poet has ever been afraid of being himself. And I doubted then that, with his desire to run away spiritually from his race, this boy would ever be a great poet. But this is the mountain standing in the way of any true Negro art in America —this urge within the race toward whiteness, the desire to pour racial individuality into the mold of American standardization, and to be as little Negro and as much American as possible.

Middle vs. Lower Class

But let us look at the immediate background of this young poet. His family is of what I suppose one would call the Negro middle class: people who are by no means rich yet never uncomfortable nor hungry—smug, contented, respectable folk, members of the Baptist church. The father goes to work every morning. He is a chief steward at a large white club. The mother sometimes does fancy sewing or supervises parties for the rich families of the town. The children go to a mixed school. In the home they read white papers and magazines. And the mother often says "Don't be like niggers" when the children are bad. A frequent phrase from the father is, "Look how well a white man does things." And so the word white comes to be unconsciously a symbol of all the virtues. It holds for the children beauty, morality, and money. The whisper of "I want to be white" runs silently through their minds. This young poet's home is, I believe, a fairly typical home of the colored middle class. One sees immediately how difficult it would be for an artist born in such a home to interest himself in interpreting the beauty of his own people. He is never taught to see that beauty. He is taught rather not to see it, or if he does, to be ashamed of it when it is not according to Caucasian patterns.

For racial culture the home of a self-styled "high-class" Negro has nothing better to offer. Instead there will perhaps be more aping of things white than in a less cultured or less wealthy home. The father is perhaps a doctor, lawyer, landowner, or politician. The mother may be a social worker, or a teacher, or she may do nothing and have a maid. Father is often dark but he has usually married the lightest woman he could find. The family attend a fashionable church where few really colored faces are to be found. And they themselves draw a color line. In the North they go to white theaters and white movies. And in the South they have at least two cars and a house "like white folks." Nordic manners, Nordic faces, Nordic hair, Nordic art (if any), and an Episcopal heaven. A very high mountain indeed for the would-be racial artist to climb in order to discover himself and his people.

But then there are the low-down folks, the so-called common element, and they are the majority—may the Lord be praised! The people who have their nip of gin on Saturday nights and are not too important to themselves or the community, or too well fed, or too learned to watch the lazy world go round. They live on Seventh Street in Washington or State Street in Chicago and they do not particularly care whether they are like white folks or anybody else. Their joy runs, bang! into ecstasy. Their religion soars to a shout. Work maybe a little today, rest a little tomorrow. Play awhile. Sing awhile. O, let's dance! These common people are not afraid of spirituals, as for a long time their more intellectual brethren were, and jazz is their child. They furnish a wealth of colorful, distinctive material for any artist because they still hold their own individuality in the face of American standardizations. And perhaps these common people will give to the world its truly great Negro artist, the one who is not afraid to be himself. Whereas the better-class Negro would tell the artist what to do, the people at least let him alone when he does appear. And they are not ashamed of him—if they know he exists at all. And they accept what beauty is their own without question.

Unused Material

Certainly there is, for the American Negro artist who can escape the restrictions the more advanced among his own group would put upon him, a great field of unused material ready for his art. Without going outside his race, and even among the better classes with their "white" culture and conscious American manners, but still Negro enough to be different, there is sufficient matter to furnish a black artist with a lifetime of creative work. And when he chooses to touch on the relations between Negroes and whites in this country with their innumerable overtones and undertones, surely, and especially for literature and the drama, there is an inexhaustible supply of themes at hand. To these the Negro artist can give his racial individuality, his heritage of rhythm and warmth, and his incongruous humor that so often, as in the Blues, becomes ironic laughter mixed with tears. But let us look again at the mountain.

A prominent Negro clubwoman in Philadelphia paid eleven dollars to hear Raquel Meller sing Andalusian popular songs. But she told me a few weeks before she would not think of going to hear "that woman," Clara Smith, a great black artist, sing Negro folksongs. And many an upper-class Negro church, even now, would not dream of employing a spiritual in its services. The drab melodies in white folks' hymnbooks are much to be preferred. "We want to worship the Lord correctly and quietly. We don't believe in 'shouting.' Let's be dull like the Nordics," they say, in effect.

"Minstrel Man"

Several of Langston Hughes's poems, including "Minstrel Man," were featured in The New Negro, *an anthology of writings on the Harlem Renaissance edited by Alain Locke and published in 1925.*

> Because my mouth
> Is wide with laughter
> And my throat
> Is deep with song,
> You do not think
> I suffer after
> I have held my pain
> So long.
>
> Because my mouth
> Is wide with laughter,
> You do not hear
> My inner cry,
> Because my feet
> Are gay with dancing,
> You do not know
> I die.

The road for the serious black artist, then, who would produce a racial art is most certainly rocky and the mountain is high. Until recently he received almost no encouragement for his work from either white or colored people. The fine novels of [Charles W.] Chestnutt go out of print with neither race noticing their passing. The quaint charm and humor of [Paul Lawrence] Dunbar's dialect verse brought to him, in his day, largely the same kind of encouragement one would give a sideshow freak (A colored man writing poetry! How odd!) or a clown (How amusing!).

The present vogue in things Negro, although it may do as much harm as good for the budding colored artist, has at least done this: it has brought him forcibly to the attention of his own people among whom for so long, unless the other race had noticed him beforehand, he was a prophet with little honor. I understand that Charles Gilpin acted for years in Negro theaters without any special acclaim from his own, but when Broadway gave him eight curtain calls, Negroes, too, began to beat a tin pan in his honor. I know a young colored writer, a manual worker by day, who had been writing well for the colored magazines for some years, but it was not until he recently broke into the white publications and his first book was accepted by a prominent New York publisher that the "best" Negroes in his city took the trouble to discover that he lived there. Then almost immediately they decided to give a grand dinner for him. But the society ladies were careful to whisper to his mother that perhaps she'd better not come. They were not sure she would have an evening gown.

The Negro artist works against an undertow of sharp criticism and misunderstanding from his own group and unintentional bribes from the whites. "O, be respectable, write about nice people, show how good we are," say the Negroes. "Be stereotyped, don't go too far, don't shatter our illusions about you, don't amuse us too seriously. We will pay you," say the whites. Both would have told Jean Toomer not to write "Cane." The colored people did not praise it. The white people did not buy it. Most of the colored people who did read "Cane" hate it. They are afraid of it. Although the critics gave it good reviews the public remained indifferent. Yet (excepting the work of [W.E.B.] DuBois) "Cane" contains the finest prose written by a Negro in America. And like the singing of [Paul] Robeson, it is truly racial.

But in spite of the Nordicized Negro intelligentsia and the desires of some white editors we have an honest American Negro literature already with us. Now I await the rise of the Negro theater. Our folk music, having achieved world-wide fame, offers itself to the genius of the great individual American Negro composer who is to come. And within the next decade I expect to see the work of a growing-school of colored artists who paint and model the beauty of dark faces and create with new technique the expressions of their own soul-world. And the Negro dancers who will dance like flame and the singers who will continue to carry our songs to all who listen—they will be with us in even greater numbers tomorrow.

Most of my own poems are racial in theme and treatment, derived from the life I know. In many of them I try to grasp and hold some of the meanings and rhythms of jazz. I am sincere as I know how to be in these poems and yet after every reading I answer questions like these from my own people: Do you think Negroes should always write about Negroes? I wish you wouldn't read some of your poems to white folks. How do you find anything interesting in a place like a cabaret? Why do you write about black people? You aren't black. What makes you do so many jazz poems?

But jazz to me is one of the inherent expressions of Negro life in America: the eternal tom-tom beating in the Negro soul—the tom-tom of revolt against weariness in a white world, a world of subway trains, and work, work, work; the tom-tom of joy and laughter, and pain swallowed in a smile. Yet the Philadelphia clubwoman is ashamed to say that her race created it and she does not like me to write about it. The old subconscious "white is best" runs through her mind. Years of study under white teachers, a lifetime of white books, pictures, and papers, and white manners, morals, and Puritan standards made her dislike the spirituals. And now she turns up her nose at jazz and all its manifestations—likewise almost everything else distinctly racial. She doesn't care for the Winold Reiss portraits of Negroes because they are "too Negro." She does not want a true picture of herself from anybody. She wants the artist to flatter her, to make the white world believe that all Negroes are as smug and as near white in soul as she wants to be. But, to my mind, it is the duty of the younger Negro artist, if he accepts any duties at all from outsiders, to change through the force of his art that old whispering "I want to be white," hidden in the aspirations of his people, to "Why should I want to be white? I am a Negro—and beautiful!"

So I am ashamed for the black poet who says, "I want to be a poet, not a Negro poet," as though his own racial world were not as interesting as any other world. I am ashamed, too, for the colored artist who runs from the painting of Negro faces to the painting of sunsets after the manner of the academicians because he fears the strange un-whiteness of his own features. An artist must be free to choose what he does, certainly, but he must also never be afraid to do what he might choose.

Let the blare of Negro jazz bands and the bellowing voice of Bessie Smith singing Blues penetrate the closed ears of the colored near-intellectuals until they listen and perhaps understand. Let Paul Robeson singing Water Boy and Rudolph Fisher writing about the streets of Harlem and Jean Toomer holding the heart of Georgia in his hands, and Aaron Douglas drawing strange black fantasies cause the smug Negro middle class to turn from their white, respectable, ordinary books and papers to catch a glimmer of their own beauty. We younger Negro artists who create now intend to express our individual dark-skinned selves without fear or shame. If white people are pleased we are glad. If they are not, it doesn't matter. We know we are beautiful. And ugly too. The tom-tom cries and the tom-tom laughs. If colored people are pleased we are glad. If they are not, their displeasure doesn't matter either. We build our temples for tomorrow, strong as we know how, and we stand on top of the mountain, free within ourselves.

VIEWPOINT 4

"Negro art there has been, is, and will be among the numerous black nations of Africa; but to suggest the possibility of any such development among the ten million colored people in this republic is self-evident foolishness."

African-American Artists Should Not Emphasize Their Black Heritage

George S. Schuyler (1895–1977)

The significant attention received by African-American writers and artists in the 1920s in Harlem and other American cities was viewed by many African-American leaders as an important and positive development. Many argued that blacks had unique contributions to make to American culture and that such demonstrations of cultural worth would help the cause of equality for blacks in American society. A more skeptical view of the arts and black Americans is presented in the following viewpoint, taken from a 1926 editorial by George S. Schuyler, then a columnist for the *Pittsburgh Courier*. A first lieutenant in World War I, Schuyler later wrote the novel *Black No More* and an autobiography entitled *Black and Conservative*. In the *Nation* article he argues that the clamor for "Negro art" is based on and is perpetuating negative racial stereotypes.

From George S. Schuyler, "Negro-Art Hokum," *Nation*, June 16, 1926. Reprinted with permission from the *Nation* magazine; © The Nation Company, L.P.

Negro art "made in America" is as non-existent as the widely advertised profundity of Cal Coolidge, the "seven years of progress" of Mayor Hylan, or the reported sophistication of New Yorkers. Negro art there has been, is, and will be among the numerous black nations of Africa; but to suggest the possibility of any such development among the ten million colored people in this republic is self-evident foolishness. Eager apostles from Greenwich Village, Harlem, and environs proclaimed a great renaissance of Negro art just around the corner waiting to be ushered on the scene by those whose hobby is taking races, nations, peoples, and movements under their wing. New art forms expressing the "peculiar" psychology of the Negro were about to flood the market. In short, the art of Homo Africanus was about to electrify the waiting world. Skeptics patiently waited. They still wait.

True, from dark-skinned sources have come those slave songs based on Protestant hymns and Biblical texts known as the spirituals, work songs and secular songs of sorrow and tough luck known as the blues, that outgrowth of ragtime known as jazz (in the development of which whites have assisted), and the Charleston, an eccentric dance invented by the gamins around the public market-place in Charleston, S.C. No one can or does deny this. But these are contributions of a caste in a certain section of the country. They are foreign to Northern Negroes, West Indian Negroes, and African Negroes. They are no more expressive or characteristic of the Negro race than the music and dancing of the Appalachian highlanders or the Dalmatian peasantry are expressive or characteristic of the Caucasian race. If one wishes to speak of the musical contributions of the peasantry of the South, very well. Any group under similar circumstances would have produced something similar. It is merely a coincidence that this peasant class happens to be of a darker hue than the other inhabitants of the land. One recalls the remarkable likeness of the minor strains of the Russian mujiks to those of the Southern Negro.

As for the literature, painting, and sculpture of Aframericans—such as there is—it is identical in kind with the literature, painting, and sculpture of white Americans: that is, it shows more or less evidence of European influence. In the field of drama little of any merit has been written by and about Negroes that could not have been written by whites. The dean of the Aframerican literati is W.E.B. Du Bois, a product of Harvard and German universities; the foremost Aframerican sculptor is Meta Warwick Fuller, a graduate of leading American art schools and former student of

Rodin; while the most noted Aframerican painter, Henry Ossawa Tanner, is dean of American painters in Paris and has been decorated by the French Government. Now the work of these artists is no more "expressive of the Negro soul"—as the gushers put it—than are the scribblings of Octavus Cohen. . . .

Just Plain American

This, of course, is easily understood if one stops to realize that the Aframerican is merely a lampblacked Anglo-Saxon. If the European immigrant after two or three generations of exposure to our schools, politics, advertising, moral crusades, and restaurants becomes indistinguishable from the mass of Americans of the older stock (despite the influence of the foreign-language press), how much truer must it be of the sons of Ham who have been subjected to what the uplifters call Americanism for the last three hundred years. Aside from his color, which ranges from very dark brown to pink, your American Negro is just plain American. Negroes and whites from the same localities in this country talk, think, and act about the same. Because a few writers with a paucity of themes have seized upon imbecilities of the Negro rustics and clowns and palmed them off as authentic and characteristic Aframerican behavior, the common notion that the black American is so "different" from his white neighbor has gained wide currency. The mere mention of the word "Negro" conjured up in the average white American's mind a composite stereotype of Bert Williams, Aunt Jemima, Uncle Tom, Jack Johnson, Florian Slappey, and the various monstrosities scrawled by the cartoonists. Your average Aframerican no more resembles this stereotype than the average American resembles a composite of Andy Gump, Jim Jeffries, and a cartoon by Rube Goldberg.

Again, the Aframerican is subject to the same economic and social forces that mold the actions and thought of the white Americans. He is not living in a different world as some whites and a few Negroes would have us believe. When the jangling of his Connecticut alarm clock gets him out of his Grand Rapids bed to a breakfast similar to that eaten by his white brother across the street, when he toils at the same or similar work in mills, mines, factories, and commerce alongside the descendants of Spartacus, Robin Hood, and Erik the Red; when he wears similar clothing and speaks the same language with the same degree of perfection; when he reads the same Bible and belongs to the Baptist, Methodist, Episcopal, or Catholic church; when his fraternal affiliations also include the Elks, Masons, and Knights of Pythias; when he gets the same or similar schooling, lives in the same kind of houses, owns the same makes of cars (or rides in them) and nightly sees the same Hollywood version of life on the screen; when he smokes the same brands of tobacco and avidly peruses the same puerile periodicals; in short, when he responds to the same political, social, moral, and economic stimuli in precisely the same manner as his white neighbor, it is sheer nonsense to talk about "racial differences" as between the American black man and the American white man. Glance over a Negro newspaper (it is printed in good Americanese) and you will find the usual quota of crime news, scandal, personals, and uplift to be found in the average white newspaper—which, by the way, is more widely read by the Negroes than is the Negro press. In order to satisfy the cravings of an inferiority complex engendered by the colorphobia of the mob, the readers of the Negro newspapers are given a slight dash of racialistic seasoning. In the homes of the black and white Americans of the same cultural and economic level one finds similar furniture, literature, and conversation. How, then, can the black American be expected to produce art and literature dissimilar to that of the white American?

Consider Coleridge-Taylor, Edward Wilmot Blyden, and Claude McKay, the Englishmen; Pushkin, the Russian; Bridgewater, the Pole; Antar, the Arabian; Latino, the Spaniard; Dumas, père and fils, the Frenchmen; and Paul Laurence Dunbar, Charles W. Chestnut, and James Weldon Johnson, the Americans. All Negroes; yet their work shows the impress of nationality rather than race. They all reveal the psychology and culture of their environment—their color is incidental. Why should Negro artists of America vary from the national artistic norm when Negro artists in other countries have not done so? If we can foresee what kind of white citizens will inhabit this neck of the woods in the next generation by studying the sort of education and environment the children are exposed to now, it should not be difficult to reason that the adults of today are what they are because of the education and environment they were exposed to a generation ago. And that education and environment were about the same for blacks and whites. One contemplates the popularity of the Negro-art hokum and murmurs, "How come?"

The Old Myth of Racial Differences

This nonsense is probably the last stand of the old myth palmed off by Negrophobists for all these many years, and recently rehashed by the sainted [President Warren G.] Harding, that there are "fundamental, eternal, and inescapable differences" between white and black Americans. That there are Negroes who will lend this myth a helping hand need occasion no surprise. It has been broadcast all over the world by the vociferous scions of slaveholders, "scientists" like Madison Grant and Lothrop Stoddard, and the patriots who flood the treasury of the Ku Klux Klan; and is believed, even today, by the majority of free, white citizens. On this baseless premise, so flattering to the white mob, that the blackamoor is inferior and fundamentally different, is erected the postulate that he must needs be peculiar; and when he attempts to portray life through the medium of art, it must of necessity be a peculiar art. While such reasoning may seem conclusive to the majority of Americans, it must be rejected with a loud guffaw by intelligent people.

VIEWPOINT 5

"There should never be an opposition to segregation pure and simple unless that segregation does involve discrimination."

Self-Segregation Might Benefit African Americans

W.E.B. Du Bois (1868–1963)

From 1910 to 1934 W.E.B. Du Bois, a former professor of sociology at Atlanta University, was a high-ranking official of the National Association for the Advancement of Colored People (NAACP) and editor of the *Crisis*, its official publication. Du Bois left the civil rights organization in 1934 because of controversy over several editorials he wrote on racial segregation, two of which are reprinted here. The first appeared in the January 1934 issue of the *Crisis*. Written at a time when blacks were suffering greatly because of the Great Depression, Du Bois argues that years of agitation for social equality and civil rights have had limited results. He insists that segregation is not always the result of discrimination and that black self-segregation can help blacks build up their own institutions and improve their lives. Du Bois's views were criticized by many, including other leaders of the NAACP. The second part of this viewpoint is from a June 1934 piece written by Du Bois in response to his critics. The disagreement between Du Bois and the NAACP leadership over segregation resulted in Du Bois's resignation from the organization. Du Bois resumed his teaching career at Atlanta University and later rejoined the NAACP as a research director from 1944 to 1948. Ultimately disillusioned with the prospects for blacks in America, in 1961 he immigrated to Ghana, Africa, where he died two years later.

From W.E.B. Du Bois, editorials, *The Crisis*, January and June 1934. Reprinted by permission.

I

The thinking colored people of the United States must stop being stampeded by the word segregation. The opposition to racial segregation is not or should not be any distaste or unwillingness of colored people to work with each other, to co-operate with each other, to live with each other. The opposition to segregation is an opposition to discrimination. The experience in the United States has been that usually when there is racial segregation, there is also racial discrimination.

Segregation and Discrimination

But the two things do not necessarily go together, and there should never be an opposition to segregation pure and simple unless that segregation does involve discrimination. Not only is there no objection to colored people living beside colored people if the surroundings and treatment involve no discrimination, if streets are well lighted, if there is water, sewerage and police protection, and if anybody of any color who wishes, can live in that neighborhood. The same way in schools, there is no objection to schools attended by colored pupils and taught by colored teachers. On the contrary, colored pupils can by our own contention be as fine human beings as any other sort of children, and we certainly know that there are no teachers better than trained colored teachers. But if the existence of such a school is made reason and cause for giving it worse housing, poorer facilities, poorer equipment and poorer teachers, then we do object, and the objection is not against the color of the pupils' or teachers' skins, but against the discrimination.

In the recent endeavor of the United States government to redistribute capital so that some of the disadvantaged groups may get a chance for development, the American Negro should voluntarily and insistently demand his share. Groups of communities and farms inhabited by colored folk should be voluntarily formed. In no case should there be any discrimination against white and blacks. But, at the same time, colored people should come forward, should organize and conduct enterprises, and their only insistence should be that the same provisions be made for the success of their enterprise that is being made for the success of any other enterprise. It must be remembered that in the last quarter of a century, the advance of the colored people has been mainly in the lines where they themselves working by and for themselves, have accomplished the greatest advance.

There is no doubt that numbers of white people, perhaps the majority of Americans, stand ready to take the most distinct advantage of voluntary segregation and cooperation among colored people. Just as soon as they get a group of black folk segregated, they use it as a point of attack and discrimination. Our counter attack should be, therefore, against this discrimination; against the refusal of the South to spend the same amount of money on the black child as on the white child for its education; against the inability of black groups to use public capital; against the monopoly of credit by white groups. But never in the world should our fight be against association with ourselves because by that very token we give up the whole argument that we are worth associating with.

Doubtless, and in the long run, the greatest human development is going to take place under experiences of widest individual contact. Nevertheless, today such individual contact is made difficult and almost impossible by petty prejudice, deliberate and almost criminal propaganda and various survivals from prehistoric heathenism. It is impossible, therefore, to wait for the millennium of free and normal intercourse before we unite, to cooperate among themselves in groups of like-minded people and in groups of people suffering from the same disadvantages and the same hatreds.

It is the class-conscious working man uniting together who will eventually emancipate labor throughout the world. It is the race-conscious black man cooperating together in his own institutions and movements who will eventually emancipate the colored race, and the great step ahead today is for the American Negro to accomplish his economic emancipation through voluntary determined cooperative effort.

II

Many persons have interpreted my reassertion of our current attitude toward segregation as a counsel of despair. We can't win, therefore, give up and accept the inevitable. Never, and nonsense. Our business in this world is to fight and fight again, and never to yield. But after all, one must fight with his brains, if he has any. He gathers strength to fight. He gathers knowledge, and he raises children who are proud to fight and who know what they are fighting about. And above all, they learn that what they are fighting for is the opportunity and the chance to know and associate with black folk. They are not fighting to escape themselves. They are fighting to say to the world: the opportunity of knowing Negroes is worth so much to us and is so appreciated, that we want you to know them too.

Negroes are not extraordinary human beings. They are just like other human beings, with all their foibles and ignorance and mistakes. But they are human beings, and human nature is always worth knowing, and withal, splendid in its manifestations. Therefore, we are fighting to keep open the avenues of human contact; but in the meantime, we are taking every advantage of what opportunities of contact are already open to us, and among those opportunities which are open, and which are splendid and inspiring, is the opportunity of Negroes to work together in the twentieth century for the uplift and development of the Negro race. It is no counsel of despair to emphasize and hail the opportunity for such work.

Faulty Assumptions

The assumptions of the anti-segregation campaign have been all wrong. This is not our fault, but it is our misfortune. When I went to Atlanta University to teach in 1897, and to study the Negro problem, I said, confidently, that the basic problem is our racial ignorance and lack of culture. That once Negroes know civilization, and whites know Negroes, then the problem is solved. This proposition is still true, but the solution is much further away than my youth dreamed. Negroes are still ignorant, but the disconcerting thing is that white people on the whole are just as much opposed to Negroes of education and culture, as to any other kind, and perhaps more so. Not all whites, to be sure, but the overwhelming majority.

Our main method, then, falls flat. We stop training ability. We lose our manners. We swallow our pride, and beg for things. We agitate and get angry. And with all that, we face the blank fact: Negroes are not wanted; neither as scholars nor as business men; neither as clerks nor as artisans; neither as artists nor as writers. What can we do about it? We cannot use force. We cannot enforce law, even if we get it on the statute books. So long as overwhelming public opinion sanctions and justifies and defends color segregation, we are helpless, and without remedy. We are segregated. We are cast back upon ourselves, to an Island Within; "To your tents Oh Israel!"

Surely then, in this period of frustration and disappointment, we must turn from negation to affirmation, from the ever-lasting "No" to the ever-lasting "Yes." Instead of sitting, sapped of all initiative and independence; instead of drowning our originality in imitation of mediocre white folks; instead of being afraid of ourselves and cultivating the art of skulking to escape the Color Line; we have got to renounce a program that always involves humiliating self-stultifying scrambling to crawl somewhere where we are not wanted; where we crouch panting like a whipped dog. We have got to stop this and learn that on such a program they cannot build manhood. No, by God, stand erect in a mud-puddle and tell the white world to go to hell, rather than lick boots in a parlor.

Affirm, as you have a right to affirm, that the Negro race is one of the great human races, inferior to none in its accomplishment and in its ability. Different, it is true, and for most of the difference, let us reverently thank God. And this race, with its vantage grounds in modern days, can go forward of its own will, of its own power, and its own initiative. It is led by twelve million American Negroes of average modern intelligence, three or four million educated African Negroes are their full equals, and several million Negroes in the West Indies and South America. This body of at least twenty-five million modern men are not called upon to commit suicide because somebody doesn't like their complexion or their hair. It is their opportunity and their day to stand up and make themselves heard and felt in the modern world.

The 15th Street Presbyterian Church

In a May 1934 Crisis *piece responding to criticism by Francis J. Grimké, W.E.B. Du Bois cites Grimké's successful leadership of the black 15th Street Presbyterian Church to support his own argument that blacks should build and develop their own segregated institutions in order to ultimately discredit segregation.*

Why, in an argument on segregation, has Dr. Grimke said *nothing* of the 15th Street Presbyterian Church? This church is a result of segregation. It was founded because white Presbyterians could not listen to a pastor of Dr. Grimke's learning and character and would not sit in the same pews with the distinguished people who belonged to this church. There is no use trying to salve our logic by saying that this church represents "voluntary" segregation. It represents compulsion and compulsion of the most despicable sort. Not the compulsion of sticks and stone and fists but that withdrawal of skirts and "brotherly" advice, and unbending and unending pressure that would make an upright human being worship in Hell rather than try to be a member of a white Presbyterian Church. And yet, the separation of this class of colored people from white people was ridiculous. And what proves it is ridiculous, is the success, the outstanding success of this church. And it is only by making our segregated institutions successful and conspicuously successful, that we are going to get into our hands a weapon which in the long run is bound to kill and discredit segregation if human reason lasts. And this is the point, and the only point, where I differ with Dr. Grimke.

Indeed, there is nothing else we can do. If you have passed your resolution, "No segregation, Never and Nowhere," what are you going to do about it? Let me tell you what you are going to do. You are going back to continue to make your living in a Jim-

Crow school; you are going to dwell in a segregated section of the city; you are going to pastor a Jim-Crow Church; you are going to occupy political office because of Jim-Crow political organizations that stand back of you and force you into office. All these things and a thousand others you are going to do because you have got to.

If you are going to do this, why not say so? What are you afraid of? Do you believe in the Negro race or do you not? If you do not, naturally, you are justified in keeping still. But if you do believe in the extraordinary accomplishment of the Negro church and the Negro college, the Negro school and the Negro newspaper, then say so and say so plainly, not only for the sake of those who have given their lives to make these things worthwhile, but for those young people whom you are teaching, by that negative attitude, that there is nothing that they can do, nobody that they can emulate, and no field worthwhile working in. Think of what Negro art and literature has yet to accomplish if it can only be free and untrammeled by the necessity of pleasing white folks! Think of the splendid moral appeal that you can make to a million children tomorrow, if once you can get them to see the possibilities of the American Negro today and now, whether he is segregated or not, or in spite of all possible segregation.

"Segregation is to be fought . . . now and always."

All Segregation Harms African Americans

Francis J. Grimké (1850–1937)

Francis J. Grimké, born a slave and educated at Lincoln University and Princeton Theological Seminary, was the pastor at the 15th Street Presbyterian Church in Washington, D.C., for many years. A noted defender of the civil rights of blacks, he was one of several African-American leaders who contributed rebuttals to W.E.B. Du Bois's 1934 editorials in the *Crisis*, the journal of the National Association for the Advancement of Colored People (NAACP), in which Du Bois had questioned whether blacks should automatically be opposed to racial segregation. In the following viewpoint, which was first published in the June 1934 issue of the *Crisis*, Grimké argues that segregation is fundamentally immoral and degrading to whites and blacks and should be steadfastly fought.

Why Dr. DuBois has reopened the question of segregation in THE CRISIS I am at a loss to know. Can it be possible that in the remotest part of his brain he is beginning to think, after all, that it is a condition that ought to be accepted, a condition that we ought to stop fussing about? If so, then his leadership among us is at an end; we can follow no such leader. That is what I wrote after reading Dr. DuBois' initial article in THE CRISIS.

If we have any doubt, if we are not quite clear in our own minds in regard to it, it is well to reopen it. But if we are already

From Francis J. Grimké, "Segregation," *The Crisis*, June 1934. Reprinted with permission.

convinced that we are right, why reopen it? Do we need to be more thoroughly convinced, more firmly persuaded than we are that we are right? Or, will the reopening of it help to convince the white man that he is wrong? If so, well.

Segregation a Badge of Inferiority

Underlying the idea of race segregation is that of inferiority. It is always a badge of inferiority, and is so intended by those who impose it. It is one way of expressing contempt for the segregated, on the part of those who impose the segregation. In sheer self-respect, therefore, on the part of the segregated, it should be resented. It may be necessary for a time to endure it, but it should never be accepted as a finality.

Segregation produces a condition that is not conducive to the best interest of either race. It tends to build up a false or artificial sense of superiority in the one, and is sure to create or engender in the other, feelings of resentment, of hatred, of discontent, out of which no good can come to either, but will continue to be a source of friction, of irritation.

No race, with any self-respect, can accept the status of a segregated group for itself. To do so is virtually to admit its inferiority, to be content to have limits placed upon its possibilities by another race. The whole thing is wrong, wrong in principle, wrong in spirit. It violates every principle of right and is contrary to the spirit of Jesus Christ and to the noble ideal of brotherhood.

No race has a right to force upon another race the status of inferiority. And no race, however humble, however far behind in the process of development, should accept from another race such a status as its right and proper place in the Divine order of things. No limits can be placed upon the progress of a race except that which it places upon itself. Segregation is to be fought, therefore, now and always. One of the great evils of segregation is, that when a race has been segregated, when people have been taught to look down upon its members as inferiors, they are thus exposed to all kinds of brutality, to all kinds of injustice and oppression. The feeling is, they are inferior, and are not entitled therefore to the treatment that would be proper to accord to those of a superior brand. It is this sense of the inborn inferiority of the Negro, so deeply ingrained in the Southern white man, especially of the lower classes, that is responsible for much of the brutality that is manifested towards him in the South. The feeling is, "He is only a nigger." And being only a nigger anything is good enough for him, nothing is too mean or contemptible to visit upon him. This fact is very forcibly brought out in "The Tragedy of Lynching," by Arthur Raper.

Page 13, we read: "Do you think I am going to risk my life protecting a nigger?" said a county sheriff.

Page 19: "Most apologists for lynching, like the lynchers themselves, seem to assume that the Negro is irredeemably inferior by reason of his race—that it is a plan of God that the Negro and his children shall forever be 'hewers of wood and drawers of water.' With this weighty emphasis upon the essential racial inferiority of the Negro, it is not surprising to find the mass of whites ready to justify any and all means to 'keep the Negro in his place.'"

Page 22: "The most fundamental way in which the church is related to mob violence is that, not infrequently, the local church leaves unchallenged the general assumption that the Negro is in-

---

Blacks Must Oppose Arbitrary Segregation

Walter White, executive secretary of the NAACP from 1931 until his death in 1955, argues against segregation in this excerpt from a May 1934 article in the Crisis.

To accept the status of separateness, which almost invariably in the case of the submerged, exploited and marginal groups means inferior accommodations and a distinctly inferior position in the national and communal life, means spiritual atrophy for the group segregated. When Negroes, Jews, Catholics or Nordic white Americans voluntarily choose to live or attend church or engage in social activity together, that is their affair and no one else's. But Negroes and all other groups must without compromise and without cessation oppose in every possible fashion any attempt to impose from without the establishment of pales and ghettoes. Arbitrary segregation of this sort means almost without exception that less money will be expended for adequate sewerage, water, police and fire protection and for the building of a healthful community. It is because of this that the N.A.A.C.P. has resolutely fought such segregation, as in the case of city ordinances and state laws in the Louisville, New Orleans and Richmond segregation cases; has opposed restrictive covenants written into deeds of property, and all other forms, legal and illegal, to restrict the areas in which Negroes may buy or rent and occupy property.

This principle is especially vital where attempts are made to establish separate areas which are financed by moneys from the federal or state governments for which black people are taxed at the same rate as white. No self-respecting Negro can afford to accept without vigorous protest any such attempt to put the stamp of federal approval upon discrimination of this character. Though separate schools do exist in the South and though for the time being little can be done towards ending the expensive and wasteful dual educational system based upon caste and color prejudice, yet no Negro who respects himself and his race can accept these segregated systems without at least inward protest.

---

nately inferior and of little importance. Upon this assumption ultimately rests the justification of lynching."

The Negro, therefore, for his own sake, as well as for the sake of the white man, must resent segregation. It exposes him to all kinds of brutality, and develops in the white man, more and more, the traits of the brute. Segregation is bad for the black man. It is bad for the white man. There must be no let up therefore in the steady protest against it. As I said before, it may be necessary for a time to endure it, but never should it be accepted as a finality. Mr. Monroe Trotter is right, in publishing week after week in the [*Boston*] *Guardian*, in large letters, the ringing words "Segregation for Colored is the Real, Permanent, Damning Degradation in the U.S.A." And the thought must not be allowed to drop out of the consciousness of the race, must not be allowed to be forgotten or minimized by it. If we are content to be a segregated group, our self-respect is sadly in need of repairs. The consciousness of the fact that we are men, created in the image of God, with all the possibilities open to us that are open to other race groups, needs to be quickened, to be stimulated afresh and kept vigorously alive.

A Shameful Spectacle

The attempt of one race to put the stamp of inferiority upon another is the most shameful spectacle of which I can conceive: and is evidence, not of superiority, of which the white man is so prone to boast, but of inferiority, and inferiority of the most contemptible kind. To seek to destroy the self-respect of a race, and to beget in others contempt for it, is as despicable a thing as poor, fallen human nature is capable of. The test of true nobility, of real greatness of soul is not to be found in that kind of conduct. And the white man will one day, let us hope, come to see the heinousness of it, and repent, and show himself to be a *man*,—a *true* man, in the highest and best sense of the term.

CHAPTER 6

The Civil Rights Revolution and Beyond

Chapter Preface

Since World War II, African Americans have witnessed enormous changes in their country and their role in American society. They have made significant gains in both participation and recognized achievement in government, business, the military, entertainment, sports, and other fields. Migration has continued to transform the black population from one concentrated in the rural South to one distributed throughout the nation. The population of African Americans grew from approximately 13 million in 1940 (9.8 percent of the total U.S. population) to almost 30 million in 1990 (12 percent of the U.S. population).

The civil rights movement was perhaps the most important development in African-American history of the past half century. Many historians mark its beginnings in 1954, when the Supreme Court in *Brown v. Board of Education* reversed a decades-old legal precedent by banning "separate but equal" racially segregated schools. Over the next decade African Americans, led by Martin Luther King Jr., Fannie Lou Hamer, and others, engaged in a campaign of nonviolent demonstrations protesting their second-class citizenship status. Their efforts succeeded in removing most visible signs of discrimination, including legalized segregation, disfranchisement, and lynching. Laws ensuring blacks' right to vote enlarged their participation in the American political process, while laws against discrimination in employment and housing helped pave the way for millions of blacks to enter the middle class.

However, victories in achieving legal and political equality did not ensure social or economic equality. African Americans as a group have remained poorer than whites, and many have continued to feel alienated from American society. Numerous people—white and black—have questioned whether the civil rights movement, for all its triumphs, has lived up to its promise for African Americans. The following viewpoints provide some differing perspectives on the civil rights movement and on one of the movement's controversial legacies—affirmative action.

Viewpoint 1

"America is essentially a dream, a dream as yet unfulfilled. It is a dream of a land where men of all races . . . can live together as brothers."

Blacks Should Strive to Be Part of the American Dream

Martin Luther King Jr. (1929–1968)

In December 1955 African-American residents of Montgomery, Alabama, launched a boycott of the city's buses in response to racial segregation and mistreatment of blacks. A young Baptist minister was tapped to lead the movement. The boycott, which lasted over a year and resulted in the integration of the bus service, is viewed by many today as the opening chapter of the civil rights movement. The minister—Martin Luther King Jr.—found himself a national figure renowned for his eloquence, for his courage in facing threats of violence, and for his idea that nonviolent resistance was the way for black Americans to attain equality in the United States.

King was not directly involved in the next significant passages of the burgeoning civil rights movement. In 1960 black college students in the South initiated "sit-in" demonstrations to desegregate lunch counters, libraries, and other public facilities. In 1961 the Congress of Racial Equality (CORE) sponsored "Freedom Rides" in which interracial groups traveled on previously segregated interstate buses. Both the students and the Freedom Riders embraced King's philosophy of nonviolence and gained national attention for their willingness to be beaten and arrested. In the minds of many Americans, King remained the personification of the civil rights movement—an impression strengthened by his "I

Have a Dream" speech at the 1963 March on Washington and his receiving the 1964 Nobel Peace Prize. His assassination in 1968 shocked and saddened the nation.

The following viewpoint is excerpted from a commencement address King gave on June 6, 1961, at Lincoln University, a historically black college in Pennsylvania. It provides a good summation of King's views regarding the place of African Americans in U.S. history, the necessity for nonviolence, and the progress of the civil rights movement. It is essential, he argues, for both blacks and whites to embrace the American dream of equality and brotherhood and to reject both white and black supremacy.

Today you bid farewell to the friendly security of this academic environment, a setting that will remain dear to you as long as the cords of memory shall lengthen. As you go out today to enter the clamorous highways of life, I should like to discuss with you some aspects of the American dream. For in a real sense, America is essentially a dream, a dream as yet unfulfilled. It is a dream of a land where men of all races, of all nationalities and of all creeds can live together as brothers. The substance of the dream is expressed in these sublime words, words lifted to cosmic proportions: "We hold these truths to be self-evident, that all men are created equal, that they are endowed by their Creator with certain unalienable rights, that among these are life, liberty, and the pursuit of happiness." This is the dream.

One of the first things we notice in this dream is an amazing universalism. It does not say some men, but it says all men. It does not say all white men, but it says all men, which includes black men. It does not say all Gentiles, but it says all men, which includes Jews. It does not say all Protestants, but it says all men, which includes Catholics.

And there is another thing we see in this dream that ultimately distinguishes democracy and our form of government from all of the totalitarian regimes that emerge in history. It says that each individual has certain basic rights that are neither conferred by nor derived from the state. To discover where they came from it is necessary to move back behind the dim mist of eternity, for they are God-given. Very seldom if ever in the history of the world has a sociopolitical document expressed in such profoundly eloquent and unequivocal language the dignity and the worth of human personality. The American dream reminds us that every man is heir to the legacy of worthiness.

Ever since the Founding Fathers of our nation dreamed this noble dream, America has been something of a schizophrenic personality, tragically divided against herself. On the one hand we have proudly professed the principles of democracy, and on the other hand we have sadly practiced the very antithesis of those principles. Indeed slavery and segregation have been strange paradoxes in a nation founded on the principle that all men are created equal. This is what the Swedish sociologist, Gunnar Myrdal, referred to as the American dilemma.

But the shape of the world today does not permit us the luxury of an anemic democracy. The price America must pay for the continued exploitation of the Negro and other minority groups is the price of its own destruction. The hour is late; the clock of destiny is ticking out. It is trite, but urgently true, that if America is to remain a first-class nation she can no longer have second-class citizens. Now, more than ever before, America is challenged to bring her noble dream into reality, and those who are working to implement the American dream are the true saviors of democracy.

Now may I suggest some of the things we must do if we are to make the American dream a reality. First I think all of us must develop a world perspective if we are to survive. The American dream will not become a reality devoid of the larger dream of a world of brotherhood and peace and good will. The world in which we live is a world of geographical oneness and we are challenged now to make it spiritually one.

Man's scientific genius and technological ingenuity has dwarfed distance and placed time in chains. Jet planes have compressed into minutes distances that once took days and months to cover. It is not common for a preacher to be quoting Bob Hope, but I think he has aptly described this jet age in which we live. If, on taking off on a nonstop flight from Los Angeles to New York City, you develop hiccups, he said, you will hic in Los Angeles and cup in New York City. That is really *moving*. If you take a flight from Tokyo, Japan, on Sunday morning, you will arrive in Seattle, Washington, on the preceding Saturday night. When your friends meet you at the airport and ask you when you left Tokyo, you will have to say, "I left tomorrow." This is the kind of world in which we live. Now this is a bit humorous but I am trying to laugh a basic fact into all of us: the world in which we live has become a single neighborhood.

Through our scientific genius we have made of this world a neighborhood; now through our moral and spiritual development we must make of it a brotherhood. In a real sense, we must all learn to live together as brothers, or we will all perish together as fools. We must come to see that no individual can live alone; no nation can live alone. We must all live together; we must all be

230

concerned about each other. . . .

We are caught in an inescapable network of mutuality; tied in a single garment of destiny. Whatever affects one directly, affects all indirectly. As long as there is poverty in this world, no man can be totally rich even if he has a billion dollars. As long as diseases are rampant and millions of people cannot expect to live more than twenty or thirty years, no man can be totally healthy, even if he just got a clean bill of health from the finest clinic in America. Strangely enough, I can never be what I ought to be until you are what you ought to be. You can never be what you ought to be until I am what I ought to be. This is the way the world is made. I didn't make it that way, but this is the interrelated structure of reality. John Donne caught it a few centuries ago and could cry out, "No man is an island entire of itself; every man is a piece of the continent, a part of the main . . . any man's death diminishes me, because I am involved in mankind, and therefore never send to know for whom the bell tolls; it tolls for thee." If we are to realize the American dream we must cultivate this world perspective.

There is another thing quite closely related to this. We must keep our moral and spiritual progress abreast with our scientific and technological advances. This poses another dilemma of modern man. We have allowed our civilization to outdistance our culture. Professor MacIver follows the German sociologist, Alfred Weber, in pointing out the distinction between culture and civilization. Civilization refers to what we use; culture refers to what we are. Civilization is that complex of devices, instrumentalities, mechanisms and techniques by means of which we live. Culture is that realm of ends expressed in art, literature, religion and morals for which at best we live.

The great problem confronting us today is that we have allowed the means by which we live to outdistance the ends for which we live. We have allowed our civilization to outrun our culture, and so we are in danger now of ending up with guided missiles in the hands of misguided men. This is what the poet [Henry David] Thoreau meant when he said, "Improved means to an unimproved end." If we are to survive today and realize the dream of our mission and the dream of the world, we must bridge the gulf and somehow keep the means by which we live abreast with the ends for which we live.

No Inferior Races

Another thing we must do is to get rid of the notion once and for all that there are superior and inferior races. Now we know that this view still lags around in spite of the fact that many great anthropologists, Margaret Mead and Ruth Benedict and Melville Herskovits and others have pointed out and made it clear through scientific evidence that there are no superior races and there are no inferior races. There may be intellectually superior individuals within all races. In spite of all this evidence, however, the view still gets around somehow that there are superior and inferior races. The whole concept of white supremacy rests on this fallacy.

We Believe in the American Dream

The Birmingham Manifesto, written by local civil rights leaders Fred L. Shuttlesworth and N.L. Smith, was issued to the public on April 3, 1963, at the start of a massive campaign of nonviolent protests in Birmingham, Alabama. Birmingham police shocked the nation in May by using police dogs and fire hoses against the marchers. Birmingham reappeared in the news in September 1963 when a bomb planted in a church killed four black children.

The patience of an oppressed people cannot endure forever. The Negro citizens of Birmingham for the last several years have hoped in vain for some evidence of good faith resolution of our just grievances.

Birmingham is part of the United States and we are *bona fide* citizens. Yet the history of Birmingham reveals that very little of the democratic process touches the life of the Negro in Birmingham. We have been segregated racially, exploited economically, and dominated politically. Under the leadership of the Alabama Christian Movement for Human Rights, we sought relief by petition for repeal of city ordinances requiring segregation and the institution of a merit hiring policy in city employment. We were rebuffed. We then turned to the system of the courts. We weathered set-back after set-back. . . .

We have always been a peaceful people, bearing our oppression with super-human effort. Yet we have been the victims of repeated violence, not only that inflicted by the hoodlum element but also that inflicted by the blatant misuse of police power. . . .

We believe in the American Dream of democracy, in the Jeffersonian doctrine that "all men are created equal and are endowed by their Creator with certain inalienable rights, among these being life, liberty and the pursuit of happiness.". . .

We act today in full concert with our Hebraic-Christian tradition, the law of morality and the Constitution of our nation. The absence of justice and progress in Birmingham demands that we make a moral witness to give our community a chance to survive. We demonstrate our faith that we believe that The Beloved Community can come to Birmingham.

You know, there was a time when some people used to argue the inferiority of the Negro and the colored races generally on the basis of the Bible and religion. They would say the Negro was inferior by nature because of Noah's curse upon the children of Ham. And then another brother had probably read the logic of Aristotle. You know Aristotle brought into being the syllogism which had a major premise and a minor premise and a conclusion, and one brother had probably read Aristotle and he put his argument in the framework of an Aristotelian syllogism. He could say that all men are made in the image of God. This was a major premise. Then came his minor premise: God, as everybody knows, is not a Negro; therefore the Negro is not a man. And that was called logic!

But we don't often hear these arguments today. Segregation is now based on "sociological and cultural" grounds. "The Negro is not culturally ready for integration, and if integration comes into being it will pull the white race back a generation. It will take fifty or seventy-five years to raise these standards." And then we hear that the Negro is a criminal, and there are those who would almost say he is a criminal by nature. But they never point out that these things are environmental and not racial; these problems are problems of urban dislocation. They fail to see that poverty, and disease, and ignorance breed crime whatever the racial group may be. And it is a tortuous logic that views the tragic results of segregation and discrimination as an argument for the continuation of it.

If we are to implement the American dream we must get rid of the notion once and for all that there are superior and inferior races. This means that members of minority groups must make it clear that they can use their resources even under adverse circumstances. We must make full and constructive use of the freedom we already possess. We must not use our oppression as an excuse for mediocrity and laziness. For history has proven that inner determination can often break through the outer shackles of circumstance. Take the Jews, for example, and the years they have been forced to walk through the long and desolate night of oppression. This did not keep them from rising up to plunge against cloud-filled nights of oppression, new and blazing stars of inspiration. Being a Jew did not keep Einstein from using his genius-packed mind to prove his theory of relativity.

Individual Achievements

And so, being a Negro does not have to keep any individual from rising up to make a contribution as so many Negroes have done within our own lifetime. Human nature cannot be catalogued, and we need not wait until the day of full emancipation. So from an old clay cabin in Virginia's hills, Booker T. Washington rose up to be one of the nation's great leaders. He lit a torch in Alabama; then darkness fled.

From the red hills of Gordon County, Georgia, from an iron foundry at Chattanooga, Tennessee, from the arms of a mother who could neither read nor write, Roland Hayes rose up to be one of the nation's and the world's greatest singers. He carried his melodious voice to the mansion of the Queen Mother of Spain and the palace of King George V. From the poverty-stricken areas of Philadelphia, Pennsylvania, Marian Anderson rose up to be the world's greatest contralto, so that Toscanini could say that a voice like this comes only once in a century. Sibelius of Finland could say, "My roof is too low for such a voice."

From humble, crippling circumstances, George Washington Carver rose up and carved for himself an imperishable niche in the annals of science. There was a star in the sky of female leadership. Then came Mary McLeod Bethune to let it shine in her life. There was a star in the diplomatic sky. Then came Ralph Bunche, the grandson of a slave preacher, and allowed it to shine in his life with all of its radiant beauty. There were stars in the athletic sky. Then came Joe Louis with his educated fists, Jesse Owens with his fleet and dashing feet, Jackie Robinson with his powerful bat and calm spirit. All of these people have come to remind us that we need not wait until the day of full emancipation. . . .

Creative Protest

Finally, if we are to implement the American dream, we must continue to engage in creative protest in order to break down all of those barriers that make it impossible for the dream to be realized. Now I know there are those people who will argue that we must wait on something. They fail to see the necessity for creative protest, but I say to you that I can see no way to break loose from an old order and to move into a new order without standing up and resisting the unjust dogma of the old order.

To do this, we must get rid of two strange illusions that have been held by the so-called moderates in race relations. First is the myth of time advanced by those who say that you must wait on time; if you "just wait and be patient," time will work the situation out. They will say this even about freedom rides. They will say this about sit-ins: that you're pushing things too fast—cool off—time will work these problems out. Well, evolution may hold in the biological realm, and in that area Darwin was right. But when a Herbert Spencer [nineteenth-century philosopher and formulator of "Social Darwinism"] seeks to apply "evolution" to the whole fabric of society, there is no truth in it. Even a superficial look at history shows that social progress never rolls in on the wheels of inevitability. It comes through the tireless effort and the persistent work of dedicated individuals. Without this hard work, time itself becomes an ally of the primitive forces of irrational emotionalism and social stagnation. And we must get rid of the myth of time.

Education and Legislation

There is another myth, that bases itself on a species of educational determinism. It leads one to think that you can't solve this problem through legislation; you can't solve this problem through judicial decree; you can't solve this problem through executive orders on the part of the president of the United States. It must be solved by education. Now I agree that education plays a great role, and it must continue to play a great role in changing attitudes, in getting people ready for the new order. And we must also see the importance of legislation.

It is not a question either of education or of legislation. Both legislation and education are required. Now, people will say, "You can't legislate morals." Well, that may be true. Even though morality may not be legislated, behavior can be regulated. And this is very important. We need religion and education to change attitudes and to change the hearts of men. We need legislation and federal action to control behavior. It may be true that the law can't make a man love me, but it can keep him from lynching me, and I think that's pretty important also.

And so we must get rid of these illusions and move on with determination and with zeal to break down the unjust systems we find in our society, so that it will be possible to realize the American dream. As I have said so often, if we seek to break down discrimination, we must use the proper methods. I am convinced more than ever before that, as the powerful, creative way opens, men and women who are eager to break the barriers of oppression and of segregation and discrimination need not fall down to the levels of violence. They need not sink into the quicksands of hatred. Standing on the high ground of noninjury, love and soul force, they can turn this nation upside down and right side up.

Nonviolent Resistance

I believe, more than ever before, in the power of nonviolent resistance. It has a moral aspect tied to it. It makes it possible for the individual to secure moral ends through moral means. This has been one of the great debates of history. People have felt that it is impossible to achieve moral ends through moral means. And so a Machiavelli could come into being and so force a sort of duality within the moral structure of the universe. Even communism could come into being and say that anything justifies the end of a classless society—lying, deceit, hate, violence—anything. And this is where nonviolent resistance breaks with communism and with all of those systems which argue that the end justifies the means, because we realize that the end is preexistent in the means. In the long run of history, destructive means cannot bring about constructive ends.

The practical aspect of nonviolent resistance is that it exposes the moral defenses of the opponent. Not only that, it somehow arouses his conscience at the same time, and it breaks down his morale. He has no answer for it. If he puts you in jail, that's all right; if he lets you out, that's all right too. If he beats you, you accept that; if he doesn't beat you—fine. And so you go on, leaving him with no answer. But if you use violence, he does have an answer. He has the state militia; he has police brutality.

Nonviolent resistance is one of the most magnificent expressions going on today. We see it in the movement taking place among students in the South and their allies who have been willing to come in from the North and other sections. They have taken our deep groans and passionate yearnings, filtered them in their own souls, and fashioned them into the creative protest, which is an epic known all over our nation. They have moved in a uniquely meaningful orbit, imparting light and heat to a distant satellite. And people say, "Does this bring results?" Well, look at the record.

In less than a year, lunch counters have been integrated in more than 142 cities of the Deep South, and this was done without a single court suit; it was done without spending millions and millions of dollars. We think of the freedom rides, and remember that more than sixty people are now in jail in Jackson, Mississippi. What has this done? These people have been beaten; they have suffered to bring to the attention of this nation, the indignities and injustices Negro people still confront in interstate travel. It has, therefore, had an educational value. But not only that—signs have come down from bus stations in Montgomery, Alabama. They've never been down before. Not only that—the attorney general of this nation has called on ICC [Interstate Commerce Commission] to issue new regulations making it positively clear that segregation in interstate travel is illegal and unconstitutional.

And so this method can bring results. Sometimes it can bring quick results. But even when it doesn't bring immediate results, it is constantly working on the conscience; it is at all times using moral means to bring about moral ends. And so I say we must continue on the way of creative protest. I believe also that this method will help us to enter the new age with the proper attitude.

As I have said in so many instances, it is not enough to struggle for the new society. We must make sure that we make the psychological adjustment required to live in that new society. This is true of white people, and it is true of Negro people. Psychological adjustment will save white people from going into the new age with old vestiges of prejudice and attitudes of white supremacy. It will save the Negro from seeking to substitute one tyranny for another.

Against Racial Separation

I know sometimes we get discouraged and sometimes disappointed with the slow pace of things. At times we begin to talk about racial separation instead of racial integration, feeling that there is no other way out. My only answer is that the problem never will be solved by substituting one tyranny for another. Black supremacy is as dangerous as white supremacy, and God is not interested merely in the freedom of black men and brown men and yellow men. God is interested in the freedom of the whole human race and in the creation of a society where all men can live together as brothers, where every man will respect the dignity and the worth of human personality.

By following this method, we may also be able to teach our world something that it so desperately needs at this hour. In a day when Sputniks and Explorers are dashing through outer space, and guided ballistic missiles are carving highways of death through the stratosphere, no nation can win a war. The choice is no longer between violence and nonviolence; it is either nonviolence or nonexistence. Unless we find some alternative to war, we will destroy ourselves by the misuse of our own instruments. And so, with all of these attitudes and principles working together, I believe we will be able to make a contribution as men of good will to the ongoing structure of our society and toward the realization of the American dream. And so, as you go out today, I call upon you not to be detached spectators, but involved participants, in this great drama that is taking place in our nation and around the world.

Every academic discipline has its technical nomenclature, and modern psychology has a word that is used, probably, more than any other. It is the word *maladjusted*. This word is the ringing cry of modern child psychology. Certainly all of us want to live a well-adjusted life in order to avoid the neurotic personality. But I say to you, there are certain things within our social order to which I am proud to be maladjusted and to which I call upon all men of good will to be maladjusted.

A Call to Be Maladjusted

If you will allow the preacher in me to come out now, let me say to you that I never did intend to adjust to the evils of segregation and discrimination. I never did intend to adjust myself to religious bigotry. I never did intend to adjust myself to economic conditions that will take necessities from the many to give luxuries to the few. I never did intend to adjust myself to the madness of militarism, and the self-defeating effects of physical violence. And I call upon all men of good will to be maladjusted because it may well be that the salvation of our world lies in the hands of the maladjusted.

So let us be maladjusted, as maladjusted as the prophet Amos, who in the midst of the injustices of his day could cry out in words that echo across the centuries, "Let justice run down like waters and righteousness like a mighty stream." Let us be as maladjusted as Abraham Lincoln, who had the vision to see that this nation could not exist half slave and half free. Let us be maladjusted as Jesus of Nazareth, who could look into the eyes of the men and women of his generation and cry out, "Love your enemies. Bless them that curse you. Pray for them that despitefully use you."

I believe that it is through such maladjustment that we will be able to emerge from the bleak and desolate midnight of man's inhumanity to man into the bright and glittering daybreak of freedom and justice. That will be the day when all of God's children, black men and white men, Jews and Gentiles, Catholics and Protestants, will be able to join hands and sing in the words of the old Negro spiritual, "Free at last! Free at last! Thank God almighty, we are free at last!"

VIEWPOINT 2

"Not only does America have a very serious problem, but our people have a very serious problem. America's problem is us."

Blacks Can Never Be Part of the American Dream

Malcolm X (1925–1965)

While the civil rights movement was gaining momentum and visibility in the 1950s and 1960s, not all blacks were united behind its tactics of nonviolent protest and its goals of racial integration. A noteworthy and controversial alternative vision of blacks in America was expressed in the black nationalist speeches and statements by Malcolm X.

Malcolm Little was born in Nebraska in 1925. A school dropout at fifteen, he was convicted and imprisoned for burglary in 1946. While in prison he became a follower of Elijah Muhammad, the leader of the Nation of Islam, a religious sect that combined Islamic teachings with black nationalist beliefs and whose members were commonly called Black Muslims. Malcolm adopted X—a symbol of his stolen identity as a descendant of slaves—as his surname. Upon his release from prison he became a minister of the Nation of Islam and quickly rose to become one of its leading speakers. His speeches, attacking whites as "evil," gained national attention.

The following viewpoint is excerpted from a speech Malcolm X gave at a public rally at King Solomon Baptist Church in Detroit on November 10, 1963, at the conclusion of the Northern Negro Grass Roots Leadership Conference. He argues that blacks are not and never will be Americans but are instead an oppressed population that shares the same white enemy as colonized African and Asian peoples. He further contends that blacks will not achieve a true revolution unless they use violence and that blacks should strive for racial separation and self-sufficiency rather than integration. Malcolm X specifically criticizes Martin Luther King Jr. and other established black civil rights leaders for not truly representing most black Americans and for cooperating with whites. He belittles civil rights movement activities such as the 1963 March on Washington, in which King and others led 200,000 people of different races in a peaceful demonstration calling for racial equality and civil rights.

Shortly after this speech Malcolm X broke with Elijah Muhammad and the Nation of Islam. Moving away from some of his separatist and antiwhite views, he founded the Muslim Mosque, Inc. and the secular Organization for African-American Unity. His ideas and example became a powerful influence on African-American thought following his assassination in February 1965.

We want to have just an off-the-cuff chat between you and me, us. We want to talk right down to earth in a language that everybody here can easily understand. We all agree tonight, all of the speakers have agreed, that America has a very serious problem. Not only does America have a very serious problem, but our people have a very serious problem. America's problem is us. We're her problem. The only reason she has a problem is she doesn't want us here. And every time you look at yourself, be you black, brown, red or yellow, a so-called Negro, you represent a person who poses such a serious problem for America because you're not wanted. Once you face this as a fact, then you can start plotting a course that will make you appear intelligent, instead of unintelligent.

What you and I need to do is learn to forget our differences. When we come together, we don't come together as Baptists or Methodists. You don't catch hell because you're a Baptist, and you don't catch hell because you're a Methodist. You don't catch hell because you're a Methodist or Baptist, you don't catch hell because you're a Democrat or a Republican, you don't catch hell because you're a Mason or an Elk, and you sure don't catch hell because you're an American; because if you were an American, you wouldn't catch hell. You catch hell because you're a black man. You catch hell, all of us catch hell, for the same reason.

So we're all black people, so-called Negroes, second-class citizens, ex-slaves. You're nothing but an ex-slave. You don't like to be told that. But what else are you? You are ex-slaves. You didn't come here on the "Mayflower." You came here on a slave ship. In chains, like a horse, or a cow, or a chicken. And you were brought here by the people who came here on the "Mayflower," you were brought here by the so-called Pilgrims, or Founding Fathers. They were the ones who brought you here.

A Common Enemy

We have a common enemy. We have this in common: We have a common oppressor, a common exploiter, and a common discriminator. But once we all realize that we have a common enemy, then we unite—on the basis of what we have in common. And what we have foremost in common is that enemy—the white man. He's an enemy to all of us. I know some of you all think that some of them aren't enemies. Time will tell.

In Bandung back in, I think, 1954, was the first unity meeting in centuries of black people. And once you study what happened at the Bandung conference, and the results of the Bandung conference, it actually serves as a model for the same procedure you and I can use to get our problems solved. At Bandung all the nations came together, the dark nations from Africa and Asia. Some of them were Buddhists, some of them were Muslims, some of them were Christians, some were Confucianists, some were atheists. Despite their religious differences, they came together. Some were communists, some were socialists, some were capitalists—despite their economic and political differences, they came together. All of them were black, brown, red or yellow.

The number-one thing that was not allowed to attend the Bandung conference was the white man. He couldn't come. Once they excluded the white man, they found that they could get together. Once they kept him out, everybody else fell right in and fell in line. This is the thing that you and I have to understand. And these people who came together didn't have nuclear weapons, they didn't have jet planes, they didn't have all of the heavy armaments that the white man has. But they had unity.

They were able to submerge their little petty differences and agree on one thing: That there one African came from Kenya and was being colonized by the Englishman, and another African came from the Congo and was being colonized by the Belgian, and another African came from Guinea and was being colonized by the French, and another came from Angola and was being colonized by the Portuguese. When they came to the Bandung conference, they looked at the Portuguese, and at the Frenchman, and at the Englishman, and at the Dutchman, and learned or realized the one thing that all of them had in common—they were all from Europe, they were all Europeans, blond, blue-eyed and white skins. They began to recognize who their enemy was. The same man that was colonizing our people in Kenya was colonizing our people in the Congo. The same one in the Congo was colonizing our people in South Africa, and in Southern Rhodesia, and in Burma, and in India, and in Afghanistan, and in Pakistan. They realized all over the world where the dark man was being oppressed, he was being oppressed by the white man; where the dark man was being exploited, he was being exploited by the white man. So they got together on this basis—that they had a common enemy.

And when you and I here in Detroit and in Michigan and in America who have been awakened today look around us, we too realize here in America we all have a common enemy, whether he's in Georgia or Michigan, whether he's in California or New York. He's the same man—blue eyes and blond hair and pale skin—the same man. So what we have to do is what they did. They agreed to stop quarreling among themselves. Any little spat that they had, they'd settle it among themselves, go into a huddle—don't let the enemy know that you've got a disagreement.

Instead of airing our differences in public, we have to realize we're all the same family. And when you have a family squabble, you don't get out on the sidewalk. If you do, everybody calls you uncouth, unrefined, uncivilized, savage. If you don't make it at home, you settle it at home; you get in the closet, argue it out behind closed doors, and then when you come out on the street, you pose a common front, a united front. And this is what we need to do in the community, and in the city, and in the state. We need to stop airing our differences in front of the white man, put the white man out of our meetings, and then sit down and talk shop with each other. That's what we've got to do.

The Black Revolution

I would like to make a few comments concerning the difference between the black revolution and the Negro revolution. Are they both the same? And if they're not, what is the difference? What is the difference between a black revolution and a Negro revolution? First, what is a revolution? Sometimes I'm inclined to believe that many of our people are using this word "revolution" loosely, without taking careful consideration of what this word actually means, and what its historic characteristics are. When you study the historic nature of revolutions, the motive of a revolution, the objective of a revolution, the result of a revolution, and the methods used in a revolution, you may change words. You may devise another program, you may change your goal and you may change your mind.

Look at the American Revolution in 1776. That revolution was for what? For land. Why did they want land? Independence. How was it carried out? Bloodshed. Number one, it was based on land, the basis of independence. And the only way they could get it was bloodshed. The French Revolution—what was it based on? The landless against the landlord. What was it for? Land. How did they get it? Bloodshed. Was no love lost, was no compromise, was no negotiation. I'm telling you—you don't know what a revolution is. Because when you find out what it is, you'll get back in the alley, you'll get out of the way.

Following the March on Washington on August 28, 1963, President John F. Kennedy meets with the leaders of the march. From left to right are: Whitney Young, Martin Luther King Jr., John Lewis, Rabbi Joachim Prinz, Eugene C. Blake, A. Philip Randolph, Kennedy, Walter Reuther, Vice President Lyndon B. Johnson, and Roy Wilkins. Young, King, Lewis, Randolph, and Wilkins are five of the "Big Six" civil rights leaders who were criticized by Malcolm X for being too cooperative with the president and other whites (the sixth being James Farmer).

The Russian Revolution—what was it based on? Land; the landless against the landlord. How did they bring it about? Bloodshed. You haven't got a revolution that doesn't involve bloodshed. And you're afraid to bleed. I said, you're afraid to bleed.

As long as the white man sent you to Korea, you bled. He sent you to Germany, you bled. He sent you to the South Pacific to fight the Japanese, you bled. You bleed for white people, but when it comes to seeing your own churches being bombed and little black girls murdered, you haven't got any blood. You bleed when the white man says bleed; you bite when the white man says bite; and you bark when the white man says bark. I hate to say this about us, but it's true. How are you going to be nonviolent in Mississippi, as violent as you were in Korea? How can you justify being nonviolent in Mississippi and Alabama, when your churches are being bombed, and your little girls are being murdered, and at the same time you are going to get violent with Hitler, and Tojo, and somebody else you don't even know?

If violence is wrong in America, violence is wrong abroad. If it is wrong to be violent defending black women and black children and black babies and black men, then it is wrong for America to draft us and make us violent abroad in defense of her. And if it is right for America to draft us, and teach us how to be violent in defense of her, then it is right for you and me to do whatever is necessary to defend our own people right here in this country.

The Chinese Revolution—they wanted land. They threw the British out, along with the Uncle Tom Chinese. Yes, they did. They set a good example. When I was in prison, I read an article—don't be shocked when I say that I was in prison. You're still in prison. That's what America means: prison. When I was in prison, I read an article in *Life* magazine showing a little Chinese girl, nine years old; her father was on his hands and knees and she was pulling the trigger because he was an Uncle Tom Chinaman. When they had the revolution over there, they took a whole generation of Uncle Toms and just wiped them out. And within ten years that little girl became a full-grown woman. No more Toms in China. And today it's one of the toughest, roughest, most feared countries on this earth—by the white man. Because there are no Uncle Toms over there.

Of all our studies, history is best qualified to reward our research. And when you see that you've got problems, all you have to do is examine the historic method used all over the world by others who have problems similar to yours. Once you see how they got theirs straight, then you know how you can get yours straight. There's been a revolution, a black revolution, going on in Africa. In Kenya, the Mau Mau were revolutionary; they were the ones who brought the word "Uhuru" to the fore. The Mau Mau, they were revolutionary, they believed in scorched earth, they knocked everything aside that got in their way, and their revolution also was based on land, a desire for land. In Algeria, the northern part of Africa, a revolution took place. The Algerians were revolutionists, they wanted land. France offered to let them be integrated into France. They told France, to hell with France, they wanted some land, not some France. And they engaged in a bloody battle.

Nonviolence Is No Revolution

So I cite these various revolutions, brothers and sisters, to show you that you don't have a peaceful revolution. You don't have a turn-the-other-cheek revolution. There's no such thing as a nonviolent revolution. The only kind of revolution that is nonviolent is the Negro revolution. The only revolution in which the goal is loving your enemy is the Negro revolution. It's the only revolution in which the goal is a desegregated lunch counter, a desegregated theater, a desegregated park, and a desegregated public toilet; you can sit down next to white folks—on the toilet. That's no revolution. Revolution is based on land. Land is the basis of all independence. Land is the basis of freedom, justice, and equality.

The white man knows what a revolution is. He knows that the black revolution is world-wide in scope and in nature. The black revolution is sweeping Asia, is sweeping Africa, is rearing its head in Latin America. The Cuban Revolution—that's a revolution. They overturned the system. Revolution is in Asia, revolution is in Africa, and the white man is screaming because he sees revolution in Latin America. How do you think he'll react to you when you learn what a real revolution is? You don't know what a revolution is. If you did, you wouldn't use that word.

Revolution is bloody, revolution is hostile, revolution knows no compromise, revolution overturns and destroys everything that gets in its way. And you, sitting around here like a knot on the wall, saying, "I'm going to love these folks no matter how much they hate me." No, you need a revolution. Whoever heard of a revolution where they lock arms, as Rev. [Albert B.] Cleage was pointing out beautifully, singing "We Shall Overcome"? You don't do that in a revolution. You don't do any singing, you're too busy swinging. It's based on land. A revolutionary wants land so he can set up his own nation, an independent nation. These Negroes aren't asking for any nation—they're trying to crawl back on the plantation.

When you want a nation, that's called nationalism. When the white man became involved in a revolution in this country against England, what was it for? He wanted this land so he could set up another white nation. That's white nationalism. The American Revolution was white nationalism. The French Revolution was white nationalism. The Russian Revolution too—yes, it was—white nationalism. You don't think so? Why do you think Khrushchev and Mao can't get their heads together? White nationalism. All the revolutions that are going on in Asia and Africa today are based on what?—black nationalism. A revolutionary is a black nationalist. He wants a nation. I was reading some beautiful words by Rev. Cleage, pointing out why he couldn't get together with someone else in the city because all of them were afraid of being identified with black nationalism. If you're afraid of black nationalism, you're afraid of revolution. And if you love revolution, you love black nationalism.

To understand this, you have to go back to what the young brother here referred to as the house Negro and the field Negro back during slavery. There were two kinds of slaves, the house Negro and the field Negro. The house Negroes—they lived in the house with master, they dressed pretty good, they ate good because they ate his food—what he left. They lived in the attic or the basement, but still they lived near the master; and they loved the master more than the master loved himself. They would give their life to save the master's house—quicker than the master would. If the master said, "We got a good house here," the house Negro would say, "Yeah, we got a good house here." Whenever the master said "we," he said "we." That's how you can tell a house Negro.

If the master's house caught on fire, the house Negro would fight harder to put the blaze out than the master would. If the master got sick, the house Negro would say, "What's the matter, boss, *we* sick?" *We* sick! He identified himself with his master, more than his master identified with himself. And if you came to the house Negro and said, "Let's run away, let's escape, let's separate," the house Negro would look at you and say, "Man, you crazy. What you mean, separate? Where is there a better house than this? Where can I wear better clothes than this? Where can I eat better food than this?" That was that house Negro. In those days he was called a "house nigger." And that's what we call them today, because we've still got some house niggers running around here.

This modern house Negro loves his master. He wants to live near him. He'll pay three times as much as the house is worth just to live near his master, and then brag about "I'm the only Negro out here." "I'm the only one on my job." "I'm the only one in this school." You're nothing but a house Negro. And if someone comes to you right now and says, "Let's separate," you say the same thing that the house Negro said on the plantation. "What you mean, separate? From America, this good white man? Where you going to get a better job than you get here?" I mean, this is what you say. "I ain't left nothing in Africa," that's what you say. Why, you left your mind in Africa.

On that same plantation, there was the field Negro. The field Negroes—those were the masses. There were always more Negroes in the field than there were Negroes in the house. The Negro in the field caught hell. He ate leftovers. In the house they ate high up on the hog. The Negro in the field didn't get anything but what was left of the insides of the hog. They call it "chitt'lings" nowadays. In those days they called them what they were—guts. That's what you were—gut-eaters. And some of you are still gut-eaters.

The field Negro was beaten from morning to night; he lived in a shack, in a hut; he wore old, castoff clothes. He hated his master. I say he hated his master. He was intelligent. That house Negro loved his master, but that field Negro—remember, they were in the majority, and they hated the master. When the house caught on fire, he didn't try to put it out; that field Negro prayed for a wind, for a breeze. When the master got sick, the field Negro prayed that he'd die. If someone came to the field Negro and said, "Let's separate, let's run," he didn't say "Where we going?" He'd say, "Any place is better than here." You've got field Negroes in America today. I'm a field Negro. The masses are the field Negroes. When they see this man's house on fire, you don't hear the little Negroes talking about "*our* government is in trouble." They say, "*The* government is in trouble." Imagine a Negro: "*Our* government"! I even heard one say "*our* astronauts." They won't even let him near the plant—and "*our* astronauts"! "*Our* Navy"—that's a Negro that is out of his mind, a Negro that is out of his mind.

Just as the slavemaster of that day used Tom, the house Negro, to keep the field Negroes in check, the same old slavemaster today has Negroes who are nothing but modern Uncle Toms, twentieth-century Uncle Toms, to keep you and me in check, to keep us under control, keep us passive and peaceful and nonviolent. That's Tom making you nonviolent. It's like when you go to the dentist, and the man's going to take your tooth. You're going to fight him when he starts pulling. So he squirts some stuff in your jaw called novocaine, to make you think they're not doing anything to you. So you sit there and because you've got all of that novocaine in your jaw, you suffer—peacefully. Blood running all down your jaw, and you don't know what's happening. Because someone has taught you to suffer—peacefully.

The white man does the same thing to you in the street, when he wants to put knots on your head and take advantage of you and not have to be afraid of your fighting back. To keep you from fighting back, he gets these old religious Uncle Toms to teach you and me, just like novocaine, to suffer peacefully. Don't stop suffering—just suffer peacefully. As Rev. Cleage pointed out, they say you should let your blood flow in the streets. This is a shame. You know he's a Christian preacher. If it's a shame to him, you know what it is to me.

There is nothing in our book, the Koran, that teaches us to suffer peacefully. Our religion teaches us to be intelligent. Be peaceful, be courteous, obey the law, respect everyone; but if someone puts his hand on you, send him to the cemetery. That's a good religion. In fact, that's that old-time religion. That's the one that Ma and Pa used to talk about: an eye for an eye, and a tooth for a tooth, and a head for a head, and a life for a life. That's a good religion. And nobody resents that kind of religion being taught but a wolf, who intends to make you his meal.

This is the way it is with the white man in America. He's a wolf—and you're sheep. Any time a shepherd, a pastor, teaches you and me not to run from the white man and, at the same time, teaches us not to fight the white man, he's a traitor to you and me. Don't lay down a life all by itself. No, preserve your life, it's the best thing you've got. And if you've got to give it up, let it be even-steven.

Civil Rights Leaders

The slavemaster took Tom and dressed him well, fed him well and even gave him a little education—a *little* education; gave him a long coat and a top hat and made all the other slaves look up to him. Then he used Tom to control them. The same strategy that was used in those days is used today, by the same white man. He takes a Negro, a so-called Negro, and makes him prominent, builds him up, publicizes him, makes him a celebrity. And then he becomes a spokesman for Negroes—and a Negro leader.

I would like to mention just one other thing quickly, and that is the method that the white man uses, how the white man uses the "big guns," or Negro leaders, against the Negro revolution. They are not a part of the Negro revolution. They are used against the Negro revolution.

When Martin Luther King failed to desegregate Albany, Georgia, the civil-rights struggle in America reached its low point. King became bankrupt almost, as a leader. The Southern Christian Leadership Conference was in financial trouble; and it was in trouble, period, with the people when they failed to desegregate Albany, Georgia. Other Negro civil-rights leaders of so-called national stature became fallen idols. As they became fallen idols, began to lose their prestige and influence, local Negro leaders began to stir up the masses. In Cambridge, Maryland, Gloria Richardson; in Danville, Virginia, and other parts of the country, local leaders began to stir up our people at the grass-roots level. This was never done by these Negroes of national stature. They control you, but they have never incited you or excited you. They control you, they contain you, they have kept you on the plantation.

As soon as King failed in Birmingham, Negroes took to the streets. King went out to California to a big rally and raised I don't know how many thousands of dollars. He came to Detroit and had a march and raised some more thousands of dollars. And recall, right after that Roy Wilkins attacked King. He accused King and CORE [Congress Of Racial Equality] of starting trouble everywhere and then making the [Wilkins-led] NAACP [National Association for the Advancement of Colored People] get them out of jail and spend a lot of money; they accused King and CORE of raising all the money and not paying it back. This happened; I've got it in documented evidence in the newspaper. Roy started attacking King, and King started attacking Roy, and [CORE leader James] Farmer started attacking both of them. And as these Negroes of national stature began to attack each other, they began to lose their control of the Negro masses.

The Negroes were out there in the streets. They were talking about how they were going to march on Washington. Right at that time Birmingham had exploded, and the Negroes in Birmingham—remember, they also exploded. They began to stab the crackers in the back and bust them up 'side their head—yes, they did. That's when [President John F.] Kennedy sent in the troops, down in Birmingham. After that, Kennedy got on the television and said "this is a moral issue." That's when he said he was going to put out a civil-rights bill. And when he mentioned civil-rights bill and the Southern crackers started talking about how they were going to boycott or filibuster it, then the Negroes started talking—about what? That they were going to march on Washington, march on the Senate, march on the White House, march on the Congress, and tie it up, bring it to a halt, not let the government proceed. They even said they were going out to the airport and lay down on the runway and not let any airplanes land. I'm telling you what they said. That was revolution. That was revolution. That was the black revolution.

It was the grass roots out there in the street. It scared the white man to death, scared the white power structure in Washington, D.C., to death; I was there. When they found out that this black steamroller was going to come down on the capital, they called in Wilkins, they called in [A. Philip] Randolph, they called in these national Negro leaders that you respect and told them, "Call it off." Kennedy said, "Look, you all are letting this thing go too far." And Old Tom said, "Boss, I can't stop it, because I didn't start it." I'm telling you what they said. They said, "I'm not even in it, much less at the head of it." They said, "These Negroes are doing things on their own. They're running ahead of us." And that old shrewd fox, he said, "If you all aren't in it, I'll put you in it. I'll put you at the head of it. I'll endorse it. I'll welcome it. I'll help it. I'll join it."

A matter of hours went by. They had a meeting at the Carlyle Hotel in New York City. The Carlyle Hotel is owned by the Kennedy family; that's the hotel Kennedy spent the night at, two nights ago; it belongs to his family. A philanthropic society headed by a white man named Stephen Currier called all the top civil-rights leaders together at the Carlyle Hotel. And he told them, "By you all fighting each other, you are destroying the civil-rights movement. And since you're fighting over money from white liberals, let us set up what is known as the Council for United Civil Rights Leadership. Let's form this council, and all the civil-rights organizations will belong to it, and we'll use it for fund-raising purposes." Let me show you how tricky the white man is. As soon as they got it formed, they elected Whitney Young as its chairman, and who do you think became the co-chairman? Stephen Currier, the white man, a millionaire. . . . Wilkins knows it happened. King knows it happened. Every one of that Big Six—they know it happened.

Once they formed it, with the white man over it, he promised them and gave them $800,000 to split up among the Big Six; and told them that after the march was over they'd give them $700,000 more. A million and a half dollars—split up between leaders that you have been following, going to jail for, crying crocodile tears for. And they're nothing but Frank James and Jesse James and the what-do-you-call-'em brothers.

The March on Washington

As soon as they got the setup organized, the white man made available to them top public-relations experts; opened the news media across the country at their disposal, which then began to project these Big Six as the leaders of the march. Originally they weren't even in the march. You were talking this march talk on Hastings Street, you were talking march talk on Lenox Avenue, and on Fillmore Street, and on Central Avenue, and 32nd Street and 63rd Street. That's where the march talk was being talked. But the white man put the Big Six at the head of it; made them the march. They became the march. They took it over. And the first move they made after they took it over, they invited Walter Reuther, a white man; they invited a priest, a rabbi, and an old white preacher, yes, an old white preacher. The same white element that put Kennedy into power—labor, the Catholics, the Jews, and liberal Protestants; the same clique that put Kennedy in power, joined the march on Washington.

It's just like when you've got some coffee that's too black, which means it's too strong. What do you do? You integrate it with cream, you make it weak. But if you pour too much cream in it, you won't even know you ever had coffee. It used to be hot, it becomes cool. It used to be strong, it becomes weak. It used to wake you up, now it puts you to sleep. This is what they did with the march on Washington. They joined it. They didn't integrate it, they infiltrated it. They joined it, became a part of it, took it over. And as they took it over, it lost its militancy. It ceased to be angry, it ceased to be hot, it ceased to be uncompromising. Why, it even ceased to be a march. It became a picnic, a circus. Nothing but a circus, with clowns and all. You had one right here in Detroit—I saw it on television—with clowns leading it, white clowns and black clowns. I know you don't like what I'm saying, but I'm going to tell you anyway. Because I can prove what I'm saying. If you think I'm telling you wrong, you bring me Martin Luther King and A. Philip Randolph and James Farmer and those other three, and see if they'll deny it over a microphone.

No, it was a sellout. It was a takeover. When James Baldwin came in from Paris, they wouldn't let him talk, because they couldn't make him go by the script. Burt Lancaster read the speech that Baldwin was supposed to make; they wouldn't let Baldwin get up there, because they know Baldwin is liable to say anything. They controlled it so tight, they told those Negroes what time to hit town, how to come, where to stop, what signs to carry, what song to sing, what speech they could make, and what speech they couldn't make; and then told them to get out of town by sundown. And every one of those Toms was out of town by sundown. Now I know you don't like my saying this. But I can back it up. It was a circus, a performance that beat anything Hollywood could ever do, the performance of the year. Reuther and those other three devils should get an Academy Award for the best actors because they acted like they really loved Negroes and fooled a whole lot of Negroes. And the six Negro leaders should get an award too, for the best supporting cast.

"The overriding issue . . . is whether there is a national commitment to equity and parity. Either we affirm that, or we reject that by law."

Affirmative Action Programs Benefit African Americans

Jesse Jackson (b. 1941)

Affirmative action refers to various public laws and private programs designed to increase educational and employment opportunities for blacks and other potential victims of discrimination. Gaining initial prominence in the 1960s in the wake of the civil rights movement, affirmative action programs became increasingly controversial in the 1970s and 1980s. Many African Americans viewed affirmative action as necessary to redress past injustices and offset current discrimination. Critics of affirmative action labeled it "reverse discrimination" (discrimination against whites) and argued that it betrayed and cheapened the ideals of the civil rights movement.

Jesse Jackson has been a consistent supporter of affirmative action. Jackson, who worked for Martin Luther King Jr. in the late 1960s, became perhaps the nation's most prominent black civil rights activist and political leader of the 1970s and 1980s. In 1984 and 1988 he ran for the Democratic presidential nomination, finishing third and second, respectively, in the Democratic primaries.

In 1978 Jackson was the featured speaker at a symposium on African-American issues sponsored by the American Enterprise Institute, a public policy research organization based in Washington, D.C. The following viewpoint includes excerpts from his

From *A Conversation with the Reverend Jesse Jackson*, held on May 16, 1978, at the American Enterprise Institute for Public Policy Research, Washington, D.C., AEI Studies #209; ©1978 by American Enterprise Institute for Public Policy Research, reprinted courtesy of AEI.

opening statement and a question-and-answer session featuring Jackson and a panel of journalists. Jackson strongly rejects the argument that affirmative action programs are unfair to whites and argues that the United States needs a national commitment to equality for blacks, in part to compensate for past injustices.

Affirmative action was then in the nation's headlines because of several legal cases involving affirmative action programs, including *DeFunis v. Odegaard* and *The Regents of the University of California v. Bakke*. The latter case, which in May 1978 had been argued before the U.S. Supreme Court but had not yet been decided, was initiated by Allen Bakke, a white applicant who was denied admission to the University of California at Davis Medical School. Bakke sued the university, claiming that he had been passed over in favor of less-qualified minority applicants admitted to sixteen places set aside for them under an affirmative action program. In June 1978 the Supreme Court, in a 5-4 decision, ruled that Bakke's constitutional rights had been violated and ordered his enrollment, but the Court did not invalidate all affirmative action programs.

I would like to express to you how delighted I am to have this opportunity today to engage in dialogue. I will try to make my presentation as brief as I can and to open up the meeting for as much discussion as possible.

The difference between where we are now and where we were ten years ago, when there was a tremendous pressure upon us to demonstrate and to engage in forms of drama, is that at that time we called our movement a freedom movement. That was an accurate description, because segregation eliminated our options—we did not have freedom. We did not have the freedom to use public accommodations; we did not have the freedom to vote; we did not have the freedom of open housing; our options were reduced. In some sense, in the 1960s the public accommodations bill, the voting rights bill, and the open housing bill gave us freedom. But beyond freedom, the goal must be equity and parity, or equality.

Freedom and Equality

Many people use the words "freedom" and "equality" interchangeably, but they're not interchangeable terms because equality can be measured—it can be turned into numbers. Now we are free to register and to vote; now our challenge is, indeed, to register and to vote, and to vote according to our vested interest. There are 16 million blacks eligible to vote, and only 9 million are registered to vote. So there is a challenge for us to take full advantage of that measure of political freedom and then to vote according to our vested interest, freedom.

When we speak about equity and parity, we begin to talk about issues such as quotas, which brought about the *DeFunis* versus *Odegaard* suit in Washington, or we begin to talk about affirmative action, which has brought about, of course, the *Bakke* case. *DeFunis* versus *Odegaard* or *Bakke* would not have been issues in 1960, because they deal with something other than what we were dealing with in 1960 or, indeed, in 1968. The goal of our struggle now has to be educational equity and parity, and economic equity and parity. We must measure our relationships with our allies by how willing they are to help us achieve equality and parity, which really is beyond freedom.

In economics, the income gap is getting wider. We're not achieving equity and parity. The reason we focus on education is that this gap is getting wider.

In the last few years the term "reverse discrimination" has been used. It gives the impression that whites are losing ground because the white majority has made a decision against its best interest, which has not happened. It gives the impression that some whites are not moving as fast as they want to move because they have been held back, while blacks catch up. The fact is, there are 48 percent more whites in medical school today than there were in 1970; there are 64 percent more whites in law school now than there were then. If on a scale of 100, sixteen seats are set aside for blacks—and I might add that those sixteen would be split up among various ethnic groups—more than sixteen seats have been added to the 100 for whites.

No Reverse Discrimination

There is no reverse discrimination. If white America feels its expansion is slowing down, the pressure is not coming from black America and the drive for affirmative action. The jobs that the white workers had at the Zenith plant in Chicago have gone to Mexicans, not to Watts. The steel workers' jobs that were lost in Youngstown, Ohio, have not gone to Harlem. They've gone to Tokyo.

The money that many white Americans expected to be available for investment has gone to the Pacific rim. Last year, out of $160 billion for capital investment, $32 billion went abroad. One dollar out of every five dollars now goes abroad, and with those dollars goes a tremendous number of jobs. Therefore much of the pressure that white America feels is not coming from black America. We've become a rather visible scapegoat, and when terms like reverse discrimination are used, they give a false impression.

Bakkeism is really not against preferential treatment; that's not the issue that's being raised. There's no resistance to the rich having preferential acceptance in universities—it's called cultural mix, and nobody resists sitting next to the rich. Nobody's resisting the super athletes' coming to the major white universities; nobody resists the children of faculty or alumni having preferential acceptance. In a real sense, Bakkeism is racism; it is resistance to our mobility. It is saying "You may have freedom, but you cannot have equity and parity." What is at stake in the Supreme Court now is whether or not the culture will support our urge for equity and power. . . .

The challenge of self-reliance for black and poor America cannot be overlooked. Someone has given out the mistaken notion the last few years that self-reliance is a kind of conservative idea. In fact, it is rather radical and revolutionary. Dependency belongs with the slavery syndrome. Self-reliance is resistance to domination and occupation. It's what Jesus meant when he said, "The Kingdom of God is within." Freedom is not going to come from some chariot from the sky, which is superstitious; it's going to come from our own will to organize and break out from under oppression. . . .

Questions and Answers

Ms. Charlene Hunter-Gault, "McNeil Lehrer Report": What impact do you think a pro-Bakke decision would have on the larger issues of equity and parity, not only in education but in employment and other areas?

Reverend Jackson: A pro-Bakke decision would simply give dignity and official status to the hard-hat movement. It would be, in some sense, the official stopping of the reconstruction movement of the century. The affirmative action provisions are like the presence of the federal troops in the South in the last century. To take that away would be like pulling out the troops again, and some of the same kinds of things would begin to happen. It would have the effect of making many people more cynical than they are, which would be unfortunate.

I would hope that we would not lose the decision, that at worst it would be sent back to the state of California, which it never should have left, in my judgment. But if we do come to have an obligation to rebel, that rebellion may take the form of major sit-ins on college campuses, showing that we will rebel nonviolently until we are protected with provisions for our share, to assure our orderly growth and development. It may take the form of street demonstrations in selected cities; it may take the form of selected boycotts against major companies that want our consumer dollars but do not want to hire and promote us. We cannot simply stand by and feel bad about the fact that the judges did not rule in our favor. . . .

Jim Weighart, *New York Daily News:* Some of the people who have expressed reservations about the principles involved in the *Bakke* case have done so even though they say they approve affirmative action. They feel there's something intrinsically wrong with the situation where a man who otherwise meets qualifications for admittance is excluded because there are too many of his kind. I would like to have you comment on that, but I would like to turn it around. What if there was a more rigid quota system that would be satisfactory to blacks—say, 20 percent or whatever. If a black qualified but was excluded because he was one over that quota, would you feel the same way about that instance as you feel about Bakke?

Defending Affirmative Action

John E. Jacob was president of the National Urban League from 1982 to 1994. He was a strong defender of affirmative action programs when they came under attack during the presidencies of Ronald Reagan and George Bush. In this passage from a speech made in New Orleans on July 31, 1983, Jacob defends affirmative action as a necessary means toward the creation of a color-blind society.

I want to talk a little about affirmative action. It is an issue of primary importance. Too many people, including many of our friends, have been brainwashed into thinking it amounts to harmful reverse discrimination. Too many agree with the [Reagan] Administration when it says it wants color-blind policies that are racially neutral.

Well, black people too, want a society that is color-blind and racially neutral. Our four hundred year history of protest and struggle has tried to move society to treat the races equally. If there were parity in the distribution of society's rewards and responsibilities there would be no need for affirmative action; for numerical goals, for compliance timetables.

But there is no parity. We have a racial spoils system, but it is a spoils system that favors white males and excludes blacks, other minorities and women. We face not only the results of historic discrimination, but the effects of persistent present discrimination. That discrimination exists despite the laws forbidding it—laws the Justice Department is not enforcing.

We are a nation still gripped by racial and group prejudices. It is a fantasy to suppose we can act as if race were not a factor. The only way we can create a truly color-blind society in the long run is by positive, race-conscious affirmative action policies in the short run.

Affirmative action is not a preference system or a reparations system. It is a sensible tool to bring into the mainstream groups that have always been excluded from it and who are today relegated to the margins of our society.

REVEREND JACKSON: Well, that's almost abstract. We've never had that situation. Further evidence is that Bakke's age was too high and his grades were too low—I mean, we ain't rejected no genius;

America ain't lost no great statesman. [Laughter.]

When America lost Bakke, it ain't lost no potential President, you know—nothing like that. I think that's the first thing we need to get out.

MR. WEIGHART: He is a man who does have rights. His marks were much higher than many of those who were accepted, especially among the minority—

REVEREND JACKSON: Let me put this another way. I can only try to explain it by example because I'm not a lawyer or a judge—I'm just a country preacher, trying to share with you what I see.

An Unfair Contest

Suppose two men were running a one-mile race, and it was discovered at the halfway point that the man that was behind had weights on his ankles. The referee said, "This is wrong," and shot the gun and stopped the race, but each man retained his relative position. Then the referee said, "Now that the weights are off your ankles, start again." Unless there was some basis for determining merit based upon the speed of the last two laps, we might ask why anyone bothered to stop the event in the first place? We can understand that in track; we know that's unfair because we're not dealing with a racial issue.

The holocaust of 60 million blacks getting killed, two hundred years of slavery, and another hundred years of official segregation isn't any joke. We have no obligation to take it lightly. We are not behind because of any resistance to work or any lack of intelligence. We were absolutely set behind by national policy. If this nation has any commitment to justice, it cannot judge the race from the end, according to how the people are coming in; it must also judge it by how the people started off. That is the overriding issue. If there is one white doctor for every 649 whites, and one black doctor for every 5,000 blacks, it isn't because we have an aversion to medicine. If there is one white dentist to every 1,900 whites, and one black dentist to every 8,400 blacks, that is the result of our holocaust. . . .

This is a very hot and emotional subject. But the overriding issue, from where I sit, is whether there is a national commitment to equity and parity. Either we affirm that, or we reject that by law. There is no evidence that the American business community, or the American labor community, or the American educational community will voluntarily commit itself to such goals without pressure and leverage. Furthermore, there is no evidence that blacks are behind because of genes. The nation's agenda, our national policies—and not any laziness in blacks—have set us back. . . .

The latest statistics show that a white high school dropout, without giving him a name, has more job options than a black high school graduate, without giving him a name. As late as 1950, when

I was growing up in the South, and they were telling me how qualified we had to be, 65 to 70 percent of the labor force in this country, skilled and semiskilled, were white males without a high school diploma. At that time, a black with a college degree couldn't be a policeman. As late as 1960, 46 percent of the skilled and semiskilled labor force in high-paying union jobs were white males without a high school diploma. It's in a new book called *Protest, Politics and Prosperity*, by Dorothy K. Newman and funded by the Carnegie Corporation. The evidence is there. Our crisis is essentially not a class one, as some people now want to say; it is essentially a caste one.

Blacks Rejected Because of Race

There is substantial evidence that many blacks are still categorically rejected because of race, whereas our character and intelligence are not even tested. There is no evidence that there are no black coaches in the National Football League because we can't figure out X's and O's. There is no evidence that there are no black baseball managers because we don't understand baseball. The real evidence is something very different from that.

This society cannot run from its shame, which is race, and from the black man's burden, which is shame. I'm not saying that anyone should feel guilty about what one writer called "The White Man's Shame and the Black Man's Burden," because I don't think guilt is a solution. I think we ought to be responsible about it. To be responsible about it is to accept it as real and do something about it.

Now, I go another step. There is no evidence that the white runner is in front because he has innate speed. He is there in fact because of unfair advantages. To be sure, some white folks can outrun some black folks, and some white folks have got more soul than some black folks. Some black folks haven't got any rhythm, and some white folks can't think, so we don't need to play any funny old games with little individual analogies. The question really is not whether America can stop and support Bakke. The question is how it will adjudge itself and appraise itself if it supports a policy that does not take into account a commitment to overcome its most horrible sin.

Germany killed 6 million Jews, and that was its sin; it was wrong. This country and others have forced Germany to keep paying money for it, which is not any substitute, but the reparations represent some evidence that Germany was wrong and ought to pay for it, and we support that.

If we're going to justify compensation for the extermination of 6 million Jews—and I think we ought to; I keep repeating that—then we ought to support compensation for 60 million blacks, 200 years of slavery, 100 years of segregation.

Do you realize that this is just the twenty-fourth year after the 1954 Supreme Court decision? As late as twenty-four years ago I had to go to an inferior school, by law. Black teachers had to receive inferior salaries, by law. If, in fact, blacks were up in that race, it would not prove that we are equal, it would prove that we are superior. It would not prove that white people are fair.

VIEWPOINT 4

"Affirmative action must be re-evaluated. . . . It has created new protected classes, made victim status desirable and forced society to question the accomplishments of its children."

Affirmative Action Programs Harm African Americans

Clarence Pendleton (1930–1988)

Clarence Pendleton was the first black chairman of the U.S. Commission on Civil Rights. Appointed in November 1981 by President Ronald Reagan, he served in that capacity until his death in 1988. Pendleton was a controversial choice for civil rights commissioner because of his opposition to affirmative action, school busing, and other government-mandated programs. During his tenure as chairman he was often at odds with other commission members and with most black civil rights leaders, who favored such civil rights measures.

The following viewpoint is taken from a 1985 article in which Pendleton argues that affirmative action programs run counter to the ideals and goals of the Civil Rights Act of 1964. These ideals include equality of opportunity and the end of all racial discrimination, he argues, not the hiring of African Americans in order to fulfill affirmative action goals or quotas.

From Clarence Pendleton, "Opportunity," part 1 of "Equality of Opportunity or Equality of Results," *Human Rights*, Fall 1985; ©1985 by American Bar Association. Reprinted with permission.

It has been more than 20 years since the Civil Rights Act of 1964 was passed, and the debate over what Congress intended still rages.

During the last 21 years, the question has remained: Was the intent of Congress to provide equality of opportunity or equality of results?

For 84 days, the longest debate in its history, the Senate tried to resolve the issue in 1964. We still have not answered the question.

Many leading civil rights organizations at that time, led by Senator Hubert Humphrey, argued the equality of opportunity side. Humphrey assured his colleagues time and again that group preferences were not to be tolerated.

There is nothing in Title VII of the bill, he insisted, "that will give any power to the (Equal Employment Opportunity) Commission or to any court to require hiring, firing or promotion of employees in order to meet a racial 'quota' or to achieve a certain racial balance. That bugaboo has been brought up a dozen times; but it is nonexistent."

The opposition believed that, despite the intent of the bill, the effect would be to insure equality of results, as interpreted by the enforcing agencies of government.

The act was passed to substantiate the rights of blacks. However, the bill's language insisted that race, color, religion, and national origin were to limit no one's rights.

The act followed the language and spirit of the 13th, 14th, and 15th amendments to the Constitution. It spoke of "citizens, individuals, and persons," not blacks, not Hispanics, native Americans, Asians, or any other group that might be subject to discrimination.

It seemed as though Justice John Marshall Harlan's famous dissent in Plessy v. Ferguson would be the law at last: "In view of the Constitution, in the eye of the law, there is in this country no superior, dominant ruling class of citizens. There is no caste here. Our Constitution is color-blind, and neither knows nor tolerates classes among its citizens.

"In respect of civil rights, all citizens are equal before the law. The humblest is the peer of the most powerful. The law regards man as man, and takes no account of his surroundings or of his color when his civil rights as guaranteed by the supreme law of the Land are involved."

Americans thought the eloquent words spoken by Dr. Martin Luther King Jr. from the steps of the Lincoln Memorial were cast in stone. All people, he said, were "to be judged by the content of their character not by the color of their skin."

One would be sadly and grossly mistaken to believe that a

color-blind society has been obtained. The implementation and enforcement of this law, as columnist George Will once described, succeeded in dividing "the majestic national river into little racial and ethnic creeks."

Affirmative Action Creates Discrimination

Shelby Steele, an English professor at San Jose State University in California, gained prominence in the late 1980s as a black conservative writer. In this passage from an article published in the May 13, 1990, issue of the New York Times Magazine, *he argues that affirmative action actually contributes to discrimination against African Americans in the workplace.*

Several blacks I spoke with said they were still in favor of affirmative action because of the "subtle" discrimination blacks were subject to once they were on the job. One photojournalist said, "They have ways of ignoring you." A black female television producer said: "You can't file a lawsuit when your boss doesn't invite you to the insider meetings without ruining your career. So we still need affirmative action." Others mentioned the infamous "glass ceiling" through which blacks can see the top positions of authority but never reach them. But I don't think racial preferences are a protection against this subtle discrimination; I think they contribute to it.

In any workplace, racial preferences will always create two-tiered populations composed of preferreds and unpreferreds. In the case of blacks and whites, for instance, racial preferences imply that whites are superior just as they imply that blacks are inferior. They not only reinforce America's oldest racial myth but, for blacks, they have the effect of stigmatizing the already stigmatized.

I think that much of the "subtle" discrimination that blacks talk about is often (not always) discrimination against the stigma of questionable competence that affirmative action marks blacks with. In this sense, preferences make scapegoats of the very people they seek to help. And it may be that at a certain level employers impose a glass ceiling, but this may not be against the race so much as against the race's reputation for having advanced by color as much as by competence. This ceiling is the point at which corporations shift the emphasis from color to competency and stop playing the affirmative-action game. Here preference backfires for blacks and becomes a taint that holds them back.

The United States, Will wrote, became "less a nation than an angry menagerie of factions scrambling for preference."

The massive societal consensus that demanded passage of the Civil Rights Act of 1964 began to break down in the 1970s. New legislation and an executive order required increased attention to race and ethnicity in hiring by any private or public employer that received federal aid or was subject to government regulation.

It was now required to count how many minorities were recruited, interviewed, trained, hired, admitted, served or enrolled.

Twenty years later, it is still necessary "to count noses" to determine if there is discrimination.

That equality of opportunity so ardently fought for and won in 1964 has given way to equality of results through such bureaucratic devices as fair share, proportional representation, special preferences, quotas, goals, timetables, and set-asides.

Today, many blacks believe that the laws were passed to ensure only their civil rights, and that blacks are due a special preference from the government to make up for the despicable institution of slavery. They sincerely believe that the government has not yet made up for past atrocities.

This is where I part company with some of my people. I believe that blacks were only due the granting of equal status, equal protection. I also believe that many of the laws and court decisions that occurred since 1964 were necessary to reassert the constitutional guarantees expressed by the 13th, 14th, and 15th amendments.

Insistence on group preference is a role reversal. Those who marched, struggled and died for equality now want separation.

In enforcing the Civil Rights Act, the government perpetuated and worsened the situation with a myriad of artificial allotments, considered incentives to assist and propel minorities into America's mainstream.

Those artificial allotments included goals, timetables, quotas and other numerical devices imposed by government to suit its notion of how society should be organized—a society where a person's standing is determined by pigment, ethnicity or gender.

Allocating social benefits on the basis of race or gender has led to bitterness and disharmony. Economist Thomas Sowell expressed a cause for concern when he stated, "There is much reason to fear the harm that (a racial preference) is doing to its supposed beneficiaries, and still more reason to fear the long-run consequences of polarizing the nation. Resentments do not accumulate indefinitely without consequences.". . .

Equality of Opportunity

It is equality of opportunity that allows one to advance toward that laudable goal of a color-blind, race and gender neutral society. Only equality of opportunity will facilitate each individual or group to achieve to the limit of their creativity, imagination and enthusiasm.

Congress and the courts should make a commitment to pursue the moral and constitutional high ground and reject any notion that discrimination can be eliminated or minimized by racial balancing in the form of proportional representation. Nor should Congress condone equality of results in the form of preferential treatment such as quotas, goals, timetables or set-asides.

The main objective of the federal, state and local government must be to provide equal opportunity based upon individual merit. Each of us has an obligation to make sure that our children can compete based upon merit. This means they must be prepared.

A quality education must be available to all children. This nation cannot afford another generation of illiterates of any color.

Derrick Bell, dean of the University of Oregon Law School and a leading force in early court cases to end segregation, has concluded that while "there is potential strength in the argument that school desegregation is needed to improve society, the danger is that this societal personification of the benefit reduces the priority for correction of the harm suffered directly by blacks to a secondary importance when it should be the primary concern."

As W.E.B. DuBois said years ago, "The black child needs neither segregated schools nor mixed schools. What he needs is an education."

I myself survived and prospered without the so-called benefits of affirmative action and integration. The reason for my survival and success is preparation. I attended the all-black Dunbar High School in Washington, D.C. and was given a special gift.

Those black teachers demanded excellence and I left prepared to go forward. I obtained both post secondary degrees from a black college, Howard University, which gave me the tools necessary to achieve success.

We must encourage black people to support black institutions: the black church, black colleges, banks, fraternities, service organizations and countless others. We cannot depend upon philanthropy and charity to save our institutions.

We must create innovative and effective public policy that opens doors and keeps them open. We should be advocating the relaxation and repeal of various regulations that restrict entry and access to the marketplace.

Not only black Americans would benefit from such advocacy. Is it necessary for a barber or beautician to know the name of every bone in the hand to adequately cut hair? Why should a New York City taxi medallion cost $85,000 when a license in Washington, D.C. is only $200? Licensing only serves to restrict access to the market. How many people have $85,000?

Minimum wage also restricts entry into the market by black teenagers. Even the black mayors in the United States believe this to be true, yet many of us continue to work against initiation of legislation to reduce minimum wage.

Finally, affirmative action must be re-evaluated. A program

which began with the best intentions and highest ideals has ended up setting white against black. It has created new protected classes, made victim status desirable and forced society to question the accomplishments of its children.

Most tragically, it has created a generation which sees no need to take risk and will never see its rewards. No quota will make any of us successful. No program of quotas will prevent the last of us from failing. Risk taking should be the engine that propels us to success.

Solving the problem of discrimination with more laws and regulations is not the answer. We have a moral responsibility to remove the barriers that deny people access to equal opportunity. We should get rid of special protections that can place more barriers to opportunity.

A passage in *The Essential Rousseau*, "Discourse on Inequality Among Men," written in 1755, sums up the situation:

"Peoples once accustomed to masters are no longer in condition to do without them. If they try to shake off the yoke, they move still farther away from freedom because they confuse it with an unbridled license that is opposed to it, and their revolutions nearly always deliver them into the hands of seducers who only make their chains heavier than before."

CHAPTER 7

Two Reflections on Racism Against African Americans

Chapter Preface

African Americans have had to cope with white racial prejudice and discrimination for virtually all of the group's history. This assertion is, for most historians, a matter beyond dispute. In the March 28, 1991, *New York Review of Books*, historical writer Garry Wills argues that African Americans' overall experience with racism makes their past far different from that of other ethnic groups, even those who have been victims of some form of prejudice.

> No other group in America has been subject to racism in the full sense—to xenophobia, to chauvinism, to ethnic stereotypes, yes; but not to the radical sense of otherness that racism presents in its full virulence. Blacks have been alien, not only in national or cultural or social terms, but in the deepest human sense of worth that can make intermarriage more a blasphemy than a social comedown where blacks—as opposed, say, to those of different religions, or nationalities—are concerned.

Most Americans would agree that racism against African Americans has been a major problem in the past. However, whether racism *remains* such a problem is for some a debatable issue. Those who argue that racism in America has decreased point to the gains made by African Americans since the 1960s, many of which directly resulted from the civil rights movement. Federal civil rights laws have banned racial discrimination in employment, education, and voting registration. The number of African Americans in public office has jumped from about 100 in 1965 to more than 7,300 in 1990. Similar increases have occurred in city police forces, businesses, and the professions, resulting in the emergence of a large new black middle class. By the 1990s almost half of black married couples earned more than $40,000 a year.

Despite these gains, black poverty continues to be a serious problem. The ratio of blacks to whites below the poverty line in 1959 was approximately three to one—a ratio that has remained unchanged despite the victories of the civil rights movement. In 1992, 42.7 percent of African-American households earned less than $15,000 (compared to 21.6 percent of white households). Some observers blame this persistence of poverty on continuing racial discrimination as well as on what historian George M. Fredrickson describes as "the accumulated disadvantages inherited from more than three hundred years of white domination and exploitation." But others have argued that social pathologies within the black community, including crime, lack of education, and single-parent families, are the real barriers to black progress. "Even if racism were to disappear overnight," writes conservative scholar Dinesh D'Souza,

> the worst problems facing black America would persist. Single parenthood and welfare dependency among the black underclass would not cease. Crack and AIDS would continue to ravage black communities. The black crime rate . . . would still extract a terrible toll. . . . Racism is hardly the most serious problem facing African Americans in the United States today.

Many people believe, however, that racism remains the primary obstacle African Americans face, whether they are among the black poor or the black middle class. Ellis Cose, in his 1993 book *The Rage of a Privileged Class*, interviewed highly successful African Americans and documented the disillusionment and anger they felt toward their country and what they perceived as continuing slights and signs of racial discrimination and prejudice. "The bottom line is you're black," said one corporate executive profiled, "and that's still a negative in this society."

Race has long been the "bottom line" for many African Americans throughout American history. The viewpoints in this chapter reflect on this history and present two dramatically different visions of the 1960s civil rights movement and the extent of racism in American society.

VIEWPOINT 1

"Despite what we designate as progress wrought through struggle over many generations, we remain . . . a dark and foreign presence, always the designated 'other.'"

Racism Remains the Primary Obstacle Facing African Americans

Derrick Bell (b. 1931)

Derrick Bell is a legal scholar, writer, and civil rights activist. He supervised school desegregation cases in the South during the civil rights movement while working for the NAACP Legal Defense and Education Fund. The first African-American professor hired by Harvard Law School, Bell left his tenured position in 1990 in protest over the institution's failure to hire and grant tenure to African-American women faculty members. He later became a visiting professor at New York University in New York City. Bell is the author of several books, including *And We Are Not Saved* and *Faces at the Bottom of the Well*, from which the following viewpoint is excerpted.

Bell argues that despite the decline of visible signs of racial discrimination, racism against blacks is a permanent and defining feature of American life. Throughout American history, he argues, whites have used racism against blacks as a social bond and stabilizer. Civil rights legislation and other steps toward racial equality made during the civil rights movement have proven shallow and temporary, he asserts. He concludes that African Americans must accept the fact that racism will remain a central aspect of their existence in the United States.

When I was growing up in the years before the Second World War, our slave heritage was more a symbol of shame than a source of pride. It burdened black people with an indelible mark of difference as we struggled to be like whites. In those far-off days, survival and progress seemed to require moving beyond, even rejecting slavery. Childhood friends in a West Indian family who lived a few doors away often boasted—erroneously as I later learned—that their people had never been slaves. My own more accurate—but hardly more praiseworthy—response was that my forebears included many free Negroes, some of whom had Choctaw and Blackfoot Indian blood.

Self-Delusion

In those days, self-delusion was both easy and comforting. Slavery was barely mentioned in the schools and seldom discussed by the descendants of its survivors, particularly those who had somehow moved themselves to the North. Emigration, whether from the Caribbean islands or from the Deep South states, provided a geographical distance that encouraged and enhanced individual denial of our collective, slave past. We sang spirituals but detached the songs from their slave origins. As I look back, I see this reaction as no less sad, for being very understandable. We were a subordinate and mostly shunned portion of a society that managed to lay the onus of slavery neatly on those who were slaves while simultaneously exonerating those who were slaveholders. All things considered, it seemed a history best left alone.

Then, after the Second World War and particularly in the 1960s, slavery became—for a few academics and some militant Negroes—a subject of fascination and a sure means of evoking racial rage as a prelude to righteously repeated demands for "Freedom Now!" In response to a resurrection of interest in our past, new books on slavery were written, long out-of-print volumes republished. The new awareness reached its highest point in 1977 with the television version of Alex Haley's biographical novel, *Roots*. The highly successful miniseries informed millions of Americans—black as well as white—that slavery in fact existed and that it was awful. Not, of course, as awful as it would have been save for the good white folks the television writers had created to ease the slaves' anguish, and the evil ones on whose shoulders they placed all the guilt. Through the magic of literary license, white viewers could feel revulsion for slavery without necessarily recognizing American slavery as a burden on the nation's history, certainly not a burden requiring reparations in the present.

Even so, under pressure of civil rights protests, many white Americans were ready to accede to if not applaud Supreme Court rulings that the Constitution should no longer recognize and validate laws that kept in place the odious badges of slavery.

As a result, two centuries after the Constitution's adoption, we did live in a far more enlightened world. Slavery was no more. Judicial precedent and a plethora of civil rights statutes formally prohibited racial discrimination. Compliance was far from perfect, but the slavery provisions in the Constitution did seem lamentable artifacts of a less enlightened era.

The Fact of Slavery

But the fact of slavery refuses to fade, along with the deeply embedded personal attitudes and public policy assumptions that supported it for so long. Indeed, the racism that made slavery feasible is far from dead in the last decade of twentieth-century America; and the civil rights gains, so hard won, are being steadily eroded. Despite undeniable progress for many, no African Americans are insulated from incidents of racial discrimination. Our careers, even our lives, are threatened because of our color. Even the most successful of us are haunted by the plight of our less fortunate brethren who struggle for existence in what some social scientists call the "underclass." Burdened with life-long poverty and soul-devastating despair, they live beyond the pale of the American Dream. What we designate as "racial progress" is not a solution to that problem. It is a regeneration of the problem in a particularly perverse form.

According to data compiled in 1990 for basic measures of poverty, unemployment, and income, the slow advances African Americans made during the 1960s and 1970s have definitely been reversed. The unemployment rate for blacks is 2.5 times the rate for whites. Black per-capita income is not even two thirds of the income for whites; and blacks, most of whom own little wealth or business property, are three times more likely to have income below the poverty level than whites. If trends of the last two decades are allowed to continue, readers can safely—and sadly—assume that the current figures are worse than those cited here.

Statistics cannot, however, begin to express the havoc caused by joblessness and poverty: broken homes, anarchy in communities, futility in the public schools. All are the bitter harvest of race-determined unemployment in a society where work provides sustenance, status, and the all-important sense of self-worth. . . . Poverty is less the source than the status of men and women who, despised because of their race, seek refuge in self-rejection. Drug-related crime, teenaged parenthood, and disrupted and disrupting family life all are manifestations of a despair that feeds on self. That despair is bred anew each day by the images on ever-playing television sets, images confirming that theirs is the disgraceful form of living, not the only way people live.

Few whites are able to identify with blacks as a group—the essential prerequisite for feeling empathy with, rather than aversion from, blacks' self-inflicted suffering. . . . Unable or unwilling to perceive that "there but for the grace of God, go I," few whites are ready to actively promote civil rights for blacks. Because of an irrational but easily roused fear that any social reform will unjustly benefit blacks, whites fail to support the programs this country desperately needs to address the ever-widening gap between the rich and the poor, both black and white.

Lulled by comforting racial stereotypes, fearful that blacks will unfairly get ahead of them, all too many whites respond to even the most dire reports of race-based disadvantage with either a sympathetic headshake or victim-blaming rationalizations. Both responses lead easily to the conclusion that contemporary complaints of racial discrimination are simply excuses put forward by people who are unable or unwilling to compete on an equal basis in a competitive society.

For white people who both deny racism and see a heavy dose of the Horatio Alger myth as the answer to blacks' problems, how sweet it must be when a black person stands in a public place and condemns as slothful and unambitious those blacks who are not making it. Whites eagerly embrace black conservatives' homilies to self-help, however grossly unrealistic such messages are in an economy where millions, white as well as black, are unemployed and, more important, in one where racial discrimination in the workplace is as vicious (if less obvious) than it was when employers posted signs "no negras need apply."

The Persistence of Racism

Whatever the relief from responsibility such thinking provides those who embrace it, more than a decade of civil rights setbacks in the White House, in the courts, and in the critical realm of media-nurtured public opinion has forced retrenchment in the tattered civil rights ranks. We must reassess our cause and our approach to it, but repetition of time-worn slogans simply will not do. As a popular colloquialism puts it, it is time to "get real" about race and the persistence of racism in America.

To make such an assessment—to plan for the future by reviewing the experiences of the past—we must ask whether the formidable hurdles we now face in the elusive quest for racial equality are simply a challenge to our commitment, whether they are the latest variation of the old hymn "One More River to Cross." Or, as we once again gear up to meet the challenges posed by these unexpected new setbacks, are we ignoring a current message with implications for the future which history has already taught us about the past?

The Persistence of Racism

In a review of Dinesh D'Souza's book The End of Racism *published in the October 2, 1995, edition of the* New Yorker, *historian Sean Wilentz disputes D'Souza's arguments that racism has largely faded from American life.*

White attitudes toward race have certainly improved since the nineteen-sixties, more than some liberals admit. Still, centuries-old patterns of prejudice usually take more than a few decades to uproot. One reason D'Souza is so optimistic about the decline of white racism is that he defines racism very narrowly, as a belief in the genetic inferiority of blacks. Because far fewer white Americans today publicly endorse that belief than did so in the nineteen-forties, D'Souza sees white racism as nearing extinction. Actually, numerous reliable studies show that even while whites voice egalitarian sentiments about integrated schools and workplaces, they continue to discriminate against blacks in hiring and (especially) housing, and still show a propensity to regard blacks as lazier, less intelligent, and more violent than any other ethnic group. D'Souza's reply is: What of it? These discriminations are rational and justified responses to genuine black pathologies. It is a matter, he writes, of "better safe than sorry." Or, to put it more bluntly, that's the way blacks really are. . . .

In any case, racial inequity is not simply a matter of attitudes. D'Souza is quick to dismiss institutional racism as "a nonsense phrase," mainly because he seems never to have learned what the phrase actually means. The Social Security system is a fair example of the broader phenomenon. In designing the system, during the nineteen-thirties, Congress, at the explicit insistence of Southern representatives, excluded certain occupational categories in which blacks were heavily represented—most notably, agricultural labor and domestic service—and the system remained that way into the fifties. To this day, a generation of laborers and servants and their families are paying the cumulative price for that exclusion.

Such assessment is hard to make. On the one hand, contemporary color barriers are certainly less visible as a result of our successful effort to strip the law's endorsement from the hated Jim Crow signs. Today one can travel for thousands of miles across this country and never see a public facility designated as "Colored" or "White." Indeed, the very absence of visible signs of discrimination creates an atmosphere of racial neutrality and encourages whites to believe that racism is a thing of the past. On the other hand, the general use of so-called neutral standards to continue exclusionary practices reduces the effectiveness of traditional civil rights laws, while rendering discriminatory actions more oppressive than ever. Racial bias in the pre-*Brown* era was stark, open, unalloyed with hypocrisy and blank-faced lies. We blacks, when rejected, knew who our enemies were. They were not us! Today, because bias is masked in unofficial practices and "neutral" standards, we must wrestle with the question whether race or some individual failing has cost us the job, denied us the promotion, or prompted our being rejected as tenants for an apartment. Either conclusion breeds frustration and alienation— and a rage we dare not show to others or admit to ourselves.

Modern discrimination is, moreover, not practiced indiscriminately. Whites, ready and willing to applaud, even idolize black athletes and entertainers, refuse to hire, or balk at working with, blacks. Whites who number individual blacks among their closest friends approve, or do not oppose, practices that bar selling or renting homes or apartments in their neighborhoods to blacks they don't know. Employers, not wanting "too many of them," are willing to hire one or two black people, but will reject those who apply later. Most hotels and restaurants who offer black patrons courteous—even deferential—treatment, uniformly reject black job applicants, except perhaps for the most menial jobs. When did you last see a black waiter in a really good restaurant?

Racial schizophrenia is not limited to hotels and restaurants. As a result, neither professional status nor relatively high income protects even accomplished blacks from capricious acts of discrimination that may reflect either individual "preference" or an institution's bias. The motivations for bias vary; the disadvantage to black victims is the same.

Careful examination reveals a pattern to these seemingly arbitrary racial actions. When whites perceive that it will be profitable or at least cost-free to serve, hire, admit, or otherwise deal with blacks on a nondiscriminatory basis, they do so. When they fear—accurately or not—that there may be a loss, inconvenience, or upset to themselves or other whites, discriminatory conduct usually follows. Selections and rejections reflect preference as much as prejudice. A preference for whites makes it harder to prove the discrimination outlawed by civil rights laws. This difficulty, when combined with lackluster enforcement, explains why discrimination in employment and in the housing market continues to prevail more than two decades after enactment of the Equal Employment Opportunity Act of 1965 and the Fair Housing Act of 1968.

Racial policy is the culmination of thousands of these individual practices. Black people, then, are caught in a double bind. We are, as I have said, disadvantaged unless whites perceive that nondiscriminatory treatment for us will be a benefit for them. In addition, even when nonracist practices might bring a benefit, whites may rely on discrimination against blacks as a unifying factor and a safety valve for frustrations during economic hard times.

Racism and Impoverished Whites

Almost always, the injustices that dramatically diminish the rights of blacks are linked to the serious economic disadvantage suffered by many whites who lack money and power. Whites, rather than acknowledge the similarity of their disadvantage, particularly when compared with that of better-off whites, are easily detoured into protecting their sense of entitlement vis-à-vis blacks for all things of value. Evidently, this racial preference expectation is hypnotic. It is this compulsive fascination that seems to prevent most whites from even seeing—much less resenting—the far more sizable gap between their status and those who occupy the lofty levels at the top of our society.

Race consciousness of this character, as Professor Kimberlè Crenshaw suggested in 1988 in a pathbreaking *Harvard Law Review* article, makes it difficult for whites "to imagine the world differently. It also creates the desire for identification with privileged elites. By focusing on a distinct, subordinate 'other,' whites include themselves in the dominant circle—an arena in which most hold no real power, but only their privileged racial identity."

The Stabilizing Role of Blacks

The critically important stabilizing role that blacks play in this society constitutes a major barrier in the way of achieving racial equality. Throughout history, politicians have used blacks as scapegoats for failed economic or political policies. Before the Civil War, rich slave owners persuaded the white working class to stand with them against the danger of slave revolts—even though the existence of slavery condemned white workers to a life of economic privation. After the Civil War, poor whites fought social reforms and settled for segregation rather than see formerly enslaved blacks get ahead. Most labor unions preferred to allow plant owners to break strikes with black scab labor than allow blacks to join their ranks. The "them against us" racial ploy—always a potent force in economic bad times—is working again: today whites, as disadvantaged by high-status entrance requirements as blacks, fight to end affirmative action policies that, by eliminating class-based entrance requirements and requiring widespread advertising of jobs, have likely helped far more whites than blacks. And in the 1990s, as through much of the 1980s, millions of Americans—white as well as black—face steadily worsening conditions: unemployment, inaccessible health care, inadequate housing, mediocre education, and pollution of the environment. The gap in national incomes is approaching a crisis as those in the top fifth now earn more than their counterparts in the bottom four fifths combined. The conservative guru Kevin Phillips used a different but no less disturbing comparison: the top two million income earners in this country earn more than the next one hundred million.

Shocking. And yet conservative white politicians are able to gain and hold even the highest office despite their failure to address seriously any of these issues. They rely instead on the time-tested formula of getting needy whites to identify on the basis of their shared skin color, and suggest with little or no subtlety that white people must stand together against the Willie Hortons, or against racial quotas, or against affirmative action. The code words differ. The message is the same. Whites are rallied on the basis of racial pride and patriotism to accept their often lowly lot in life, and encouraged to vent their frustration by opposing any serious advancement by blacks. Crucial to this situation is the unstated understanding by the mass of whites that they will accept large disparities in economic opportunity in respect to other whites as long as they have a priority over blacks and other people of color for access to the few opportunities available.

This "racial bonding" by whites means that black rights and interests are always vulnerable to diminishment if not to outright destruction. The willingness of whites over time to respond to this racial rallying cry explains—far more than does the failure of liberal democratic practices (re black rights) to coincide with liberal democratic theory—blacks' continuing subordinate status. This is, of course, contrary to the philosophy of Gunnar Myrdal's massive midcentury study *The American Dilemma*. Myrdal and two generations of civil rights advocates accepted the idea of racism as merely an odious holdover from slavery, "a terrible and inexplicable anomaly stuck in the middle of our liberal democratic ethos." No one doubted that the standard American policy making was adequate to the task of abolishing racism. White America, it was assumed, *wanted* to abolish racism.

Forty years later, in *The New American Dilemma*, Professor Jennifer Hochschild examined what she called Myrdal's "anomaly thesis," and concluded that it simply cannot explain the persistence of racial discrimination. Rather, the continued viability of racism demonstrates "that racism is not simply an excrescence on a fundamentally healthy liberal democratic body, but is part of what shapes and energizes the body." Under this view, "liberal democracy and racism in the United States are historically, even inherently, reinforcing; American society as we know it exists only because of its foundation in racially based slavery, and it thrives only because racial discrimination continues. The apparent anomaly is an actual symbiosis."

The Designated "Other"

The permanence of this "symbiosis" ensures that civil rights gains will be temporary and setbacks inevitable. Consider: In this last decade of the twentieth century, color determines the social and economic status of all African Americans, both those who have been highly successful and their poverty-bound brethren whose lives are grounded in misery and despair. We rise and fall less as a result of our efforts than in response to the needs of a white society that condemns all blacks to quasi citizenship as surely as it segregated our parents and enslaved their forebears. The fact is that, despite what we designate as progress wrought through struggle over many generations, we remain what we were in the beginning: a dark and foreign presence, always the designated "other." Tolerated in good times, despised when things go wrong, as a people we are scapegoated and sacrificed as distraction or catalyst for compromise to facilitate resolution of political differences or relieve economic adversity.

We are now, as were our forebears when they were brought to the New World, objects of barter for those who, while profiting from our existence, deny our humanity. It is in the light of this fact that we must consider the haunting questions about slavery and exploitation contained in Professor Linda Myers's *Understanding an Afrocentric World View: Introduction to an Optimal Psychology*, questions that serve as their own answers.

We simply cannot prepare realistically for our future without assessing honestly our past. It seems cold, accusatory, but we must try to fathom with her "the mentality of a people that could continue for over 300 years to kidnap an estimated 50 million youth and young adults from Africa, transport them across the Atlantic with about half dying unable to withstand the inhumanity of the passage, and enslave them as animals.". . .

Of course, Americans did not invent slavery. The practice has existed throughout recorded history, and Professor Orlando Patterson, a respected scholar, argues impressively that American slavery was no worse than that practiced in other parts of the world. But it is not comparative slavery policies that concern me. Slavery is, as an example of what white America has done, a constant reminder of what white America might do.

We must see this country's history of slavery, not as an insuperable racial barrier to blacks, but as a legacy of enlightenment from our enslaved forebears reminding us that if they survived the ultimate form of racism, we and those whites who stand with us can at least view racial oppression in its many contemporary forms without underestimating its critical importance and likely permanent status in this country.

To initiate the reconsideration, I want to set forth this proposition, which will be easier to reject than refute: *Black people will never gain full equality in this country. Even those herculean efforts we hail as successful will produce no more than temporary "peaks of progress," short-lived victories that slide into irrelevance as racial patterns adapt in ways that maintain white dominance. This is a hard-to-accept fact that all history verifies. We must acknowledge it, not as a sign of submission, but as an act of ultimate defiance....*

I realize that . . . many people will find it difficult to embrace my assumption that racism is a permanent component of American life. Mesmerized by the racial equality syndrome, they are too easily reassured by simple admonitions to "stay on course," which come far too easily from those—black and white—who are not on the deprived end of the economic chasm between blacks and whites.

The goal of racial equality is, while comforting to many whites, more illusory than real for blacks. For too long, we have worked for substantive reform, then settled for weakly worded and poorly enforced legislation, indeterminate judicial decisions, token government positions, even holidays. . . . We must . . . reassess the worth of the racial assumptions on which, without careful thought, we have presumed too much and relied on too long.

VIEWPOINT 2

"Racism cannot explain most of the contemporary hardships faced by African Americans, even if some of them had their historical roots in oppression."

Racism Is No Longer the Primary Obstacle Facing African Americans

Dinesh D'Souza (b. 1961)

Dinesh D'Souza is John M. Olin fellow at the American Enterprise Institute, a conservative think tank based in Washington, D.C. His works include *Illiberal Education*, a critique of college education, and *The End of Racism*, a study of U.S. history, African Americans, and racism. In the following viewpoint, excerpted from the latter work, D'Souza examines the debate between Booker T. Washington and W.E.B. Du Bois over whether economic self-development or civil rights agitation would best help African Americans, and he traces the influence of these two figures on the civil rights movement of the 1960s and on black leaders today. He contends that black leadership has mainly embraced Du Bois's emphasis on reforming white America to attain civil and legal rights, that this goal has been largely realized, and that racism no longer has the power to impede black progress. Present obstacles to black progress, he concludes, are social pathologies such as crime, lack of education, and broken families—problems that can be best addressed by reviving Washington's neglected prescription of self-help.

A generation after the civil rights movement, blacks have made remarkable progress, and Martin Luther King, Jr.'s birthday is a national holiday. Yet along with this progress, and perhaps inseparable from it, African Americans today suffer the seemingly intractable pathologies of the underclass, even the black middle class seems disgruntled, and throughout the country King's vision of a society in which we are judged as individuals on our merits appears more distant than ever. In many ways, America is a less hopeful and more race conscious society in the 1990s than in the 1960s. Derrick Bell [in *And We Are Not Saved*] offers his bitter assessment of the aftermath of the civil rights era: "We have made progress in everything, yet nothing has changed.". . .

Bell has concluded that the civil rights movement was a failure characterized by "weakly worded and poorly enforced legislation, indeterminate judicial decisions, token government position and holidays." Bell alleges that white liberals never really supported black aspirations, that "reform resulting from civil rights invariably promotes the interests of the white majority," and that American racism is ingrained and unalterable. In order to determine whether Bell's widely shared cynicism is justified, we must seek to answer a dilemma he poses: "Those most deeply involved in this struggle are at a loss for a rational explanation of how the promise of racial equality escaped a fulfillment that 30 years ago appeared assured."

A Ferocious Debate

Did the color-blind vision so eloquently articulated by Martin Luther King, Jr. unravel so quickly because it was flawed from the outset? The extensive literature on the civil rights movement offers no good answer to this question. The reason is that most of this literature is triumphalist in tone, uncritically embracing the premises which framed the civil rights agenda of the 1950s and 1960s. . . .

The civil rights movement, in the view of its cheerleading chroniclers, emerged as a spontaneous eruption of freedom-loving activism that overwhelmed the dogs and hoses of white prejudice and forced the racist establishment to capitulate to the sheer moral power of black claims for freedom and basic rights. Actually, the civil rights movement and its agenda arose out of a ferocious debate between W.E.B. Du Bois and Booker T. Washington, two men who represent contrasting black strategies of political protest and self-help. The civil rights movement represented a choice of the path outlined by Du Bois over that of Washington. By revisiting the debate between these two great men, we can discover options exercised and options foregone. Blacks, after all, would be in a different situation today if the civil rights leadership had opted for Washington instead. . . .

At the Atlanta Exposition fair in Georgia in 1895, Booker T. Washington outlined a vision of race relations in America that brought thunderous applause from the audience, and press accolades from across the country. Southern women were said to leap out of their seats. Not since the prose of Frederick Douglass electrified white abolitionist audiences in Boston was a Northern reading public so moved. And never in America over three centuries had a black man attracted the public admiration of the white South. Born a slave, Booker T. Washington overcame an almost unbelievable set of obstacles to become America's leading black educator, orator, and institution builder. Washington transcended his experience of victimization without any trace of psychological debilitation or bitterness toward whites. On the principle that "it is a hard matter to convert an individual by abusing him," he sought reconciliation and common ground even with Southern segregationists. As Washington said in his famous Atlanta speech:

> The wisest among my race understand that the agitation of questions of social equality is the extremest folly, and that progress in the enjoyment of all the privileges that will come to us must be the result of severe and constant struggle rather than of artificial forcing.

Rather than emphasize political protest and denunciations of white racism, Washington advocated that through industrial education, personal discipline, mutual aid, and racial solidarity, blacks should achieve self-reliance and at the same time contribute to society. This, he believed, would be the best practical strategy to undermine racism. . . .

To Du Bois and his group, Washington's approach seemed painfully accommodationist. In *The Souls of Black Folk* and other writings and speeches, Du Bois portrayed Washington as the original Uncle Tom, willing to embrace the slights of segregation in return for crumbs from the white man's table. Du Bois repudiated Washington's populist program of basic industrial education which he viewed as menial and degrading. Du Bois's indignation sprang in part from his own background: he was an unabashed elitist who spoke French and German; used words like "yonder," "hark," "anon," and "whence"; and was rarely seen in public without gloves and a cane. Du Bois called for a Talented Tenth of liberally educated blacks who could shepherd what he considered the ignorant masses to the blessings of full citizenship. "The Negro race," he said, "is going to be saved by its exceptional men."

While Washington spoke the older language of duty, Du Bois spoke the more modern language of rights. Rather than making deals with segregationists, whom Du Bois considered the worst enemy of blacks, Du Bois called for a militant campaign of political agitation that would expose, educate, and wrest concessions from the white oppressor. "We claim for ourselves every single right that belongs to a free American, political, civil and social, and until we get these rights we will never cease to protest and assail the ears of America." For Du Bois, blacks confronted a single and obvious enemy: white racism. Washington's view was that blacks faced two obstacles, which reinforced each other: white racism, which inferiorized blacks; and black civilizational backwardness, which strengthened white racism and prevented blacks from making advances that were possible even in the restricted orbit of segregation. Precisely because he held that racism was entrenched, unyielding, and regrettably confirmed by black behavior, Washington argued for an emphasis on black self-help. In blunt language, he criticized black profligacy, promiscuity, and crime.

> A race or an individual which has no fixed habits, no fixed place of abode, no time for going to bed, or getting up in the morning, for going to work; no arrangement, order or system in all the ordinary business of life—such a race and such individuals are lacking in self-control, lacking in some of the fundamentals of civilization.

Such criticism of his own people outraged Du Bois, who saw it as ignoring the basic causes of black disadvantage, and thus a craven surrender to the white racist adversary. He roared:

> If they accuse Negro women of lewdness, what are they doing but advertising to the world the shameless lewdness of those Southern men who brought millions of mulattoes into the world? Suppose today Negroes do steal; who was it that for centuries made stealing a virtue by stealing their labor?

Washington did not deny that black cultural pathologies were the consequence of generations of slavery and oppression. The relevant issue for him was that they existed, and had to be confronted. His argument was that as a result of ignorance, sexual irresponsibility, and crime, many blacks were simply not in a position to take full advantage of the opportunity, and to exercise the responsibility, of free citizens, and thus Du Bois's agenda was sound but premature. . . .

Booker T. Washington and W.E.B. Du Bois basically differed on the nature of racism and the nature of the white man in America. . . . Du Bois emphasized the impediments of white racism while Washington also considered the defects of black culture. Du Bois was fundamentally an idealist. As a consequence of his deep belief in the equality of racial groups, Du Bois assumed that once blacks were given legal rights they would be able to compete effectively with whites. Washington was a realist and a pragmatist.

He conceded the civilizational superiority of whites, and sought to use segregation to promote black solidarity and economic development—the first step, he believed, that blacks needed to take to raise cultural standards to the level of whites'. Du Bois believed that racism was a product of irrational antagonism, yet through education and activism whites could be made to appreciate black appeals for rights and justice. Washington insisted that whites would deal with and respect those blacks who lived decently and produced things that whites wanted. Washington argued that, even as victims, blacks should learn to get up, while Du Bois maintained that they must pressure the white oppressor to raise them up. . . .

King, Washington, and Du Bois

It was Martin Luther King, Jr. who made possible the great victories of the civil rights movement: the Civil Rights Act of 1964, forbidding discrimination in education and employment; the Voting Rights Act of 1965, removing obstacles to the right to vote; and the Fair Housing laws of 1968, granting blacks access to rent and purchase homes. The unifying principle of these laws was nondiscrimination: race was outlawed as a legitimate basis for employment, voting, and the sale of real estate. How did King succeed, almost single-handedly, in winning support for this agenda? . . .

The answer lies with King himself. King . . . combined Booker T. Washington's emphasis on personal integrity and group solidarity with W.E.B. Du Bois's emphasis on securing basic rights. . . .

King's genius was that he attacked racism with religious and political principles that many of the Southern racists themselves professed. These were not black principles but American principles, rooted in the nation's Christian and constitutional tradition. Much of what King said sounded like an elaboration of the Declaration of Independence. King frequently cited the Declaration and did not endorse the view that its author was a hypocrite; on the contrary, King realized that his uncashed "promissory note" was nothing more than the "sublime words" of Thomas Jefferson.

Like Booker T. Washington, King recognized the importance both of political right and of democratic consent. Nonviolence and civil disobedience were his calculated techniques for building that consent. . . .

Although King often spoke of the pervasiveness of American racism, all his rhetoric was based upon the contrary assumption that Americans were basically opposed to racism. After all, it is useless to accuse someone of a character trait of which they are proud. If Americans were confident in their racism, they would take King's allegations as a compliment. Only because many Americans by this time considered racism to be fundamentally wrong did King succeed in establishing the foundation for landmark changes in law and policy. The tragedy of King's life is that he was never able to pursue the second dimension of his project: a concerted effort to raise the competitiveness and civilizational level of the black population. King recognized the basic truth of Washington's argument that regardless of the cause, blacks as a group were deficient in important skills which required careful cultivation and training. King said:

> We must not let the fact that we are the victims of injustice lull us into abrogating responsibility for our own lives. We must not use our oppression as an excuse for mediocrity and laziness. Our crime rate is far too high. Our level of cleanliness is frequently far too low. We are too often loud and boisterous, and spend far too much on drink. By improving our standards here and now, we will go a long way toward breaking down the arguments of the segregationist. . . . The Negro will only be free when he reaches down to the inner depths of his own being and signs with the pen and ink of assertive manhood his own emancipation proclamation.

Yet King did not live long enough to pursue this path. . . .

African Americans Today

Racism undoubtedly exists, but it no longer has the power to thwart blacks or any other group in achieving their economic, political, and social aspirations. It cannot be denied that African Americans suffer slights in terms of taxidrivers who pass them by, pedestrians who treat them as a security risk, banks that are reluctant to invest in black neighborhoods, and other forms of continued discrimination. Some of this discrimination is irrational, motivated by bigotry or faulty generalization. Much of it . . . is behavior that is rational from the point of view of the discriminator and at the same time harmful for black individuals who do not conform to the behavioral pattern of their peers. Such incidents undoubtedly cause pain, and invite legitimate public sympathy and concern. But they do not explain why blacks as a group do worse than other groups in getting into selective colleges, performing well on tests, gaining access to rewarding jobs and professions, starting and successfully operating independent businesses, and maintaining productive and cohesive communities.

Racism cannot explain most of the contemporary hardships faced by African Americans, even if some of them had their historical roots in oppression. Activists like Derrick Bell may deny it, but America today is not the same place that it was a generation ago. African Americans now live in a country where a black man, Colin Powell, who three decades ago could not be served a hamburger in many Southern restaurants, became chairman of the

Joint Chiefs of Staff; where an African American, Douglas Wilder, was elected governor of Virginia, the heart of the Confederacy; where a former Dixiecrat like Senator Strom Thurmond supported the nomination of Clarence Thomas, a black man married to a white woman, for the Supreme Court; and where an interracial jury convicted Byron De La Beckwith for killing civil rights activist Medgar Evers a generation after two all-white juries acquitted him.

Slavery's Legacy

In his book The End of Racism, *Dinesh D'Souza examines the effects of slavery and its abolition on African Americans.*

It is understandable that American blacks, on discovering the circumstances in which their ancestors were brought to this country, would feel at best a qualified patriotism. But upon reflection this ambivalence may be unwarranted. Africans were not uniquely unfortunate to be taken as slaves; their descendants were uniquely fortunate to be born in the only civilization in the world to abolish slavery on its own initiative, without the slaves being in a position to revolt and gain their own independence. . . .

What do Americans today owe blacks because of slavery? The answer is: probably nothing. If there is a social debt, it is to the slaves, and the slaves are dead. It makes little sense to say that the United States has an obligation to place African Americans in the economic and social position they would occupy "but for" slavery, since "but for" slavery they would probably be worse off in Africa. More precisely, "but for" slavery they would not exist. Frederick Douglass, who better than anyone else understood the lasting harms inflicted by slavery, argued that it entitled blacks to nothing more than the freedom to help themselves. "Our oppressors have divested us of many valuable blessings and facilities for improvement and education, but thank heaven, they have not yet been able to take from us the privilege of being honest, industrious, sober and intelligent."

Many scholars and civil rights activists continue to blame racism for African American problems; yet if white racism controls the destiny of blacks today, how has one segment of the black community prospered so much over the past generation, while the condition of the black underclass has deteriorated? Since black women and black men are equally exposed to white bigotry, why are black women competitive with white women in the workplace, while black men lag behind all other groups? In major cities in which blacks dominate the institutions of government, is it realistic to assume that white racism is the main cause of crime, delinquency, and dilapidation? It also is not at all clear how racism could prevent the children of middle-class blacks from performing as well as whites and Asians on tests of mathematical and logical reasoning. Black pathologies such as illegitimacy, dependency, and crime are far more serious today than in the past, when racism was indisputably more potent and pervasive. "No one who supports the contemporary racism thesis," William Julius Wilson acknowledges, "has provided adequate or convincing answers to these questions."

Even if racism were to disappear overnight, the worst problems facing black America would persist. Single parenthood and welfare dependency among the black underclass would not cease. Crack and AIDS would continue to ravage black communities. The black crime rate, with its disproportionate impact on African American communities, would still extract a terrible toll. Indeed drugs and black-on-black crime kill more blacks in a year than all the lynchings in U.S. history. Racism is hardly the most serious problem facing African Americans in the United States today. Their main challenge is a civilizational breakdown that stretches across class lines but is especially concentrated in the black underclass. At every socioeconomic level, blacks are uncompetitive on those measures of achievement that are essential to modern industrial society. Many middle-class African Americans are, by their own account, distorted in their social relations by the consuming passion of black rage. And nothing strengthens racism in this country more than the behavior of the African American underclass, which flagrantly violates and scandalizes basic codes of responsibility, decency, and civility. As far as many blacks are concerned, as E. Franklin Frazier once wrote, "The travail of civilization is not yet ended."

Racism began in the West as a biological explanation for a large gap of civilizational development separating blacks from whites. Today racism is reinforced and made plausible by the reemergence of that gap within the United States. For many whites the criminal and irresponsible black underclass represents a revival of barbarism in the midst of Western civilization. If this is true, the best way to eradicate beliefs in black inferiority is to remove their empirical basis. As African American scholars Jeff Howard and Ray Hammond argue, if blacks as a group can show that they are capable of performing competitively in schools and the work force, and exercising both the rights and the responsibilities of American citizenship, then racism will be deprived of its foundation in experience. If blacks can close the civilization gap, the race problem in this country is likely to become insignificant. African Americans in particular and society in general have the daunting mission to address the serious internal problems within black culture. That is the best antiracism now. . . .

Blacks as a group stand at a historic junction. Very few people in the civil rights leadership recognize this: convinced that racism of a hundred varieties stands between African Americans and success, most of the activists are ready to do battle once again with this seemingly elusive and invincible foe. Yet the agenda of securing legal rights for blacks has now been accomplished, and there is no point for blacks to increase the temperature of accusations of racism. Historically whites have used racism to serve powerful entrenched interests, but what interests does racism serve now? Most whites have no economic stake in the ghetto. They have absolutely nothing to gain from oppressing poor blacks. Indeed the only concern that whites seem to have about the underclass is its potential for crime and its reliance on the public purse.

By contrast, it is the civil rights industry which now has a vested interest in the persistence of the ghetto, because the miseries of poor blacks are the best advertisement for continuing programs of racial preferences and set-asides. . . . Formerly a beacon of moral argument and social responsibility, the civil rights leadership has lost much of its moral credibility, and has a fair representation of charlatans who exploit the sufferings of the underclass to collect research grants, minority scholarships, racial preferences, and other subsidies for themselves. . . .

The Supreme Challenge

The supreme challenge faced by African Americans is the one that Booker T. Washington outlined almost a century ago: the mission of building the civilizational resources of a people whose culture is frequently unsuited to the requirements of the modern world. . . .

Sadly, the habits that were needed to resist racist oppression or secure legal rights are not the ones needed to exercise personal freedom or achieve success today. As urged by black reformers, both conservative and liberal, the task ahead is one of rebuilding broken families, developing educational and job skills, fostering black entrepreneurship, and curbing the epidemic of violence in the inner cities. Since the government is not in a good position to improve socialization practices among African Americans, the primary responsibility for cultural restoration undoubtedly lies with the black community itself. . . .

We can sympathize with the magnitude of the project facing African Americans. In order to succeed, they must rid themselves of aspects of their past that are, even now, aspects of themselves. The most telling refutation of racism, as Frederick Douglass once said about slavery, "is the presence of an industrious, enterprising, thrifty and intelligent free black population." For many black scholars and activists, such proposals are anathema because they seem to involve ideological sellout to the white man and thus are viewed as not authentically black. Frantz Fanon, a leading black anticolonialist writer, did not agree. What is needed after the revolution, Fanon wrote [in *Black Skin, White Masks*], is "the liberation of the man of color from himself. However painful it may be for me to accept this conclusion, I am obliged to state it: for the black man, there is only one destiny, and it is white." In this Fanon is right: for generations, blacks have attempted to straighten their hair, lighten their skin, and pass for white. But what blacks need to do is to "act white," which is to say, to abandon idiotic Back-to-Africa schemes and embrace mainstream cultural norms, so that they can effectively compete with other groups.

There is no self-esteem to be found in Africa or even in dubious ideologies of blackness. "Let the sun be proud of its achievement," Frederick Douglass said. Instead, African Americans should take genuine pride in their collective moral achievement in this country's history. Blacks as a group have made a vital contribution to the expansion of the franchise of liberty and opportunity in America. Through their struggle over two centuries, blacks have helped to make the principles of the American founding a legal reality not just for themselves but also for other groups. As W.E.B. Du Bois put it, "There are no truer exponents of the pure human spirit of the Declaration of Independence than the American Negroes."

Yet rejection in this country produced what Du Bois termed a "double consciousness," so that blacks experience a kind of schizophrenia between their racial and American identities. Only now, for the first time in history, is it possible for African Americans to transcend this inner polarization and become the first truly modern people, unhyphenated Americans. Black success and social acceptance now are both tied to rebuilding the African American community. If blacks can achieve such a cultural renaissance, they will teach other Americans a valuable lesson in civilizational restoration. Thus they could vindicate both Booker T. Washington's project of cultural empowerment and Du Bois's hope for a unique African American "message" to the world. Even more, it will be blacks themselves who will finally discredit racism, solve the American dilemma, and become the truest and noblest exemplars of Western civilization.

For Discussion

Chapter One

1. What parts of Thomas Jefferson's viewpoint seem most helpful to defenders of slavery? What parts might lend support for Benjamin Banneker's stated hope that Jefferson is "less inflexible" in his racial beliefs and "well-disposed" toward blacks?

2. Do the views of Thomas Jefferson, as expressed in his viewpoint, lend support to the argument that the Declaration of Independence should be interpreted as referring to whites only? Why or why not?

Chapter Two

1. How does Nathaniel Paul resolve the "palpable inconsistencies" between America's ideals of freedom and the existence of slavery? Do you agree with his explanation? Why or why not?

2. How important is the belief in the racial inferiority of blacks to the arguments of John C. Calhoun and William Harper defending slavery? Would their arguments retain their integrity if the authors conceded equality? Why or why not? Does Nathaniel Paul argue for or simply assume racial equality?

3. Summarize what you perceive to be the fundamental differences between the arguments of Martin R. Delany and Frederick Douglass concerning the future of blacks in America. What would be sufficient cause to convince you to leave the United States? Explain your answer.

Chapter Three

1 Does Richard H. Cain argue for "social equality" for blacks? Explain your answer. What claims does Cain make regarding the place of blacks in American history?

2. The viewpoints by James D.B. De Bow and Thomas Conway were made at a time when the political and racial situation in the South was in flux. The viewpoints of Thomas Nelson Page and Mary Church Terrell were written several decades later, when whites were firmly in control over blacks in the South. How are these changing circumstances reflected in the arguments and observations of the writers, all of whom deal to some extent with white violence against blacks?

Chapter Four

1. Judging from the arguments expressed in their viewpoints, was the rupture between Booker T. Washington and W.E.B. Du Bois inevitable or avoidable? What do you believe to be their fundamental areas of disagreement? In what areas do they agree?

2. Booker T. Washington argued that through individual achievements and economic advancement, African Americans could overcome the racial prejudice of whites. What statements of Thomas Dixon Jr. call this argument into question?

3. What importance does Thomas Dixon Jr. attach to the question of "racial amalgamation"? What arguments does Kelly Miller make on the matter?

Chapter Five

1. A significant portion of Marcus Garvey's viewpoint consists of direct attacks against the National Association for the Advancement of Colored People (NAACP); William Pickens of the NAACP responds in kind. Separate and list the personal attacks and the disagreements over the issues found in the two viewpoints. Does such sorting help in understanding the viewpoints and the issues? Why or why not?

2. William Pickens argues that some of Marcus Garvey's beliefs derive from his Jamaican background. What differences does Pickens say exist between the situations facing blacks in the West Indies and blacks in America? What parts of Garvey's program does Pickens find strange to Americans?

3. What point is George S. Schuyler making when he describes the African American as "lampblacked Anglo-Saxon"? Do you agree with his description? Why or why not?

4. Compare and contrast the black-culture arguments of Langston Hughes with the black nationalism of Marcus Garvey. Do Hughes's calls for "racial art" spring from the same source as Garvey's call for "pride and purity of race"? Why or why not?

Chapter Six

1. How do the rhetorical styles of Martin Luther King Jr. and Malcolm X differ? Which do you find more effective? Explain.

2. Both Clarence Pendleton and Jesse Jackson claim to be arguing for the ideals of Martin Luther King Jr. and the civil rights movement. What accounts for their disagreements? Who do you think makes the better claim? Why?

Chapter Seven

1. Do Derrick Bell and Dinesh D'Souza have different conceptions of what racism is? Explain your answer.

2. How might Dinesh D'Souza respond to Langston Hughes's comparisons of upper- and lower-class blacks in Hughes's viewpoint in chapter five? Do D'Souza's arguments boil down to the prescription that African Americans should "act white"? Explain your answer.

General Questions

1. In light of the viewpoints presented in this volume, which issues and questions facing African Americans have remained constant? Which have changed the most?

2. Describe some of the common arguments of Martin R. Delany, Marcus Garvey, and Malcolm X. Are they in fundamental agreement with the views of Thomas Dixon Jr. and other white supremacists? Why or why not?

Chronology

1619	Twenty Africans are deposited at Jamestown, Virginia, by a Dutch frigate.
1641	Massachusetts is the first colony to legally recognize the institution of slavery.
1671	The Maryland legislature enacts a law holding that conversion to Christianity does not alter one's slave status.
1672	Virginia passes a law rewarding the killing of "Maroons"—runaway slaves who maintain a nomadic existence on the western frontier. Between 1672 and 1864 dozens of Maroon communities are formed in the forests and swamps of South Carolina, Florida, Virginia, and other colonies and states.
1688	Quakers in Germantown, Pennsylvania, denounce slavery in America's first recorded formal protest against the institution.
1705	A Virginia law forbids free blacks to hold public office or to be witnesses in court cases.
1739	Forty-four black slaves and thirty white colonists are killed in the Stono Rebellion near Charleston, South Carolina.
1770	Crispus Attucks is killed by British soldiers in the Boston Massacre.
November 1775	The royal governor of Virginia, Lord Dunmore, issues a proclamation declaring those slaves free who join "his Majesty's troops."
January 1776	Reversing earlier policy, George Washington enlists free blacks in the Continental Army. During the Revolutionary War an estimated nine thousand free and enslaved blacks serve in the colonial war effort. An estimated fifty thousand slaves escape to join the British; some fight against the Americans.
July 1776	The Declaration of Independence is adopted by the Continental Congress after references condemning slavery have been removed.
1777	Vermont abolishes slavery.
1780	Pennsylvania passes a law to gradually abolish slavery.
1781	Blacks make up more than half of the forty-four settlers who found Los Angeles.

1783	The American Revolution ends; the state of Virginia grants freedom to all slaves who served in the war.
1787	Congress enacts the Northwest Ordinance, banning slavery in the western territory acquired from England in the Revolutionary War.
	Absalom Jones and Richard Allen form the Free African Society in Philadelphia.
1788	The Constitution, which sanctions slavery and extends the slave trade for twenty more years, is ratified by the states.
1794	Richard Allen founds the African Methodist Episcopal Church in Philadelphia.
1800	Gabriel Prosser is captured and hung after his planned slave rebellion in Virginia was betrayed and thwarted.
1804	Ohio passes "black laws" restricting the immigration and rights of African Americans; other western states follow suit.
1807	Congress forbids the importation of slaves into the United States.
1812–1815	Free and enslaved blacks serve in the War of 1812.
1816	The American Colonization Society is founded.
1820	Blacks are banned from service in the U.S. armed forces.
1822	Free black Denmark Vesey is executed after his five-year effort to organize a slave rebellion in Charleston, South Carolina, is betrayed by an informant.
1827	*Freedom's Journal*, America's first black newspaper, is founded.
1829	Free black David Walker publishes *An Appeal to the Colored People of the World*, calling for slave revolution.
September 1830	The first National Negro Convention meets in Philadelphia.
January 1831	William Lloyd Garrison publishes the first issue of the *Liberator*, his abolitionist newspaper.
August 1831	Nat Turner leads a slave rebellion in Virginia; sixty whites and more than two hundred blacks die. Turner is executed; southern states pass new security measures.
1833	The American Anti-Slavery Society is founded by black and white abolitionists.
1834	Mobs riot against free blacks in Philadelphia and New York.

1838	Frederick Douglass escapes from slavery to New York City where he begins his career as a leading black abolitionist.
1849	Harriet Tubman escapes from slavery in Maryland to freedom in Philadelphia; she will return to the South nineteen times to help slaves escape via the "Underground Railroad."
	The Maryland Supreme Court establishes a "separate but equal" doctrine in rejecting a suit for a black girl to attend a white school.
1853	The nation's first college for African Americans, Ashmun Institute (later Lincoln University), is established in Pennsylvania.
1857	The U.S. Supreme Court rules in *Dred Scott v. Sandford* that blacks "had no rights the white man was bound to respect" and abrogates all restrictions on slavery in the territories.
1861–1865	The Civil War is fought after southern states secede amidst concerns over the preservation of slavery. Thousands of slaves who escape during the conflict are declared "contraband of war" and serve the Union war effort; 250,000 African Americans serve as soldiers.
January 1, 1863	President Lincoln's Emancipation Proclamation, announced in September 1862, takes effect; it frees slaves held in the states of the Confederacy.
1865	Wisconsin, Minnesota, and Connecticut vote to deny suffrage to blacks.
March 1865	The Freedmen's Bureau is established.
December 1865	The Thirteenth Amendment to the Constitution, abolishing slavery, is ratified.
1866	The Ku Klux Klan is organized.
April 1866	Congress passes the Civil Rights Act.
July 1866	Race riots take place in Memphis and New Orleans.
1867	Congress extends the vote to blacks in Washington, D.C.
July 1868	The Fourteenth Amendment, defining national citizenship to include blacks, is ratified.
February 1870	Hiram Revels of Mississippi is appointed to replace Jefferson Davis, becoming the first African American in the U.S. Senate.
March 1870	The Fifteenth Amendment, forbidding states to deprive citizens of the right to vote because of race, is ratified.
1874	The Freedmen's Savings and Trust Company fails,

	wiping out the savings of thousands of African Americans.
March 1875	Congress passes the Civil Rights Act of 1875; it prohibits discrimination in places of public accommodation.
1877	The Compromise of 1877 withdraws federal troops from the South, ending the era of Reconstruction.
1879–1881	About fifty-five thousand blacks move to Kansas and other western states in the "Exodus Movement."
1881	Booker T. Washington opens the Tuskegee Institute in Alabama.
	Tennessee enacts the first "Jim Crow" law segregating railroad passenger cars.
October 1883	The U.S. Supreme Court declares the Civil Rights Act of 1875 unconstitutional.
August 1890	A state constitutional convention in Mississippi adopts a literacy test in order to restrict black suffrage; other southern states follow suit.
September 18, 1895	Booker T. Washington speaks at the Atlanta Exposition.
May 1896	The U.S. Supreme Court upholds the practice of segregation when it rules in *Plessy v. Ferguson* that "separate but equal" facilities are constitutional.
July 1896	The National Association of Colored Women is organized by Mary Church Terrell in Washington, D.C.
1898	Black regiments participate in the Spanish-American War.
July 1905	W.E.B. Du Bois and other black delegates gather on the Canadian side of Niagara Falls to adopt resolutions demanding equality in the United States.
February 1909	The National Association for the Advancement of Colored People (NAACP) is founded in New York City, partly in response to race riots the previous year in Springfield, Illinois.
1910	Black migration northward begins to increase; between 1910 and 1920, 330,000 African Americans will leave the South.
1911	The National Urban League is founded to assist black migrants from the South.
June 1915	The U.S. Supreme Court outlaws grandfather clauses used by southern states to disfranchise black voters.
April 6, 1917	The United States enters World War I; 300,000 blacks serve in the U.S. armed forces during the war, including 1,400 commissioned as officers.
1919	Twenty-five race riots take place in the "Red Summer" of 1919.

August 1920	Marcus Garvey presides over the national convention of the Universal Negro Improvement Association in New York City.
1922–1927	The Harlem Renaissance flourishes in New York City.
December 1927	Marcus Garvey, convicted of mail fraud, is deported after being released from prison.
1936	President Franklin D. Roosevelt appoints Mary McLeod Bethune to head the Division of Negro Affairs of the National Youth Administration. In the 1936 elections blacks abandon their traditional allegiance to the Republican Party to vote for Roosevelt and his New Deal.
1937	William H. Hastie becomes the first black federal judge.
October 1940	Benjamin O. Davis becomes the first African American promoted to general in the U.S. armed forces.
June 1941	A. Philip Randolph threatens a massive march on Washington unless the Roosevelt administration takes measures to ensure black employment in defense industries; Roosevelt agrees to establish the Fair Employment Practices Committee (FEPC).
December 1941	The United States enters World War II; about one million African Americans serve in the armed forces in segregated units.
1943	President Roosevelt declares a state of emergency and dispatches six thousand troops to Detroit following race riots in that city.
April 1944	The U.S. Supreme Court rules in *Smith v. Allwright* that blacks cannot be excluded from primary elections.
April 1947	Jackie Robinson breaks the color line in major league baseball.
May 1948	The U.S. Supreme Court holds that lower courts cannot enforce restrictive covenants used to maintain segregated housing in the United States.
July 26, 1948	President Harry S. Truman issues an executive order desegregating the armed services.
December 1952	The Tuskegee Institute reports that for the first time in seventy-one years no lynching has been reported in the United States.
May 1954	In *Brown v. Board of Education* the U.S. Supreme Court declares separate educational facilities "inherently unequal."
December 1, 1955	Rosa Parks is arrested for refusing to give up her bus seat to a white person; the action triggers a bus

	boycott in Montgomery, Alabama, led by Martin Luther King Jr.
August 1957	Congress passes the Civil Rights Act of 1957, the first such legislation to be passed since Reconstruction.
September 1957	President Dwight D. Eisenhower orders federal troops to Little Rock, Arkansas, to ensure the peaceful integration of Central High School.
February 1, 1960	Four black students stage a sit-in at a Woolworth's lunch counter in Greensboro, North Carolina; the sit-in movement to desegregate restaurants, hotels, movie theaters, libraries, and parks spreads to other southern states.
September 1962	Under federal protection, James Meredith becomes the first black admitted to the University of Mississippi.
April 1963	Civil rights activists led by Martin Luther King Jr. begin a protest campaign to desegregate Birmingham, Alabama.
August 28, 1963	Over 250,000 Americans gather at the Lincoln Memorial to urge passage of civil rights legislation and hear Martin Luther King Jr. deliver his "I Have a Dream" speech.
September 15, 1963	Four black girls are killed when a bomb rips through a Birmingham Baptist church.
July 1964	Congress passes civil rights legislation designed to end discrimination in public accommodations and employment.
February 21, 1965	Black nationalist and former Nation of Islam spokesperson Malcolm X is assassinated in New York City.
August 6, 1965	President Lyndon B. Johnson signs the Voting Rights Act.
August 11–16, 1965	Rioting in the black ghetto of Watts in Los Angeles leads to 35 deaths, 900 injuries, and over 3,500 arrests.
June 1966	Civil rights activist Stokely Carmichael popularizes the "black power" slogan.
October 1966	The Black Panther Party is founded in Oakland, California.
May–October 1967	The worst summer of racial disturbances and unrest in American history takes place.
June 13, 1967	Thurgood Marshall is the first African American appointed to the U.S. Supreme Court.
November 1967	Carl B. Stokes is elected the first black mayor of a major U.S. city, Cleveland, Ohio.

March 2, 1968	The presidentially appointed Kerner Commission reports that "white racism" was at the root of the racial disturbances of 1967 and that the country is heading toward two "separate and unequal societies."
April 4, 1968	Martin Luther King Jr. is assassinated in Memphis, Tennessee.
April 11, 1968	Congress passes civil rights legislation prohibiting racial discrimination in the sale or rental of housing.
November 1968	Shirley Chisholm of New York becomes the first black woman to win a seat in Congress.
May 14, 1970	Mississippi law enforcement officials kill two black students at Jackson State College.
1978	In *Regents of the University of California v. Allan Bakke* the U.S. Supreme Court upholds the principle of affirmative action but establishes more restrictive guidelines.
1984	Jesse Jackson campaigns for the presidential nomination of the Democratic Party.
January 20, 1986	Martin Luther King Jr.'s birthday (January 15) is observed for the first time as a federal holiday.
1990	L. Douglas Wilder takes office in Virginia as the nation's first elected African-American governor.
April 1992	Riots break out in Los Angeles following the acquittal of four white police officers in the beating of a black man.
October 1995	Controversial black nationalist Louis Farrakhan organizes his Million Man March on Washington.

Annotated Bibliography

Jervis Anderson. *A. Philip Randolph: A Biographical Portrait.* New York: Harcourt Brace Jovanovich, 1973. A biography of the head of a major black union and leader of a mass movement during World War II to secure blacks equal treatment in the military and under defense contracts.

Jervis Anderson. *This Was Harlem: A Cultural Portrait, 1900–1950.* New York: Farrar, Straus, and Giroux, 1982. A history of the making of a black ghetto and home of the Harlem Renaissance of the 1920s.

Herbert Aptheker, ed. *A Documentary History of the Negro People in the United States.* New York: Citadel Press, 1969. An important collection gathered by a pioneer in the field of black history.

Lerone Bennett Jr. *Before the Mayflower: A History of Black America.* New York: Penguin, 1984. An overview of black history from pre-seventeenth-century Africa to the 1960s written for the general reader.

Lerone Bennett Jr. *The Shaping of Black America.* New York: Penguin, 1993. A "developmental history" of African Americans that examines their struggle for autonomy and power within the United States; a companion to *Before the Mayflower.*

Ira Berlin. *Slaves Without Masters.* New York: Vintage, 1974. A history of free blacks in the South from the colonial period to the Civil War.

Ira Berlin et al., eds. *Free at Last: A Documentary History of Slavery, Freedom, and the Civil War.* New York: New Press, 1992. A collection of letters, official reports, and other records depicting how slavery came to an end during the Civil War, emphasizing the role escaped slaves and black soldiers played in achieving their emancipation.

John Blassingame. *The Slave Community.* New York: Oxford University Press, 1979. A general overview of slavery employing original slave sources to illustrate the slave system and the lives of the slaves within it.

Benjamin A. Botkin, ed. *Lay My Burden Down.* Chicago: University of Chicago Press, 1945. A collection of the reminiscences of former slaves gathered during the 1930s.

John H. Bracey, August Meier, and Elliott Rudwick, eds. *Black Nationalism in America.* New York: Bobbs-Merrill, 1970. A collection of primary sources depicting the development of black nationalist thought.

Stokely Carmichael and Charles V. Hamilton. *Black Power: The Politics of Liberation in America*. New York: Vintage, 1967. Manifesto for black power cowritten by the person (Carmichael) who made the slogan famous.

Clayborne Carson. *In Struggle: SNCC and the Black Awakening of the 1960s*. Cambridge, MA: Harvard University Press, 1981. A history of the Student Nonviolent Coordinating Committee (SNCC) that examines its creation, evolution, and relationship with other civil rights organizations.

Dan Carter. *Scottsboro: A Tragedy of the American South*. Baton Rouge: Louisiana State University Press, 1969. The story of the 1931 trial of nine black Alabama youths, eight of whom were sentenced to death for raping two white women only to have the U.S. Supreme Court overturn their convictions a year later.

William Clay. *Just Permanent Interests*. New York: Amistad Press, 1992. A history of black members of Congress from Reconstruction to the late twentieth century written by a former ranking member of Congress.

Edmund Cronon. *Black Moses*. Madison: University of Wisconsin Press, 1955. A biography of Marcus Garvey, the controversial black nationalist of the 1920s.

Harold Cruse. *The Crisis of the Negro Intellectual*. New York: Morrow, 1967. An examination of the radicalization of the civil rights movement during the 1960s.

Richard Dalfiume. *The Desegregation of the U.S. Armed Forces*. Columbia: University of Missouri Press, 1969. A study of the efforts during the administrations of Presidents Franklin D. Roosevelt and Harry S. Truman to desegregate the military.

David Brion Davis. *The Problem of Slavery in Western Culture*. New York: Oxford University Press, 1988. A history of slavery and of European and American decisions to bring slavery to the New World.

John Dollard. *Caste and Class in a Southern Town*. New Haven, CT: Yale University Press, 1937. Sociological-historical study of black life and race relations in a Mississippi town during the era of segregation.

Frederick Douglass. *My Bondage and My Freedom*. New York: Arno Press, 1968. A reprint of the autobiography of the famous black abolitionist.

Dinesh D'Souza. *The End of Racism*. New York: Free Press, 1995. A history of the rise and decline of ideas of racism, an argument for Booker T. Washington-style self-help for black Americans, and an attack on affirmative action.

W.E.B. Du Bois. *The Autobiography of W.E.B. Du Bois*. New York: International Publishers, 1968. The autobiography of a leading black intellectual and civil rights activist.

W.E.B. Du Bois. *Black Reconstruction*. New York: Harcourt, Brace, 1935. An early history of reconstruction from the point of view of black Americans.

W.E.B. Du Bois. *The Souls of Black Folk*. New York: Penguin, 1989. A reissue of the 1903 collection of essays that was written in part to stimulate opposition to Booker T. Washington and his policies of accommodation to white America.

Stanley Elkins. *Slavery: A Problem in American Institutional and Intellectual Life*. Chicago: University of Chicago Press, 1976. A controversial history of slavery and its lasting effects on African Americans.

Leslie Fishel and Benjamin Quarles, eds. *The Black American*. Glenview, IL: Scott, Foresman, 1970. A documentary history of black Americans.

Philip Foner, ed. *The Life and Writings of Frederick Douglass*. New York: International Publishers, 1950. A collection of the writings of the nineteenth-century black leader.

Elizabeth Fox-Genovese. *Within the Plantation: Black and White Women of the Old South*. Chapel Hill: University of North Carolina Press, 1988. An examination of the lives of women across racial lines in a male-dominated society.

John Hope Franklin. *Race and History: Selected Essays, 1938–1988*. Baton Rouge: Louisiana State University Press, 1989. Selected articles by the recognized dean of black historians.

John Hope Franklin and Alfred A. Moss. *From Slavery to Freedom*. 7th ed. New York: Knopf, 1994. The best single-volume survey of black history.

John Hope Franklin and Isidore Starr, eds. *The Negro in 20th Century America*. New York: Vintage Books, 1967. A reader on issues relating to the struggle for black civil rights.

V.P. Franklin. *Living Our Stories, Telling Our Truths*. New York: Scribner's, 1995. A study of the roles and uses of the autobiography among black intellectuals and political leaders.

E. Franklin Frazier. *Black Bourgeoisie*. Glencoe, IL: Free Press, 1957. A study of the rise of the black middle class in post–World War II America.

Larry Gara. *The Liberty Line: The Legend of the Underground Railroad*. Lexington: University of Kentucky Press, 1961. A history of the underground railroad that stresses the role of black, rather than white, abolitionists in its operation.

Herbert Garfinkel. *When Negroes March*. New York: Atheneum, 1969. A study of the March on Washington Movement led by A. Philip Randolph during World War II.

David J. Garrow. *Bearing the Cross*. New York: Morrow, 1986. A thorough account of Martin Luther King Jr. and the organization he led, the Southern Christian Leadership Conference (SCLC).

Henry Louis Gates. *Colored People*. New York: Knopf, 1994. A memoir of growing up black in a small West Virginia town while the civil rights movement was on the march elsewhere.

Eugene Genovese. *Roll, Jordan, Roll: The World the Slaves Made*. New York: Random House, 1976. A history of slavery that emphasizes the society created by black slaves while under a paternalistic slave system.

Paula Giddings. *When and Where I Enter: The Impact of Black Women on Race and Sex in America*. New York: Morrow, 1984. A survey of the history of African-American women that includes accounts of how many fought both racial and sexual discrimination.

Herbert Gutman. *The Black Family in Slavery and Freedom, 1750–1925*. New York: Random House, 1977. A comparative and quantitative history of the evolution of the black family under conditions of both slavery and freedom.

Shirley Taylor Haizlip. *The Sweeter the Juice: A Family Memoir in Black and White*. New York: Simon & Schuster, 1994. An intimate family history that examines the phenomenon of African Americans "passing" for white.

Vincent Harding. *There Is a River: The Black Struggle for Freedom in America*. New York: Vintage, 1983. An account of the history of black rebellion from the era of slavery through the Civil War.

Louis R. Harlan. *Booker T. Washington*. 2 vols. New York: Oxford University Press, 1972, 1983. The definitive biography of the influential black leader of the early twentieth century.

Nathan Irvin Huggins. *Revelations: American History, American Myths*. New York: Oxford University Press, 1995. Posthumous collection of writings by a noted African-American scholar.

Nathan Irvin Huggins, ed. *Voices from the Harlem Renaissance*. New York: Oxford University Press, 1976. A documentary collection of important black writers associated with the Harlem Renaissance.

Jacqueline Jones. *Labor of Love, Labor of Sorrow: Black Women, Work, and the Family from Slavery to the Present*. New York: BasicBooks, 1994. A comprehensive portrait of the lives of African-American women from slavery to the late twentieth century, drawing on both demographic evidence and personal accounts.

Winthrop Jordan. *White over Black: American Attitudes Toward the Negro, 1550–1812*. New York: Norton, 1977. An intellectual history of racism and racial thinking in early America.

Nicholas Lemann. *Promised Land*. New York: Vintage Books, 1991. A history of the great black migration from the rural South to the urban North, with special emphasis on blacks who moved from Mississippi to Chicago during and after World War II.

Gerda Lerner, ed. *Black Women in White America: A Documentary History*. New York: Vintage, 1992. An anthology of historical documents by African-American women.

Lawrence Levine. *Black Culture and Black Consciousness*. New York: Oxford University Press, 1980. A history of the lasting impact of slavery on black America.

David Lewis. *W.E.B. Du Bois: Biography of a Race*. New York: Holt, 1993. The first volume of an intellectual/political biography of W.E.B. Du Bois that takes his story through World War I.

C. Eric Lincoln. *The Black Muslims in America*. Boston: Beacon Press, 1961. A sociologist's account of the origins, doctrines, and organization of the Nation of Islam.

Leon Litwack. *Been in the Storm So Long: The Aftermath of Slavery*. New York: Knopf, 1979. A history of the lives of American blacks in the first years of freedom.

Leon Litwack. *North of Slavery*. Chicago: University of Chicago Press, 1961. An examination of the lives of blacks in the free states before the Civil War.

Rayford Logan. *The Negro in American Life and Thought: The Nadir, 1877–1901*. New York: Dial Press, 1954. A political, social, and economic history of black Americans following Reconstruction.

Shirley Wilson Logan, ed. *With Pen and Voice: A Critical Anthology of Nineteenth-Century African-American Women*. Carbondale: Southern Illinois University Press, 1995. A compilation of speeches by seven women, including Sojourner Truth, who were among the first women to speak publicly about feminist issues and race relations.

Malcolm X. *The Autobiography of Malcolm X*. With the assistance of Alex Haley. New York: Grove Press, 1965. The autobiography of the influential Black Muslim leader.

Manning Marable. *Race, Reform, and Rebellion: The Second Reconstruction in Black America, 1945–1982*. 2nd ed. Jackson: University Press of Mississippi, 1991. A broad survey of the black freedom struggle.

William McFeely. *Frederick Douglass*. New York: Norton, 1991. The most recent full-scale biography of the leading nineteenth-century spokesman for black Americans.

William McFeely. *Sapelo's People: A Long Walk into Freedom*. New York: Norton, 1994. A meditation on race and an in-depth examination of the lives of African Americans under slavery and freedom on one of the barrier islands of the southeastern United States.

James McPherson. *The Abolitionist Legacy: From Reconstruction to the NAACP*. Princeton, NJ: Princeton University Press, 1975. A history of black and white abolitionists during the interval between two critical periods of civil rights activism.

James McPherson. *Marching Toward Freedom: The Negro in the Civil War, 1861–1865*. New York: Knopf, 1967. A political, social, and military history of the wartime activities of black Americans.

August Meier. *Black Historians and the Historical Profession*. Urbana: University of Illinois Press, 1986. A survey of black historians, based on interviews with 175 members of the profession, that traces divisions between assimilationists and black nationalists.

August Meier. *Negro Thought in America, 1880–1915*. Ann Arbor: University of Michigan Press, 1963. A study of various black ideologies and strategies during the time of Booker T. Washington.

August Meier and John Hope Franklin, eds. *Black Leaders of the Twentieth Century*. Urbana: University of Illinois Press, 1982. Fifteen essays on significant African Americans written by professional historians.

August Meier and Leon Litwack, eds. *Black Leaders of the Nineteenth Century*. Urbana: University of Illinois Press, 1988. Seventeen essays on key black leaders written by noted authorities on African-American history.

August Meier, Elliott Rudwick, and Francis L. Broderick, eds. *Black Protest Thought in the Twentieth Century*. New York: Bobbs-Merrill, 1971. A collection of primary source materials.

Stephen B. Oates. *The Fires of Jubilee*. New York: Harper & Row, 1975. A brief but highly readable history of the Nat Turner slave rebellion.

Gilbert Osofsky. *Harlem: The Making of a Ghetto, 1890–1930*. New York: Harper & Row, 1966. A social history of Harlem through the Harlem Renaissance.

Gilbert Osofsky, ed. *The Burden of Race*. New York: Harper & Row, 1967. A documentary history of black-white relations in the United States.

Gilbert Osofsky, ed. *Puttin' On Ole Massa*. New York: Harper & Row, 1969. The slave narratives of Henry Bibb, William Wells Brown, and Solomon Northrup.

Leslie Owens. *This Species of Property: Slave Life and Culture in the Old South*. New York: Oxford University Press, 1976. A brief history concentrating on the daily lives of slaves in the antebellum South.

Hugh Pearson. *The Shadow of the Panther: Huey Newton and the Price of Black Power in America*. Reading, MA: Addison-Wesley, 1994. A highly critical study of one of the founders of the Black Panther party.

Ulrich B. Phillips. *American Negro Slavery*. New York: D. Appleton, 1918. A history of the institution of slavery that reflects common white racial attitudes and beliefs of the early twentieth century.

Benjamin Quarles. *Black Abolitionists*. New York: Oxford University Press, 1969. A sympathetic history of black Americans involved in the abolitionist movement as well as an examination of controversies between black and white abolitionists.

Benjamin Quarles. *The Negro in the Making of America*. Rev. ed. New York: Collier, 1987. A popular general history of the subject.

Lee Rainwater and William L. Yancey. *The Moynihan Report and the Politics of Controversy*. Cambridge, MA: MIT Press, 1967. A careful analysis of the controversial government report on black families and public reaction to it.

Willie Lee Rose. Edited by William Freehling. *Slavery and Freedom*. New York: Oxford University Press, 1982. A collection of interpretive essays concerning the transition from slavery to freedom following the ratification of the Thirteenth Amendment.

Elliott Rudwick. *Race Riot at East St. Louis, July 2, 1917*. Carbondale:

Southern Illinois University Press, 1964. A painstaking examination and analysis of one of the worst race riots in all of American history.

Bayard Rustin. *Down the Line.* Chicago: Quadrangle, 1971. The collected writings of a noted civil rights leader and pacifist.

Harvard Sitkoff. *The Struggle for Black Equality.* New York: Hill & Wang, 1981. A brief general history of the modern civil rights movement from the 1954 Supreme Court school desegregation ruling to the onset of the Reagan presidency.

Thomas Sowell. *Civil Rights: Rhetoric or Reality?* New York: Morrow, 1984. A critique of black civil rights leadership from one of the most prominent conservative black scholars of the 1980s.

Kenneth Stampp. *The Peculiar Institution: Slavery in the Antebellum South.* New York: Vintage, 1956. A comprehensive history of slavery that seeks to emphasize the harshness of the system while arguing that slavery exaggerated the differences between black and white Americans.

Shelby Steele. *The Content of Our Character.* New York: St. Martin's Press, 1990. A meditation on race relations and a critique of affirmative action by a black educator.

Dorothy Sterling, ed. *The Trouble They Seen: The Story of Reconstruction in the Words of African Americans.* New York: Da Capo Press, 1994. An anthology of letters and other writings from ex-slaves and other African Americans that document the era of Reconstruction.

Clarence E. Walker. *Deromanticizing Black History: Critical Essays and Appraisals.* Knoxville: University of Tennessee Press, 1991. A reevaluation of writings on African-American history from the 1960s and 1970s by a black history professor.

James M. Washington, ed. *A Testament of Hope.* San Francisco: Harper & Row, 1986. A generous compilation of the important writings of Martin Luther King Jr. that express the civil rights leader's views on race relations and other issues.

Juan Williams. *Eyes on the Prize: America's Civil Rights Years, 1954–1965.* New York: Viking, 1987. The companion volume to the acclaimed PBS television documentary on the civil rights movement.

Joel Williamson. *The Crucible of Race: Black/White Relations in the American South Since Reconstruction.* New York: Oxford University Press, 1984. A history that presumes and demonstrates the centrality of race and racism in the post-Reconstruction South.

Joel Williamson. *New People: Miscegenation and Mulattoes in the United States.* New York: Free Press, 1980. A history of Americans of mixed black and white ancestry from the colonial period to the late twentieth century.

C. Vann Woodward. *The Strange Career of Jim Crow.* 3rd ed. New York: Oxford University Press, 1974. A brief but incisive interpretive history of the imposition of a system of legal segregation in the American South following Reconstruction.

Index